D0393885

BODIES
WE'VE
BURIED

Inside the National Forensic Academy, the World's Top

CSI Training School

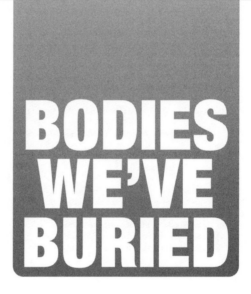

JARRETT HALLCOX and AMY WELCH

Foreword by DR. BILL BASS

BERKLEY BOOKS, NEW YORK

THE BERKLEY PUBLISHING GROUP
Published by the Penguin Group
Penguin Group (USA) Inc.
375 Hudson Street, New York, New York 10014, USA
Penguin Group (Canada), 90 Eglinton Avenue East, Suite 700, Toronto, Ontario M4P 2Y3, Canada
(a division of Pearson Penguin Canada Inc.)
Penguin Books Ltd., 80 Strand, London WC2R 0RL, England
Penguin Group Ireland, 25 St. Stephen's Green, Dublin 2, Ireland (a division of Penguin Books Ltd.)
Penguin Group (Australia), 250 Camberwell Road, Camberwell, Victoria 3124, Australia
(a division of Pearson Australia Group Pty. Ltd.)
Penguin Books India Pvt. Ltd., 11 Community Centre, Panchsheel Park, New Delhi—110 017, India
Penguin Group (NZ), Cnr. Airborne and Rosedale Roads, Albany, Auckland 1310, New Zealand
(a division of Pearson New Zealand Ltd.)
Penguin Books (South Africa) (Pty.) Ltd., 24 Sturdee Avenue, Rosebank, Johannesburg 2196,
South Africa

Penguin Books Ltd., Registered Offices: 80 Strand, London WC2R 0RL, England

This book is an original publication of The Berkley Publishing Group.

Copyright © 2006 by Jarrett Hallcox and Amy Welch.
Text design by Tiffany Estreicher.

First edition: January 2006

Library of Congress Cataloging-in-Publication Data

Hallcox, Jarrett.
    Bodies we've buried : inside the National Forensic Academy, the world's top CSI training school /
Jarrett Hallcox and Amy Welch ; foreword by Bill Bass. — 1st ed.
        p.   cm.
    Includes bibliographical references.
    ISBN 0-425-20752-8
        1. Crime scene searches—United States.   2. Criminal investigation—United States.   3. Evidence,
Criminal—United States.   4. National Forensic Academy.   I. Welch, Amy.   II. Title.
    HV8073.H223 2006
    363.25'071'5—dc22   2005024664

PRINTED IN THE UNITED STATES OF AMERICA

10   9   8   7   6   5   4   3   2   1

PUBLISHER'S NOTE: While the authors have made every effort to provide accurate Internet addresses,
at the time of publication, neither the publisher nor the authors assume any responsibility for errors, or
for changes that occur after publication. Further, the publisher does not have any control over and does
not assume any responsibility for author or third-party websites or their content.

This book is dedicated to all of the graduates and instructors of the National Forensic Academy. Let the evidence always be your guide.

Life is far too important a thing ever to talk seriously about.

—Oscar Wilde

CONTENTS

FOREWORD
Dr. Bill Bass

I know of only two areas of science in which you must destroy in order to find out what is there. The first of these is an archaeological excavation, where you must dig up the site, interpret the stratigraphy, check for intrusions, and analyze the artifacts. The second of these is a crime scene search, about which this book is a guide of what to do, and even better, what not to do. In both cases you have only one chance to do your investigation, and if it is not done correctly the first time you never have a second opportunity, because you have destroyed what you were trying to solve.

The first step in both of the above situations is photography. You must have records of what the scene looks like before it is ever touched, and you must photograph every change that you make in the investigation.

I was fortunate that early in my career as a forensic anthropologist, a Kansas Bureau of Investigation (KBI) agent, Harold Nye, gave me the best information on photography that I have ever received. Harold told me that when you arrive at a crime scene, "You shoot your way in and you shoot your way out." What Harold was saying is that for those of us who investigate crime scenes, when you arrive at the scene and get out of your car, take a picture before ever stepping into or on the scene. For example, let's take a house: When you get to the scene, take a picture of the house. Walk up to the front porch and take a picture. Open the door, and before stepping inside, take a picture of the hall or room. Never go into a room before you have taken a picture. As you leave the scene, repeat the picture-taking in reverse order.

A whole generation of investigators has worked on crime scenes since the 1959 murders of the Clutter family in western Kansas. Harold Nye was the lead KBI investigator in the Clutter murders, which led to a book about the case by Truman Capote entitled *In Cold Blood*. Harold's picture-taking led to one of the major breaks in that case. When Harold went down into the basement, he took a picture of the basement floor before ever stepping on it. After the initial crime scene investigation was over and the pictures had been developed (this was before digital cameras), Harold, while carefully inspecting the photograph, noted a shoe print that did not match any of the crime scene investigators' shoes. This became a key piece of evidence in solving the crime.

It has been a longtime hope of mine that we could put together an in-depth course that would allow hands-on experiences for police officers involved in crime scene searches. This course is the fulfillment of that dream. You will find in the pages of this book how the crime scene investigator (CSI) gains actual experience in recovering evidence and interpreting that evidence after blowing up cars and setting cars on fire. Fire scenes in houses are reproduced, with all of the students gaining valuable experiences from investigating fire scenes after watching a room or building burn. Few people, whether CSIs or not, have ever located and recovered a buried body or one scattered by animals. When a body decays on the ground, students are taught how to determine where the body first lay (where the hair mat has come off and the decay stain caused by the bodily fluids that leach out of the body during decomposition, also known as Volatile Fatty Acids).

The students in the National Forensic Academy (NFA) are taught how to locate a buried body, the proper excavation techniques, and how to recover the skeleton and artifacts left at the death scene. Prosthetic devices, such as hip and knee replacements, are handled by the

The authors, Jarrett Hallcox and Amy Welch, with Dr. Bill Bass.

(Copyright © John Williams, collection of the National Forensic Academy)

students; when found in fire scenes they can help identify the deceased. This book sheds light on what a well-trained CSI looks for.

Bodies We've Buried is a documentation of the training that goes into the education of a CSI. Most of you will be surprised and fascinated by what goes into the training of a good CSI. The authors, Jarrett and Amy, are not law enforcement officers, but are the staff members who put together the training that you will read about in the book. They have been surprised, as you will be, and have recorded their excitement for all of us to read.

For a number of years many of us in the forensic sciences and law enforcement have been concerned about the quality of training received by law enforcement officers and especially crime scene investigators. A few years ago the now-retired police chief of Knoxville, Phil Keith, and a number of us in the forensic area discussed the possibility of establishing an in-depth training program to bring the training of crime scene investigators up to the modern level of knowledge in the forensic sciences. Out of these discussions, and funded by federal grants, the NFA was born. Prior to the courses offered here, most training for CSIs was a lecture-type, one-to-five-day program, with little if any hands-on experience. This book, written by the two people who are in charge of the training of the crime scene investigators from all over the world, who are accepted into the NFA's ten-week course, will give you a day-by-day account of the trials and tribulations of finding material for the training sessions, of the humorous things in class, and of the establishment of lifelong friendships of the students and staff.

—Dr. Bill Bass

INTRODUCTION
What's in a Name?

Forensics. Who could have imagined? Not more than three years ago, we were working on master's degrees that had no relevancy to crime scene investigation whatsoever. But here we are, a city manager and a social worker, leading the biggest and best forensic program in the country. The things we see and the things we do are unbelievable to most. Yet none of it would have been possible if it wasn't for one infamous name: O. J. Simpson.

Whether you believe O. J. Simpson was guilty or not, the murder trial of the century brought to the forefront a growing problem within the law enforcement community in the shape of one little black glove. Crime scenes everywhere, both large and small, were being worked improperly, and as a result, criminals were getting away scot-free.

In the fall of 2000, in Knoxville, Tennessee, one police chief had an .idea that would forever change the way crime scenes are worked around the world. Chief Phil Keith of the Knoxville Police Department realized the desperate need to standardize and professionalize the field of crime scene investigation. And there was no better way to do that than to partner with the University of Tennessee, where the brilliant anthropologist Dr. Bill Bass had already laid the groundwork with his one-of-a-kind facility, the Body Farm.

The two entities approached the Department of Justice for seed money to start what was then called the Forensic Science Academy. They got very little. Remember, this was before the attacks of September 11, 2001, and before "CSI" was a household term. Before the TV show *CSI*, the vast majority of departments called their investigators crime scene technicians, or CSTs, and funding crime scene schools was not a priority.

Not long into the planning, we decided that we needed a better name. After much debate and a hell of a lot of politics, we settled on the National Forensics Academy. When we called forensics programs across the country asking for information, however, we were quickly connected to the heads of debate teams. It turns out that in the academic world, especially back in 2000, the word *forensics* meant the art or study of formal debate. Thus, the *s* was dropped and the National Forensic Academy was born.

Since that time, the name is not the only thing that has changed. Each class has gotten better than the one before it, making the NFA the top training ground for crime scene investigators. Nowhere else in the world can CSIs receive comprehensive hands-on forensic training and learn the most cutting-edge techniques, taught by the best practitioners in the field today.

In January, May, and September of every year, a new batch of sixteen crime scene investigators from all across the country arrives in Knoxville, Tennessee, to begin our comprehensive ten-week course.

Who would come to east Tennessee for forensic training? Well, in the beginning, hardly anybody would. We had to practically beg departments to take a chance on us and send an officer through the program. In fact, we could barely give away a seat in the class. But we were persistent because we knew we had something that would change the world of crime scene investigation training forever. And now, nearly five years later, that persistence has paid off. After that first session, word spread like wildfire—not only across Tennessee, but across the entire country—and a lot of the world for that matter. We have a three-year waiting list of CSIs, and the list gets longer every day.

Admission into the academy is now highly competitive and selective. No longer is willingness to attend the standard for admission. For

Photograph of the building where the National Forensic Academy is housed.

(Collection of the National Forensic Academy)

starters, a candidate must be employed by a law enforcement agency as a crime scene investigator, crime scene technician, or as an officer who works crime scenes. The candidate's chief or sheriff must also write a letter of recommendation stating why that particular candidate would benefit from the program and how having an NFA graduate could benefit the entire department.

Our graduates are from all different types of law enforcement agencies from all across the country. We have trained police officers, sheriff's deputies, FBI agents, U.S. Army Criminal Investigation Division (CID) agents, state troopers, and Texas Rangers. We've had CSIs from the ten largest police departments attend the academy: New York, Los Angeles, Houston, Fort Lauderdale, Chicago, Miami-Dade, Orange County, Nassau County, Detroit, and Dallas. But the academy isn't just for large departments. We also have graduates from very small departments, such as the one in Dillon, Colorado.

The thing that makes the NFA so unique is that it is dedicated only to crime scene investigators. Sure, there are other schools and programs in the country that teach crime scene investigation on some level, but those classes are taught inside of a classroom, with students ranging from CSI buffs to stay-at-home moms to defense attorneys—anybody with a buck. Each and every day, we get letters, e-mails, and phone calls from wannabes, trying their best to get into our school. And they're often weird. The strangest of all was a midnight phone call from a man who worked in a morgue and wanted to attend the academy because he liked "to cut up body parts."

At the academy, we only accept cops. We've had veteran officers with more than twenty-five years' experience and rookie cops with no experience at all. But the fact remains that only law enforcement officers are allowed to attend. Of course, that cops-only rule makes it even more ironic that the academy is run by two people without law enforcement backgrounds. When we first started, we knew absolutely nothing about crime scene investigation, but now we can identify tache noire from merely dry eyes or a Tardieu spot from a freckle with the best of them. Before the academy was created, we had seen neither a maggot-covered body nor an autopsy. Now we eat candy in front of both. Change is not always for the good, however. There are certain things you should not become accustomed to, but we have. And trust us, the things we know cause us to lock our doors at night just a little tighter than most.

Everywhere we go, people want to know what it is really like to run the toughest forensic school in the country. *How did you get to be in this position?* We ask ourselves that same question every day and still haven't figured it out. Jarrett turned down an assistant city manager's job in Colorado to be part of the grant-writing team who ultimately created the academy. As brilliant as the team was, they forgot to include one integral component in the grant—someone to run the damn thing. Jarrett, as always, drew the short straw. Instead of putting his schooling to work, behind a desk, in the clean mountain air of Colorado, Jarrett chose the backbreaking rigors (no pun intended) of starting up a *very* understaffed CSI training school—not to mention the pungent air of the Body Farm. The rest, as they say, is history. Amy

Jarrett and Amy at the arson house.
(Copyright © Joanne Devlin, collection of the National Forensic Academy)

ended up at the academy by sheer luck. She was moving to Knoxville and needed a job. After two interviews she was hired as a program coordinator for the Law Enforcement Innovation Center, the parent agency of the NFA. After only a year on the job she migrated into the world of the academy, where she's been working ever since.

Our role in the academy is to make sure it runs like a well-oiled machine. *That hardly happens, but we still like to try.* We do almost everything. Not only are we responsible for all of the administrative duties, such as managing the budgets, but we also set up the mock crime scenes, make sure the students have all of the necessary equipment, and coordinate all of the logistics that go into a ten-week course. What we don't do is teach the students. For that, we bring in the experts. Our instructors come from all across the country, in fields ranging from forensic photography to behavioral analysis. We have a cadre of instructors over thirty strong with a combined total of nearly one thousand years of forensic experience.

As you'll soon discover, crime scene investigation is nothing like what it looks like on television. We don't wear high heels and leather jackets to any scenes; we do have to crawl around in the mud; and unbelievably, we do sweat. The field of crime scene investigation is not glamorous or high-paying. What you are about to read is real. It is our uncensored recounting of what we've done and what we've seen at the National Forensic Academy—from the houses we've burned to the cars we've blown up and, yes, even the bodies we've buried.

KEEP A-KNOCKIN',
BUT YOU CAN'T COME IN

Crime Scene Management

It's always interesting to meet a new class on the first day. We try to predict who will be the leader, the partier, the quiet one, the popular one. While it may sound juvenile, the personalities of the students are a real factor in the ten weeks. Now, you might be thinking, what could that have to do with forensic training? Well, not much if this was only a one-week course and students went home in the evening and came back the next morning. But the academy isn't like that. This is a ten-week, four-hundred-hour course in which the students are forced to live and work with each other in two-bedroom apartments. It's sort of a *CSI* meets *Survivor* meets *Fear Factor* atmosphere.

Day one at the National Forensic Academy is essentially a meet and greet. We spend the morning going around the room and having everyone introduce themselves. Then we review the entire ten-week schedule so they will begin to have an idea of what they have gotten themselves into. Later that morning we hand out equipment to each student that they will use throughout the duration of the program. We give them laptops, digital cameras, 35mm cameras, and crime scene kits that include: fingerprint powder, fingerprint lift tape, a handheld alternate light source (ALS, or FLS if it is termed a forensic light source; they are one in the same), scales, a magnifying glass, a ruler, tweezers, a scalpel, goggles, a flashlight, crime scene tape, and a host of other crime scene goodies. Also on the first day, it has become a tradition that we treat the students to lunch at the local University Club, where the students get to meet the world-renowned anthropologist Dr. Bill Bass and his wonderful wife, Carol, for the first time. After about a million pictures with Dr. Bass, the class returns to the academy classroom, where they learn about the safety procedures that will be in place for the next ten weeks. It's a relatively short day, designed to ease everyone into the program. The real training begins on day two, with the basics of crime scene management.

Okay, let's play a little *Jeopardy*. We will give you the answer; you give us the question. Answer: "These small objects are the most common item found at crime scenes." Question: "What are cigarette butts?" Cigarette butts seem to be the most common item found at crime scenes. There are no scientific studies that corroborate this, but it seems that the stress of committing a crime incites people to puff away. Cigarette butts can provide a whole lot of information for the investigator in the form of DNA evidence collected from the saliva. It has been estimated, however, that as much as 30 percent of all cigarette butts found at crime scenes are not left by the perpetrator, as one might assume, but by someone who actually processed the scene. It's a little disconcerting to think that so much time and money is wasted on a potential suspect, only to find out that "suspect" is the chief officer.

In the United States alone, there are over 18,000 law enforcement departments, with over one-quarter of a million officers—that's 250,000 people who have had little to no formalized training in the area of crime scene investigation. There are those out there who come to the NFA with the brash attitude of, "I've got thirty years' experience. What can you teach me?" In reality, that usually means they have had one week of bad training and have been practicing those bad habits for the last thirty years. These problems and attitudes are universal, regardless of the size of the department or the area of the country. You certainly do not have to live in Podunk, Kentucky, to witness bad crime scene management. Take Seattle, Washington, for example.

Gun violence was rampant in 1999. The Columbine massacre was at the forefront among school shootings, not to mention a cadre of workplace shootings that happened coast to coast. On November 4, 1999, a Honolulu man, armed with two shotguns, nine rifles, and eleven pistols, entered the office where he worked and killed seven of his colleagues. Then, the very next day, a man shot and killed two of his colleagues at a boatyard in Seattle, Washington. Each case, when you wipe away the tragedy and emotion, was a complicated crime scene. But by the time of the Seattle shootings, the politics surrounding gun violence and gun control had reached a fever pitch.

The second workplace shooting in a major U.S. city in two days garnered a lot of attention. At the time, Seattle was the largest U.S. city without a dedicated CSI unit. (It wasn't until the department sent an officer through our program in 2003 that they decided to create one with the information and training gathered at the academy.) Even before officers could respond to the scene the department received a call from the White House. The White House already knew many more details than the police department, and alerted them that the president would be visiting the crime scene ASAP.

As the officers began taping off the crime scene perimeter, Seattle PD brass began to arrive in droves. Captains and deputy chiefs, with the president in tow, began ducking under crime scene tape like turnstiles at Disneyland. To their credit, the officers working the scene were irate and verbalized their frustrations, especially since the suspect had not yet been apprehended. But their complaints fell on deaf ears, and the tour of the crime scene continued. Though the suspect was eventually found, the integrity of the crime scene had clearly been violated.

If you ask any CSI what the biggest problem they face in the field is, they will almost always say crime scene contamination. Contamination of the scene can not only mislead the investigation, it can also be a defense attorney's dream come true. Proper management of the crime scene is crucial in protecting against scene contamination. It is by far the most important part of the investigation. Crime scene management (CSM) is the foundation for everything else that occurs during the investigation, and that is why the National Forensic Academy teaches CSM during the first week. Because you get only one chance to work the crime scene properly, management of that scene is crucial to solving the case. Once evidence has been moved and the scene has been released, it is too late to go back if you missed something.

Eight Steps to Working a Crime Scene

On day two the students learn the stages of basic crime scene management. Academy students are taught that there are eight steps to working a crime scene:

1. Approach the scene.
2. Secure and protect the scene.
3. Conduct a preliminary survey.
4. Photograph the scene.
5. Sketch a diagram of the scene.
6. Perform a detailed search for evidence.
7. Collect the evidence.
8. Conduct the final survey.

These steps should always be conducted in order, except for photographing the scene, which can and should be done upon arrival and all the way through the final stage of working the crime scene. In later weeks the students will learn about each step in much greater depth and scope.

APPROACH THE SCENE

Approaching the scene is the most basic of all concepts relating to crime scene investigation. Ten years ago, the approach would be to exit your vehicle and look for possible discarded evidence that might lie at the perimeter of the crime scene, such as in garbage cans or culverts, and then move right on into the crime scene area. In today's world, however, the investigator must be alert to the possibility of two very dangerous situations: a terrorist attack/weapon of mass destruction

(WMD) or a methamphetamine laboratory. Though the two are equally dangerous, the latter has become extremely common all across the nation and is of growing concern for CSIs because of the possibilities of explosives and/or hazardous materials being scattered about the scene. As an example, a recent graduate of the academy responded to a crime scene that housed a meth lab. The lab subsequently exploded, and he now has only 35 percent function in his lungs. Now a major concern to the CSI, investigators approach every crime scene as if it were a meth lab, just in case.

After safety issues are addressed, it is important that the circumstances surrounding the scene be evaluated immediately to assess the need for extra help or to prepare for the possibilities of emotional friends and relatives. Finally, personal protection equipment (PPE) is distributed, including gloves, masks, and booties to protect the CSI from infectious diseases, and to protect the integrity of the crime scene as well.

SECURE AND PROTECT THE SCENE

The next step of CSM is to secure and protect the scene. The CSI should determine how much the scene has been secured prior to his or her arrival, and then ensure that only authorized personnel are allowed access. An officer should keep a log of everyone who enters the scene, and take photographs of the soles of the shoes of everyone who is on the log to eliminate them from any footwear prints that might be found.

The golden rule of crime scene management is to not move anything! This seems like common sense, right? But how many times on TV have you seen the investigator walk into a scene and immediately pick up the murder weapon? Probably more times than you can count, and it's a huge mistake. This happens in real life as well. Not long ago, we saw scene photographs of a dead body taken from two different angles. In one picture, the body is lying on its side, facing the right. In the next picture the body is lying on its back, facing the ceiling. When the investigator was asked how this could be, the response was that the victim's mother was so upset the officers at the scene let her come into the room and hold the victim in her arms one last time. Yet another example of scene contamination.

CONDUCT A PRELIMINARY SURVEY

Once the scene is secure, the CSI can begin to work. This is basically just a walk-through in which the CSI observes what he or she sees and begins thinking of a narrative description. On the show *CSI* they walk right into a scene and begin their investigation. Wrong. This is a common mistake. Time after time, potential evidence is destroyed within the first few minutes of working a crime scene. Before the CSI even enters a residence, he or she must always shine a flashlight obliquely across the floor. What the CSI is looking for is a possible footwear impression made in dust that lies on carpet or hardwood floors. These dust prints can be lifted with an electrostatic dust lifter. This is why we teach our students to photographically document the soles of the shoes of everyone who will be working the scene and also to have them wear booties. That way, if a footprint is found, there is no question that it was not left by someone working the scene.

At this stage, the investigator learns to walk through the scene and to recognize certain areas of importance. Once the entire scene has been checked out the CSI will determine the search area that will be the focus for evidence collection. It is also during this time that the CSI needs to determine whether there is enough manpower and equipment for evidence collection. For instance, if a mattress needs to be taken to a lab for evidence, how will it be transported? This step is also a good time to look for transient evidence—evidence that might not last long or is easily lost—such as dust and hair.

This is also the point at which the investigator begins to take notes and think about the crime scene, trying to mentally reconstruct what might have happened, or determine if the scene itself might have been staged.

This step includes a narrative, which is merely the running description, supplemented by photo, video, and audio, of the condition of the crime scene in general terms. The investigator must thoroughly represent the crime scene, and nothing is insignificant. The more detail the better. Depending on the type of crime scene, it may be years before the case is adjudicated, and by that time hundreds of cases will have come and gone. All that the investigator will have to jog her memory when she goes to trial will be her narrative.

PHOTOGRAPH THE SCENE

There is nothing more important in crime scene investigation than photography, and there is nothing more underappreciated. We spend week two of the training on nothing but photography instruction, and for the rest of the course the camera is used during every single week. Most students in the class believe that they are already experts when it comes to this part of crime scene investigation because they have been taking pictures for years. The problem is that most of them take pictures like the average person—point and shoot. That is a no-no. Unfortunately, the vast majority of CSI photography courses in the United States involve CSIs going out to gardens or to marinas to take pictures of boats and flowers. These classes are predominantly taught by professional photographers who take pictures of babies on weekends—not crime scenes. At the academy, we take pictures of crime scenes.

When arriving at a scene, it is imperative to begin taking photographs as soon as possible—before anything in the scene is disturbed—and to take as many as possible thereafter. Film is cheap and you get only one chance to document the scene. If a piece of hair needs to be collected for evidence, a picture must be taken of it first so it can be documented as to where it was in the scene. Crime scene photographs will be the main documentation to refer to once everyone has left the scene, and they just might be the only piece of evidence a jury sees.

Most departments require their investigators to maintain a photo log of each picture taken. In recent years, however, it is the prevailing thought that a log limits the number of pictures that the investigator will take. We teach them to do what their department requires them to do, but to take as many as necessary and then some. It is better to photograph everything and have several pictures that turn out to be useless than not to photograph enough and to learn later that something critical was missed.

SKETCH A DIAGRAM OF THE SCENE

In addition to photographs, a sketch of the crime scene can help illustrate what the scene looked like. A diagram does not replace scene photographs. It is just another tool to help document the scene. The sketch shows the relationships of size and distance between different objects.

While at the scene a rough sketch is drawn and distance and size is recorded. Later the CSI will do a precise sketch either by hand or by computer. A CSI does not have to be an artist to draw a sketch. In fact, most use computers to sketch the scene for them. But for the many departments that do not have such high-tech tools, crime scene templates are available to aid those who sketch by hand. In order for the sketch to be legally submitted as evidence in court, it must be accurate and the testimony must actually come from the CSI who created the sketch.

PERFORM A DETAILED SEARCH FOR EVIDENCE

In step six, the search for evidence begins. Before evidence can be collected, it must be found. This, above all other steps, is the process where CSIs usually miss the mark. A detailed search involves searching every nook and cranny from top to bottom. It involves every air-conditioning vent and every light fixture. It requires CSIs to crawl on their hands and knees through the entire perimeter of the crime scene. Through the mud, through the snow, through the sewer. It is not glamorous; it is a lot of hard work. We find it extremely difficult to convince most investigators of the importance of this step, so we practice it a lot. For instance, we might throw a handful of spent cartridge casings into tall grass and have the students find them. We cannot tell you how often we hear stories of graduates who go back to their departments and find critical evidence while on their knees.

There are three things that really make a case: evidence, evidence, evidence. It is evidence that proves whether a crime has been committed; it is evidence that proves whether a particular suspect committed a crime; and it is evidence that exonerates the innocent. Think of the most famous cases of all time, and it will be the evidence or lack thereof that made or broke the case. There is an investigative theory

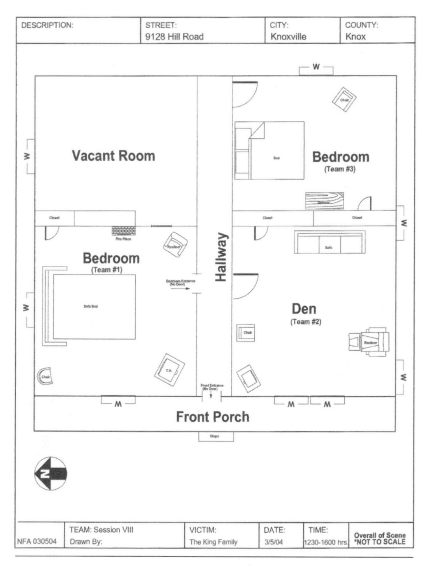

DESCRIPTION:	STREET: 9128 Hill Road	CITY: Knoxville	COUNTY: Knox

W

Vacant Room

Chair

Bed

Bedroom
(Team #3)

W

Dresser

Closet

Fire Place

Closet

Closet

W

Bedroom
(Team #1)

Recliner

Sofa

Hallway

Bedroom Entrance
(No Door)

Sofa Bed

Den
(Team #2)

W

Chair

Recliner

Chair

T.V.

Front Entrance
(No Door)

M

M

M

M

Front Porch

Steps

N

NFA 030504	TEAM: Session VIII Drawn By:	VICTIM: The King Family	DATE: 3/5/04	TIME: 1230-1600 hrs.	Overall of Scene *NOT TO SCALE

Example of a mock crime scene sketch.

(Collection of the National Forensic Academy)

called the Theory of Transfer that states that no one can enter a location without bringing in and depositing some type of evidence, and that no one can leave a location without taking some sort of evidence with them. Finding it is nearly always the key to solving the crime.

COLLECT THE EVIDENCE

What is collected at a scene is characterized in a broad category termed *physical evidence*. Physical evidence is what it sounds like—weapons, fingerprints, glass, footwear impressions, body fluids, and so on. Within that category there are two subcategories, trace evidence and impression evidence. Trace evidence is microscopic or pseudo-microscopic evidence. This type of evidence tends to be very minute. Things like hair, paint chips, DNA, and particles of dirt are examples. Impression evidence consists of items that you technically don't collect, but merely make a copy of. For example, if a footprint is found at a crime scene, a cast is made and the cast is taken back to the department. The actual footprint itself is not taken. Tool marks are another example. Let's say a hammer was used to pry open a door. That hammer will leave marks on the door. Now, that door can be taken off its hinges and sent to the lab to be analyzed, but the more practical and most common way to obtain that piece of evidence is to make an impression of the tool mark and send the impression to the lab.

This step is by far the most intensive step in crime scene management. Recording and collecting the evidence can take several hours, even days, to complete. Once all of the evidence has been photographed and documented, collection can begin. CSIs must pay special attention to detail during evidence collection. Each piece of evidence must be carefully labeled so no mix-ups occur. Sometimes this step can take the CSI away from the scene. In cases of bombings, it is common to find pieces of shrapnel still embedded in the skin of the victim, so it is necessary to go to the hospital to collect the evidence before it gets thrown away.

All evidence needs to be marked appropriately, handled sparingly, and sealed into appropriate containers with evidence tape. Appropriate containers vary, but generally speaking, light, dry items can be placed in paper bags. Insects and spent cartridge casings can be placed into plastic jars. Guns and knives should be collected into appropriate boxes. Finally, wet or contaminated debris, such as evidence from an arson scene or a vehicle explosion, should be placed in paint cans. If at all possible, someone on-site should be designated as the custodian of the evidence. This person holds the ultimate responsibility for evidence transportation and storage.

CONDUCT THE FINAL SURVEY

Conducting the final survey is the last chance the CSI will have to make a difference at the scene. There are two rules that should be considered before the scene is ultimately released upon completion. One, physical evidence can never, ever be overdocumented or overcollected. (Crime laboratories across the country will cringe upon reading that statement.) And second, there is only one chance to perform the job properly. We teach the students that even if one day they have to go back to the scene, it will never be the same as the day they arrived, so they should work it to completion. Discuss with all of those involved at the scene whether they have finished their work. The CSI should take more pictures as he or she leaves to illustrate, in case there is ever any question, how the scene looked when it was left. Finally, CSIs should be sure not to leave any tools behind—that leads to too many questions.

Footwear and Fingerprints

As the training builds from week to week, all types of evidence are dealt with. We start out slowly by dealing with two of the most basic forms of evidence: footwear and fingerprints. The first hands-on activity that we do at the academy is to learn how to properly cast a footwear impression. Casting footwear has been shown on every television show from the *Andy Griffith Show* to *Law & Order*. It is the most basic form of evidence collection. The way you properly cast is to take a large Ziploc bag and pour about sixteen ounces of dental stone into the bag with about sixteen ounces of water, zip the bag, and knead the mixture until it is the consistency of pancake batter. Once you have the proper consistency, you unzip one corner of the bag and grab a stick or a plastic spoon and pour the mixture slowly over the spoon and into the impression. The spoon keeps the liquid from splashing and disturbing the fine points that lie within the impression.

As with anything in our world today, companies have tried to complicate this simple process. The forensic supply industry is an ever-growing, multimillion-dollar-a-year industry—an industry that is always looking for ways to make more money. For instance, with very little exception, the best substance for casting footwear impressions is dental stone and water, just like what we use at the academy. But there are about as many different substances sold by these companies as there are law enforcement agencies. These compounds are typically dental stone supplemented by some other substance that needs a reactor other than water to work. So you must purchase the supply company's reactor as well as their casting material. To put it in perspective, a nine-pound box of dental stone costs about thirty dollars and gives you an average of ten castings. The other compound is about the same price, but it will make only one, very poor cast.

At the NFA, we like our students to experiment with things while they're here, and we buy various products to give them a try. Sometimes the products turn out to offer a valuable lesson. "Smurf poop," as it is affectionately known at the NFA, is a casting product that comes premeasured in a bag with about four ounces of a blue reactor. When you pour the reactor into the bag and knead the mixture, all you get is a chunky substance about the consistency of fudge. You need a stick or a spoon in order to reach back into the bag to dig out the thick mixture. It is simply expensive and unusable.

The students, once they are done playing with the Smurf poop, begin to cast their own impressions with the dental stone. Every class is the same: Eight students do it right, three mix it too thick, three mix it too thin, and two pour it on themselves—no joke. The first casts the students make are poured into an impression pressed into a product called BioFoam. It is simply a foam material in a box about as big as a shoe that you step into to make an impression. (It looks like the green foam that florists use to hold the stems of flowers, and it is used for

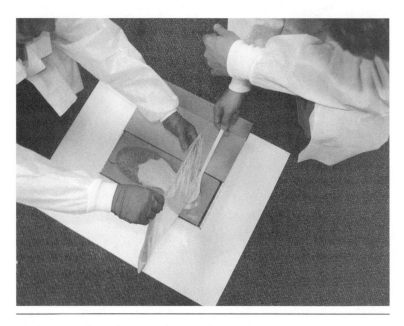

Students casting a footwear impression in BioFoam.
(Copyright © John Freeze, collection of the National Forensic Academy)

many things, including the making of orthodontics.) Then the class moves outside to cast footwear impressions made in sand, dirt, and mud using the same dental stone process.

Almost any impression can be cast, whether it is in BioFoam or dirt or even flour. Of course, the finer the material the impression is in, the more difficult it is to cast. Go ahead and try it. Take some flour and pour it onto your kitchen counter. Now, make a handprint in the flour and then pour pancake mix onto it without disturbing the print and all of the ridges. And don't sneeze, either. Here's a little trick that investigators use while making a cast, especially when the material is fine, like flour. Before the cast is poured into the impression, Aquanet hairspray (this is the only brand that is stiff enough) is sprayed onto it. This helps keep the impression intact while the cast is poured into it.

The second most basic form of evidence and probably the most well known is the fingerprint. Fingerprint collection is the cornerstone of crime scene investigation. We spend a lot of time on fingerprints, but

The blue casting product we refer to as "Smurf poop."

(Collection of the National Forensic Academy)

Session Eight graduate Eric Rish pours a cast in BioFoam.

(Collection of the National Forensic Academy)

initially we just like for the students to get acclimated to fingerprints by taking their own. We divide the class up into pairs and have students print their partners, taking major case prints. Major case prints are taken when a suspect is brought into custody during the investigation of what is considered to be a "major case" (murder, rape, or armed robbery, for example).

Most people think of fingerprints as actually that, the prints left by the finger. But the hand, on all sides, is just as unique to you as your fingers. The printing of the individual in a major case takes into account the whole hands. First, fingerprints are taken on fingerprint cards. The cards are similar to index cards, but they have been divided into five sections—one section for each finger. If you have ever had your fingerprints taken, say as part of a background check, then you are familiar with the process. Each finger is taken and pressed onto an ink pad. The CSI then takes the fingerprint by rolling the finger away from the suspect onto the card. The same is done for the thumb, except it is rolled towards the suspect. This is because of the body position of the thumb, making it easier for the person taking the print to roll. Next, the length of each finger and thumb is printed, making sure the creases are clearly visible. This is done by pressing the finger from the base to the tip, but not rolling it like before. Major case prints are extremely important because you never know what part of the hand might actually be discovered at a crime scene.

COLD FEET

Casting a footwear impression in the snow can be difficult. The cast will usually either freeze or fail to set up. One way to combat this is to use sulfur pellets. The method is simple. All the CSI needs to do is to take common sulfur pellets and heat them on a camp stove until they are dissolved. Once they are dissolved, the hot liquid can be poured slowly into the impression. The liquid sulfur cools on contact and creates a great cast of the impression.

Then the students move to the palms of the hand. Most investigators simply ink up the roller (like a small rubber paint roller), roll it up and down the hand, and have the suspect place each hand palm-down on a piece of blank white paper. But by doing it this way you cannot place a person's palm completely flat on a surface. At the academy, we are much more thorough.

Palm prints are fast becoming the new standard when it comes to latent prints. Like AFIS (Automated Fingerprint Identification System), the newly developed APIS (Automated Palmprint Identification System) will assist investigators in getting more hits by having a database that houses known palm prints of criminals. The study of palm prints is still in its infancy, and that is one of the reasons we teach it at the academy.

Essentially there are five main parts of the palm print. There is the thenar side (the fat part of the palm near the thumb). The opposite of the thenar is the hypothenar, which is the fatty part of the hand near the pinkie. Next is the interdigital part of the palm print. This is the fleshy area just below each finger. The other two parts of the palm print are the starburst (the skin flap area where the thumb connects to the hand), and the laser, or "karate chop," side of the hand.

In combination with these five areas, the major lines within the palm are also used in helping to identify a person. These lines are the distal transverse crease (the major line just under the fingers that goes across the palm), the proximal transverse crease (the line that is in the middle of the hand that moves diagonally within the palm), and the longitudinal radial crease (the diagonal line nearest the thumb).

The best way to take a palm print is to roll it, and the best way to do that is with a two-inch PVC pipe, cut about twelve to fourteen inches in length. A piece of plain white copy paper is wrapped around the pipe and secured with a rubber band. After the suspect's hand is inked, the students take the suspect's hand and roll the hand over the pipe, making sure to get the creases all the way down in the wrist. Once completed, each hand is reinked, another sheet of paper is placed on a flat surface, and the hand is rolled from the thumb to the little finger, capturing the indentations on the meaty part of the side of the hand.

What comes next is the most difficult part of taking major case

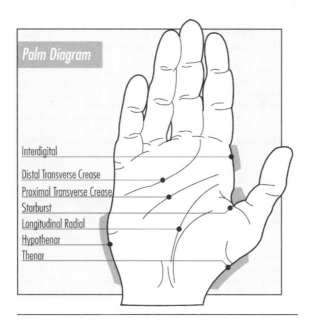

Palm Diagram

Interdigital

Distal Transverse Crease

Proximal Transverse Crease

Starburst

Longitudinal Radial

Hypothenar

Thenar

Diagram of the palm.

(Illustration by Pamela Johanns of Johanns Design)

prints. Each finger must be printed two more times from different angles. First, the finger is printed from the base and then rolled to the tip. Then the finger is printed from one side, rolled to the tip, and back down to the other side. These are all taken, starting with the finger at a forty-five-degree angle.

Only the most thorough departments take major case prints to the degree described above, and even fewer take this next print—the karate chop. Our instructors teach the students about the importance of this side of the hand. A lot of the students ask why they should care about this side of the hand because it is not a common print to take. Here's the answer.

All too often in crimes at houses, the CSI focuses on prints left inside of the house without considering what prints might exist on the outside. There are two common places to check. The first place is the light fixtures on houses, especially those that have exposed lightbulbs.

The perpetrator will invariably unscrew the bulb until the light goes out, without actually removing it, possibly leaving a print. Second, and this is where the karate chop side of the hand comes into play, the perpetrator sometimes will look into the windows of a residence the day of the crime, or even before if they have cased the residence. How do you look into the windows of a house from the outside? If you're like most people, you cup your hands around your eyes and press the sides of your hands to the window as you peer through, leaving a curled version of the karate-chop side of the hand imprinted on the window. Outside light fixtures and windows are two places that prints should always be looked for and the reason we stress the importance of major case prints. You never know what part of the hand might actually be discovered.

As week one comes to a close, we get a real sense of how the next nine weeks will go. We have not even begun to teach the components of the class that have made us famous, and yet we already start to get feedback about how much the students have learned. We are truly amazed that anyone ever catches a bad guy. Not because of the lack of good intentions, but because of the lack of training that is out there. Most of this stuff seems like common sense to us, but we live it every day, with some of the best practitioners in the country. We've learned that you cannot assume what someone should know, because everyone brings with them varying life experiences and knowledge. And you can throw out what you have seen on CSI—that's not real. The best you can hope for, the best we can hope for, is a student's willingness—a willingness to learn and a willingness to put into practice what is learned. And that's what ultimately makes a difference.

EVERY PICTURE TELLS A STORY
Photography

Do you know anyone who owns an argon laser? A Total Station? How about a cyanoacrylate fuming machine? Probably not. But how many people do you know who own a camera?

The common 35mm camera is the CSIs most important and most misused tool. Believe it or not, the same camera you use to capture the precious moments of li'l Johnny's birthday is the same camera that CSIs use to photograph all those bloody crime scenes. And unfortunately, chances are good that neither of you really knows how to use it.

When students arrive at the academy and we review the schedule for the next ten weeks, there is always a discernible groan when they find out they will spend an entire week on crime scene photography. Because the camera has become as commonplace in the home as the telephone, everyone already assumes they know how to use one. As a result, crime scene photography is treated so nonchalantly in some departments that disposable point-and-shoot cameras are standard issue. It's frightening to think that some agencies would treat the evidence surrounding your daughter's murder with no more than a $5.95 disposable camera bought at the checkout of a local drugstore.

Proper crime scene photography is a dying art, a fact that is fast becoming a recognized problem nationwide. Veteran CSIs who have mastered the art of crime scene photography are retiring to pursue other ventures in mainstream America, like photographing weddings or family portraits. All of this knowledge is leaving and not being replaced. This problem is further compounded by the pop culture movement of forensic science on television.

Forensic television shows have glamorized one-of-a-kind or extraordinarily expensive and impractical pieces of crime scene equipment. That is not to say that this equipment is not good equipment, because it is. Yet only the largest departments in the nation or national laboratories would have the money to afford them or the access to use them. If they do have enough money to buy these elaborate devices, they might only use them once every couple of years. Let's face it, the camera just ain't cool.

Here is an example of how the camera is used on *CSI*:

A dead body is discovered. The CSIs arrive and walk under the crime scene tape—without taking pictures of the soles of their shoes or wearing booties, mind you. Grissom leans over the body and quips something moderately funny as The Who blare in with the theme song. Then someone on the CSI team takes out their camera, twists the lens one time as if to focus, aims the camera directly over the top of the evidence, and snaps a picture with the flash, regardless of the lighting at the crime scene, as they drag out their laser beams and mass spectrometers to get onto the "cool and glamorous" stuff.

The National Forensic Academy, unlike *CSI*, takes crime scene photography very seriously. Each person at the NFA is issued a complete 35mm camera kit, which includes: a Nikon n80 camera body, three lenses (28-105mm, 70-300mm, and a 60mm micro lens), a detachable flash, a flash extension cord, a synchronization cord used to synchronize the flash, various filters, a Sony DSC-700 digital camera, and all of the film they can use. We use an unbelievable amount of film and batteries over the course of ten weeks—nearly one thousand rolls of film and over three hundred AA batteries. That is another thing that makes our training unique: We let the students take as many pictures as they can and develop each and every one of them. Not being a for-profit entity allows us to worry less about the bottom line and more about giving the students every opportunity to learn. The first part of the day is spent just handing out photography equipment. After lunch, the instruction begins.

Characteristics of Light

Imagine that it is midnight on the clearest night with the fullest moon you have ever seen. You have decided that you want to preserve the moment forever. So you grab your trusty 35mm camera with flash and *snap*, you take the picture. Does it turn out? It seems almost intuitive that in order to take a good picture when there is little light that you should use a flash—and the darker the night, the brighter the flash. Not exactly.

Light is the key to photography of any kind, and it is important for the class to understand some characteristics of light before they ever take the first picture. Light, or, more precisely, wavelengths of light, fall into both the visible and nonvisible spectrums. The visible spectrum of light is between roughly 400 and 700 nanometers, with the shortest visible wavelength being violet and longest visible being red. Anything below 400 nanometers is ultraviolet light, and anything above 700 nanometers is infrared. Both of these wavelengths emit radiation and can cause film to expose. Thus, it is true that the X-ray machines at airports can expose and ruin film.

Visible light will either be absorbed by an object, transmitted through an object, or, most important, reflected by an object. Reflected light is what determines the colors that we see. For example, if something looks red, then the object absorbs the majority of the green and blue wavelengths, and reflects the red. This is why white looks white and black looks black. White surfaces reflect over 95 percent of the visible spectrum, and black surfaces reflect less than 2 percent. Because light is vastly more complex than it would seem, the CSI, or anyone for that matter, should never take a picture without using a meter to measure reflected light—that is, unless you do not want the correct exposure.

The great thing about modern, single lens reflex (SLR) cameras is that they have built-in meters and an automatic shooting mode. But the automatic mode for the CSI is more of a curse than a blessing. Automatic SLR cameras are calibrated to read at 18 percent reflectance value, or essentially middle gray. Here is why that is a problem.

Most CSIs, our students included, would traditionally use the automatic mode, allowing the camera to determine the light conditions. Yet if the CSI takes a reading at a crime scene from a single luminous, white surface (remember, this is a surface that reflects 95 percent of visible light), then the camera meter will underexpose the film, making the white surface look gray. The reverse is true if the surface is black. The camera meter will overexpose the film, turning the black surface gray. While taking pictures at a crime scene, it is important to achieve the proper film exposure so that the crime scene is presented to a jury as visually accurately as possible. This ensures that what is being stated in court can be proven with a picture. For example, if a murder occurred in a residence where bloodstains were cast about onto white walls, the CSI would have a challenge making sure the pictures reflected reality. If the CSI simply takes the camera and points and shoots, without taking a meter reading, it is very possible that the white wall turns out looking gray, while the bloodstains are muted because of the color contrast. These pictures would not only fail to represent the crime scene accurately, they would also create doubt in a jury about the capabilities of the crime scene investigator working the scene. In order to achieve proper exposure of the film at a crime scene, it is imperative to turn the camera off of automatic and to take a reading at the scene, metering a Kodak 18 percent reflectance neutral gray card. This will ensure proper exposure of the film each and every time. This is done by taking the gray card and having someone hold it wherever the focus of the picture will be. Then the meter is aimed at the card and the amount of flash needed will register on the device. Armed with this new information, the class begins to practice using the camera, instead of what was true before—the camera using them.

It takes a while for the students to get used to actually using all of the features on a camera. Really, electronic gadgets come with such a wide array of features that most people never use anything more than the basic functions. We all love ease of use. If a phone rings, a VCR records, and a DVD player plays, then we are happy. Our instructors refer to it as "cashier syndrome." Years ago, before the advent of digital adding machines, a cashier could make change by doing simple math in her head. Try getting a cashier to make change today without the use of a cash register. Half the time, all you get is an open mouth and an echo. Technology might make things easier, but not necessarily better.

This exercise helps break down the habits the students have of doing things the same way they have always done them. This is still very early in the class, and remember, we are still winning over the students. Cops are no different from any other group. They think they know everything. Well, they might be a *little* different. You have to show them, show them again, prove it works, show them again, and start the process all over again. Eventually, they cave and the information sinks in.

Choosing the Correct Film

Film is the next topic of discussion. Police departments, like most people, are budget-conscious and buy whatever is on sale, no matter what the speed. Film is film, right? Film comes in 100, 200, 400, and 800 speed. This speed is calculated by an arithmetic scale, where a doubling of the sensitivity is indicated by a doubling of the speed. Thus, for each doubling of the speed, the required exposure for a given scene is cut in half. For example, if a CSI moves from 100 speed film to 200 speed film, then he or she should adjust the exposure time by one-half. Film speed also tells the grain size of a particular film. For instance, though you think of higher-speed film as being faster, it simply means that it is more sensitive to light. The number refers ultimately to the shutter speed that can be used in conjunction with the type of film. The problem with fast film is that the picture itself will suffer, because in order to be fast, color and clarity must be sacrificed. Hence, the general rule we preach at the academy is to always, always use the slowest film possible to get the job done. If CSIs carry plenty of 200 and 400 speed film, they will never face a situation they cannot properly photograph.

Up to this point, the class has been given important background information on photography and light metering, without really getting into how to properly use the camera. With boredom and fidgeting on the rise, we turn the class loose with a roll of film and allow them to take snapshots. The only directions they are given are to take some close-up shots, some outside and inside shots, and some photos in the light as well as in the dark. At the end of the day, we collect all of the film and have it processed overnight at one of the local drugstores. The instructors will take a look at each student's pictures the next morning.

After the film has been developed and distributed to the students, three words echo throughout the academy: The pictures stink. Many of the photos are underexposed or out of focus or both. That is, if the students have even remembered to put film in the camera. We had a twenty-year veteran CSI, from one of the largest agencies in the country, take pictures for an entire day without ever using the first roll of film. You would think that eventually, after about sixty pictures, you would begin to wonder why you haven't had to change the film. It is like watching an old Western movie, where nobody ever reloads their six-shooter, even though they have fired it a hundred times. Needless to say, that person was embarrassed. We can guarantee you that no one ever made that mistake again.

The Camera Lens

The lens is the "seeing eye" of the camera. We use three different lenses at the academy, and each has a specific purpose. The normal lens, or the lens that most closely resembles human vision, is the workhorse of the CSI. For a 35mm camera, a lens with a focal length between 45 and 60 millimeters is considered normal. In court these pictures will resemble how people see in real life. This lens should be used whenever feasible. Many CSIs choose to use shorter focal length lenses or wide-angle lenses all the time because it is possible to get more of the scene in one shot. But these pictures will be distorted and will need a lot of explaining in court, since everything in the foreground will appear larger and everything in the background will seem smaller. Although we issue these lenses to the students, wide-angle lenses should only be used when space limitations prevent using other lenses.

The other lens we use at the academy is the 60mm micro lens. This lens is perfect for close-ups. This is where the concept of depth of field becomes crucial. Depth of field refers to the focusing of objects within a picture. In photography, it is only possible to focus on one plane at one time. Though all images within the photo will be sharp, the areas just in front of and just in back of the primary area of focus will be what is termed as reasonably sharp, meaning some distortion will occur within these areas. These three areas combine to form the depth of field. In order to take a good close-up shot, a micro lens must be used. This is because the lens is created so that as the aperture (the diameter of the lens opening that allows light into the camera) is reduced, the depth of field increases. Apertures are measured as fractions of focal length. For example, a 60mm lens with a diameter of 30mm has a relative aperture of f/2, the focal length divided by two.

We teach our students that in order to take a great close-up shot, they must be proficient in using the copy stand in conjunction with their camera. A copy stand is a specialized tripod used for taking pictures of evidence at a micro level. The stand itself has a two-foot-by-two-foot wooden base, with a grid system outlined at the bottom. This will help the students align evidence on the base in a straight line. The stand has extension arms with lights mounted on each side of the base that can be swiveled to virtually any angle, shining light across the piece of evidence. Angling the light minimizes glaring and shadowing in the photograph. The last element of the copy stand is the camera support. The camera support is a bar that holds the camera steadily in place, with the lens facing downward. The mechanism that holds the camera rests on an interlocking wheel system that allows the operator to move the camera up and down the bar to various heights by simply turning a dial. Some great accessories we have for the copy stand are various size clamps and adjustable pedestals to rest the evidence on if it is very small. These items help hold the evidence in place and free up the CSI's hands to take the shot. Finally, before the picture is taken, a scale must be placed in close proximity to the evidence to further illustrate the size of the evidence. No evidence should ever be photographed without a scale and a direction marker.

All of this information will allow our students to be able to take good close-up shots of evidence. This is of paramount importance to be a good crime scene photographer. Oftentimes, evidence like fingerprints are found on objects such as bricks or foam cups. These items are much more difficult to lift fingerprints off of. Hence, a picture of the developed print might be the only available evidence. Close-up shots allow the investigator to take a photo of the fingerprint and run it through AFIS without actually having the print itself.

The last part of the photography lecture deals with the camera's shutter. The shutter controls the intensity of the light exposing the film inside of the camera. Most 35mm cameras have a shutter dial ranging from B to 4000. The setting B will keep the shutter open as long as it is

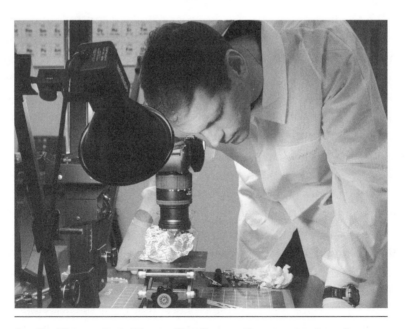

Session Five graduate Warren Hamlin uses the copy stand to take a picture of a fingerprint.

(Collection of the National Forensic Academy)

depressed. The purpose of the shutter speed is to eliminate movement of the subject and camera during exposure of the film. Playing with the various settings on the shutter will allow a photographer to take pictures that create a feeling of movement. This is not important to the CSI. What is important is to minimize movement and blurring within a photograph. This is achieved by using a shutter speed that is equal to or greater than the focal length.

Flash

We've taught the class just about everything regarding the 35mm camera except what many consider to be the most important part—the flash. The flash is an invaluable tool for the CSI. For the layperson, the flash is merely a tool to add light where there is a limited amount. Yet for the crime scene investigator, the flash is so much more. When used properly, the flash can maintain proper color representation, accentuate patterns by bringing out details, increase the depth of field, and fill in shadows. The problem with the flash is that its luminosity decreases greatly as the distance between the flash and the subject increases. This is why snapping a photo of the moon with the flash dialed up on high will do nothing to increase the quality of the picture, unless you have a flash that extends up into space. This is why the aperture, the iris of the camera, must be opened wider the farther the CSI gets from the subject.

Like many of the attributes of the 35mm camera, the flash has an automatic mode. As we have already learned, this is not necessarily the best mode for the CSI to take pictures in. Therefore, it is important for our students to have a complete understanding of the many functions of the flash unit. Here is where we stop for the day. In order to practice using the flash, we end class early, take an extended dinner break, and reconvene when the sun goes down.

The first exercise the class goes through is flash-shutter synchronization. Flash-shutter synchronization is a fun, practical exercise. We go into the auditorium and set up the camera on a tripod in the back of the room. For this exercise, it is best to have four people. One person operates the camera, one person operates the flash on an extension, one person covers the camera lens, and the other person will be the subject in the picture.

In a two-hundred-seat auditorium, one person can be shown in one photograph sitting in every single seat just by taking one picture. The way this special effect is accomplished is by first darkening the auditorium. Next, one student takes a piece of cardboard, or anything similar, and covers the lens of the camera. The aperture of the camera is left open. Then the subject sits in any seat in the auditorium. The trick in taking the picture is in the timing. With the lens covered, and the camera and flash operators in position, the picture is taken. This is accomplished by the students synchronizing the activities of moving the cover off of the lens, while at the same time firing the flash. The mystery person in the auditorium will be exposed onto the film. Immediately after the picture is taken, the lens must once again be covered back up. When this is repeated, with the subject moving all over the auditorium seat by seat, he or she will show up in multiple seats in one picture. This is a really cool trick, and yes, it does have a practical application when combined with the forensic photography technique "painting with light."

Painting with light is a forensic photography technique very few CSIs know how to perform. It is a way to literally light up the night to fully expose and colorize the scene for the photograph. This is the one task that we teach at the academy that all students rave about immediately. In order to understand this process, we teach it in the context of a crime scene. Imagine a car wreck that has occurred in the middle of the night, in a very dimly lit area. There is the car, as well as various other pieces of evidence that have been scattered about as close as twenty feet and as far away as three hundred. This process takes two sets of hands and, therefore, two students. First, the camera is set up with 400 speed film and placed on a tripod. Then one person operates the camera as the other fires the flash to light the area. The camera's aperture is turned to the setting that calculates the distance from the flash to the subject, with the shutter left wide open. One student fires the flash at a forty-five-degree angle, in the direction away from the camera, from wherever the initial picture is taken. The student operating the flash will continue to fire the flash, illuminating the scene, while the other continues to take the pictures, being very careful not to over-

Session Nine graduate Kent Warren practices trick photography during our nighttime photography class.
(Collection of the National Forensic Academy)

lap exposures. When more lighting is needed, the student operating the camera can shine his or her flashlight outward from where the camera is set up in a figure-eight motion. This helps ensure the right amount of luminescence within the scene. After each picture, the lens is covered back up. If done correctly, this will give one, very illuminated picture of the entire crime scene. It has been said by many people within the law enforcement community that painting with light cannot be performed with a digital camera. *Wrong again.* This can be done better with a digital camera, with even fewer flashes.

Contrary to popular belief, the flash is just as important in bright sunshine as it is in the dark. The class learns this the following day. Our instructors pay special attention in the early part of the photography class to see which students take pictures in the daytime and do not use the flash (none of them ever do). This is the biggest mistake amateur photographers make. The flash is invaluable even when there is plenty

LIGHTS OUT

Ambient lights make nighttime photography extremely challenging. This is especially true if the light is emanating from above in the form of a streetlight. One way the CSI can control the amount of light at a nighttime crime scene is to take the camera's flash and aim it at the streetlight's sensor and fire the flash. When the flash is fired, the streetlight will be fooled into thinking that it is daytime and go out, giving the CSI a few minutes to take the shot.

of light. The human eye can see more colors, nuances, and contrasts than the best, modern photography equipment can. Film cannot match what the human eye sees. Therefore, CSIs have got to take pictures as close to what the human eye can see as they possibly can.

The best film for taking pictures in daylight and filling in the shadows is 200 speed. This is contrary to what the back of the film box suggests. Four-hundred speed film is thought of as the best film for taking daylight pictures, and if you are using a simple point-and-shoot camera, then that's probably right. Yet for forensic photography, where extreme detail and resolution is paramount, 200 speed is best for daylight pictures. This is because the film is slower, meaning the shutter can be synchronized down to as little as 1/125th of a second.

Fill flash might be the most technical photography technique that we teach at the academy because the technique incorporates everything that the students have learned thus far. Some students in the class practice this method for the entire ten weeks before they ever master it. The scene we set up for this exercise is simple. We take a car and park it where the sunlight is hitting the car, but not the trunk of the car directly. Then we raise the trunk, which contains duffle bags and other items that are visible with the naked eye. Taking a picture of the trunk from a distance of fifteen feet with the flash will not illuminate the subtle shadows that lie in the back of the trunk. To get the best possible representation of the trunk, a fill flash should be used. Since practice makes perfect, we teach the students to fill in the shadows with the flash. First, the students take a meter reading of the light in the area of the trunk and set the camera to whatever the meter displayed. Let's assume it reads 1/60th of a second at f/16. Next, with the camera in the manual mode, the students find the distance on the flash unit that corresponds with f/11 (fifteen feet). The students then place the flash fifteen feet from the shadow portion of the trunk and take the picture. This will give the shadowed portion of the picture a one-stop reduction in exposure as compared to the rest of the picture. When the picture is developed, the scene will have the proper amount of light and closely resemble what the human eye would have seen.

As some teams work on the fill-flash exercise, others work on taking shots of footwear impressions. In the flower bed outside of the academy, to the dismay of the cadets who will have to fix our mess later, we make several different shoe impressions. Shoe impressions, like many fingerprints, cannot be easily collected. Again, pictures of the shoe impressions may be the only thing a jury ever sees. They may also be the only thing an investigator has to compare to once a suspect's actual shoe has been recovered. The students take their tripod and invert the head, so the camera can shoot straight down. The students then mount the camera onto the tripod and place the tripod perpendicular to the impression, careful to extend the legs far enough so that they do not disturb the impression. A metric footwear scale, a scale that is merely a large "L," is placed near the footprint and in the view of the camera, but not actually touching the impression itself. Most prints are three-dimensional, like those left in dirt or sand. Two-dimensional prints are those left in dust or blood. A three-dimensional print, regardless of the amount of light present, must be lit obliquely (at an angle) in order to capture the unique detail of the shoe impression. More often than not, all that is needed is for someone to shine a flashlight obliquely across the impression at a forty-five-degree angle. The camera should be set up at the maximum resolution, with one-to-one scale, in order to take this particular shot. The students press the button and

NFA instructor John Williams, along with graduates of Session Three, prepare to properly photograph a footwear impression.

(Collection of the National Forensic Academy)

A footwear impression illuminated obliquely with a flashlight.

(Collection of the National Forensic Academy)

FOOTSPRAY

Some footwear impressions are so faint that they are hardly discernible. This means that when they are photographed, the impression may be too faint to be seen in the picture. In order to bring out the highlights of the impression, all the CSI needs is a can of bright orange paint. Take the can and hold it about ten inches above the impression. Spray the paint outward, allowing it to fall gently onto the highest points in the impression. Do not spray the paint onto the impression directly. This will make the photo of the impression jump off the page, without damaging the impression itself.

presto, a great picture of the footwear impression emerges. They must be able to prove they can take this picture properly before they will be allowed to graduate from the academy.

Digital Photography

The last day of photography week is spent on digital photography. It is a common misconception by many law enforcement agencies that digital photographs are not admissible in court. The thought is that the CSI who takes the digital images might alter them in some way, which is possible. Yet all crime scene work is based on the integrity of the person working the scene. The CSI can alter anything at a crime scene, not just digital photographs. Furthermore, courts have been readily accepting digital images for years—just as often as regular 35mm pictures. We use both types of cameras at the academy, though we are currently making the move to strictly digital. The reason is that the principles of photography are the same, regardless of the camera used. Also, we think it is better for the CSI working the scene to get that immediate feedback by viewing the image on the spot, instead of waiting days for the photographs to be developed. This eliminates mistakes. Finally, it is believed by many knowledgeable people that within the next five years, many companies who currently make film will stop doing so and move solely into the digital age. We will be ready. Unfortunately, there are still those hardheads around who do not want to step into the twenty-first century. We wonder what they will do with their cameras when they can no longer buy film.

Forensic photographers are a dying breed. But they're not alone. The entire field of forensic science is about to enter a tumultuous phase that could be devastating. Roughly 80 percent of all of the forensic knowledge resides with a mere 20 percent of those practicing the craft, and many of those are approaching retirement, if they haven't retired already. The void is already being felt across the nation in the form of a staggering lack of experts in myriad fields, such as fingerprint classification, firearms examination, and yes, even forensic photography. Much of this knowledge will be taken to the graves of those who had it. Exacerbating this problem is the fact that some who have this knowledge, gained through tedious decades of on-the-job training, refuse to pass it down to the new breed of "college kid cops" taking their places. In many ways, forensic science is on the brink of a modern-day Dark Age. We're fortunate to work with a cadre of men and women, from all age groups, who altruistically believe in passing on what they know to future generations. They feel that it is their duty to do so. Let's just hope for all of our sakes that they continue to enlighten.

PHOTOGRAPHY

There are very few things on Earth that have the raw emotional power that a photograph has. Photographs preserve particular moments in time forever. They allow us not only to travel back in time, but to visit places and things without ever actually being there. Right now, you're thinking of a particularly happy time and a photo that you have that makes you smile. But some photos are not intended to be pleasant.

Certain pieces of evidence at a crime scene simply cannot be collected. The evidence is of such a fragile nature that merely attempting to bring it back to the lab will destroy it beyond any usable form. Therefore, photographs are the only way to preserve the evidence and possibly link it to a suspect. This is particularly true with certain shoe impressions, especially if they are left in blood.

One early morning in December, a manager for a gospel band was brutally murdered while preparing for an upcoming concert. The building where the victim was murdered was usually used for fashion shows, but on this particular day it would be turned into a concert hall. As the victim arrived in the morning to pick up the keys to the building, he was killed by a petty thief, who took less than five hundred dollars' worth of merchandise—a crime that was only a misdemeanor.

There was very little incriminating evidence collected at the scene. There were no fingerprints or any DNA evidence, except for what the victim had left. The only real evidence were several bloody footprints left at the scene. The crime scene investigators who worked the scene took perfect, one-to-one close-ups of the transient evidence in hopes of comparing them to a possible suspect at a later date. They would get that chance.

One of the items the suspect stole was a refrigerator, which he sold for a mere twenty dollars. The purchaser of the fridge helped lead police to the person from whom he had bought the item. Once the suspect was located, his clothes, including his shoes, were taken into custody as part of the evidence of the crime. Not only did the suspect have the victim's blood on his person, he also had a small amount of blood on his shoe, though not enough to match to the victim. A forensic expert in the field of shoe and footwear impressions identified the shoes of the suspect as those that had left the impressions at the scene, however. By taking the photos of the impressions and comparing them to the actual shoe, the expert was able to read the specific details of the shoe and make a conclusion that the impression and the shoe were a perfect match.

The suspect began to recant his original story, claiming to have been there as a thief and having stumbled across the victim, who, he said, had already been killed. At trial, all of the evidence was presented, including one color photograph of the victim lying in a pool of his own blood. The picture was used to show jurors that anyone who came in the vicinity of the victim would, in all likelihood, have left a shoe impression in the blood, which the suspect did. Furthermore, the picture shows bloodstains on the wall near the victim, indicative of projected blood, and injuries on the victim also matched cuts and abrasions associated with a stab wound. The suspect eventually led the police to the knife he had thrown into a ditch, though he still clung to his story that he did not commit the murder and was only trying to protect the person who did.

Eventually, the jury found the defendant guilty due to a preponderance of circumstantial evidence. The photographs used to connect the victim to the suspect were the key factors in determining guilt. The defendant was charged with felony murder and sentenced to life in prison. Every picture truly does tell a story.

GOODWILL HUNTING

Latent Print Development

The College of Carnage. The Harvard of Hellish Violence. These are just two of the nicknames that the National Forensic Academy has earned over the course of the last several years. These names were given to the NFA because we don't believe in sitting behind a desk and telling our students what they should do—we believe in having them do it. There is no better way to learn. Unlike at most schools, our students get to practice their newly acquired skills with the instructors nearby, so if they have a question, they can ask. It is much better for our students to make their mistakes here, where they can learn from them. Think of an airline pilot. Would you want to fly with someone if the only training he had ever had was from reading a book? Of course not. You'd want a pilot who had flown before. Solving crime shouldn't be any different. The hallmark of the academy is the amount of hands-on training the students receive. Of the 400 hours of training, 250 of those hours are outside of the classroom. Everything the students learn in the classroom is also demonstrated in the field. Of course, that means a lot more work for us.

When you graduate from college with your master's degree, all you can hope for is to put what you have learned to good use. We each have a master's degree, one in public administration and the other in social work—not typical degrees you would think of when you think of forensic science. While we have found our degrees to be very useful in *managing* the National Forensic Academy, there are no classes to prepare someone for many of the things we have had to do. You see, the academy is a program that is so outside of the box that there isn't any rule book or manual, so the university basically leaves us to our own devices. We have, shall we say, "had to wing it" when doing much of the training, and that has made for some interesting situations.

Finding the Mock Crime Scene

The hands-on activities really begin during week three. This week brings about the first mock crime scene that the students will have to "work" using the skills they have acquired over the previous two weeks. The first scene is relatively simple, but in order to set it up, we must first find a house—a house that no one lives in and that is safe enough, and sturdy enough, to walk in. Good luck.

Finding a house that we can use for free that is not an old, abandoned crack house is not an easy order to fill. Now, you might be saying to yourself, "Crimes can happen in bad houses, so why search for a nice house?" Learning is our main objective, and we have found that it is very hard to learn when you continue to fall through the floor as you work a mock crime scene. For that reason, we try to obtain decent houses.

In the beginning, though, we had to take what we could get, and believe us when we say we have seen our share of odd things in our quest for the perfect crime scene house. We have fallen through floors, been chased by rats, and been stung by our share of bees. We have moved toilets from the middle of living rooms and once cleaned up remnants of a satanic ritual. One time, we even used an old fish market that reeked of rotten shrimp and had a driveway made out of broken clamshells. In the early days, we learned to make do. But as our popularity increased within the local community, we were able to find better houses, especially with help from the Department of Transportation. As anybody who visits Knoxville will tell you, there is always road con-

A typical crime scene house currently used by the NFA.

(Collection of the National Forensic Academy)

Session Eight graduate Danny Dehyle and NFA instructor Steve Nichols stand outside an early example of an NFA crime scene residence.

(Collection of the National Forensic Academy)

struction going on, which means a lot of good homes are being torn down in the name of progress. Unlike many Knoxvillians, we are very thankful for all of those orange cones.

We always find it a little strange when we take those first steps through the door of our crime scene house. You'd think that when people move from one house to another they would take all of their belongings with them. This is far from being true. Every house, and this is no exaggeration, we mean every house we've ever used, has had some form of Christmas decorations still there. Whether it is lights on the house, a wreath on a door, or a fully decorated tree still standing in the living room, the ghosts of Christmas past seem to be very alive in these vacant houses. We still haven't figured out this eerie coincidence. We've also been in houses with clothes still folded neatly in the closet and family photos still hanging on the walls—not to mention full medicine cabinets. The strangest item we have found in a house would have to be a human leg. Imagine going through an abandoned house, with no electricity, in the middle of nowhere, choking on that overpowering musty smell that all old houses have, as the floor creaks with every step. Then, turning the corner, down a dark hallway, you see what appears to be a leg sticking out from behind a door—it's enough to make you scream. As it turned out, it was not a real leg after all, but someone's prosthesis, complete with a sock and shoe. We're not sure how you forget to take your prosthetic leg with you when you move, but for us, it only adds to the reality of our mock crime scene.

Decorating the Crime Scene

With an empty, residential home secured, the real fun begins. Even though a few personal items might still be in the house, rarely is there any furniture left. In order to have an accurate mock crime scene, we need furniture. So, we get to go shopping! Unfortunately for us, it is not shopping in the traditional sense of the word. Furniture shopping at the NFA is interesting at best and nauseating at worst. In order to set up realistic crime scene scenarios, we furnish all of the houses we use to look as if someone is living there. In all, during the course of one year of training, we use twelve houses and decorate each and every one of them as thoroughly as possible.

Because we end up destroying each house and all of its furnishings, we don't want to buy the furniture that we use. We've found that the cheapest way to furnish a crime scene is acquiring furniture from our local Goodwill drop-off center. Now, for those of you who do not know, Goodwill Industries is a charitable organization that takes donations of household goods and sells them back to the community at a very cheap price. Most people think that when they send their bags of old clothes, furniture, and toys to Goodwill that they are going to get into the hands of someone else who really needs them. That's not always the case. Goodwill will pick up just about anything that people are willing to get rid of. That means there is a lot of stuff that nobody wants—and for good reason. You'd be amazed at the number of items that just get crushed and bailed up like cardboard boxes. In other words, one man's trash is another man's trash. That's where we come in.

The treasure hunt begins as soon as we pull up to the back of the Goodwill lot. Of course, this isn't your usual treasure hunt. The back lot consists of nothing more than mounds and mounds of old, wet junk. Toys, television sets, couches, chairs, desks, clothes, shoes, the list goes on and on. For some reason, there is a never-ending supply of nasty household items being delivered every day to our local Goodwill store. We show up and just go through everything as if we own the place. They are so glad to see us arrive, because it means there will be that much less for them to crush and bail—and they don't want to touch it any more than we do. The place smells bad, too. The odor is so unbelievable that it makes the Body Farm smell like a flower garden. And since the piles of junk are outside, you never know what type of critters might go scavenging through the stuff at night. Yet we go traipsing through the piles, grabbing up mattresses, couches, chairs, and other items. The employees, keeping dry by standing under the awnings, just stare at us with their mouths agape, making "gross-out" faces, as if they have just been kicked in the groin. Then it's off to the closest bathroom for some antibacterial soap and lots of hand sanitizer.

Our goal while we're at Goodwill is to search for items that will furnish three or four rooms at the crime scene, usually a living room, an office, and two bedrooms. We always look for a couch with all of its cushions, a stuffed chair, and a TV for the living room scene. Sometimes we might get lucky and find a coffee table, too. If we're really lucky, we can even find a couch that is not stained with urine—but that isn't usually the case. We used to wonder how someone's couch could get so urine stained, but then we realized the less we wonder about why things end up at Goodwill the easier it is for us to search through them. We also look for a desk, chair, and computer monitor for the office scene. But, without question, our least favorite scene is the bedroom. For a realistic bedroom scene, you obviously need a bed, and believe us when we say that mattresses are always the worst thing to pick up at Goodwill. Not only are they old, nasty, and usually soaking wet, but think about what people do on their mattress, and we don't mean sleep. Yep, you guessed it, we have had the pleasure of hauling semen-stained mattresses to our crime scene houses. It's during times like these, when it's raining and it's cold and we're trying to unload someone else's stained mattress into a house, that we take a second to laugh, not to mention gag, because this is definitely not what we went to graduate school for.

With our DNA-soaked furniture and other finds loaded into our trailer, we go to the house to set up the scene. We arrange the furnishings in the house just as you would in yours. We set up an office, two bedrooms, a kitchen, and a living room, each room complete to include office accoutrements, electrical appliances, wall hangings, televisions, and videocassette recorders. If you ignore the smell, you might think you're at home.

Creating the Crime Scene Scenario

After we "decorate" the houses as best we can, it is time to concoct a crime scene scenario. These mock scenes are usually done after work, so everyone begins to get a little giddy. Giddiness in the forensic world usually results in humor that's, well, let's just say adult-oriented. Thus, one room in the house inevitably ends up having a mock sexual homicide. We purchased a training dummy, known affectionately as "Bendy," when the academy first started over five years ago. It's the same kind of dummy *CSI* uses, only ours always ends up bent over, butt in the air, with a tube of KY Jelly and a pack of condoms within reach—not to mention a pair of thong panties hanging from the ceiling fan (there is a real training element to the KY and condoms, we promise). Imagine the two of us, going to the local Wal-Mart, buying fifty rolls of film, twenty packs of batteries, a tube of KY Jelly, a pair of thong panties, and one pack of condoms. The cashiers can hardly contain their laughter. Unfortunately, we can't say the same for the university auditors.

At this particular scene, the students will be looking for fingerprints, footwear impressions, tool marks, even blood. This is when we get to think like criminals. Well, like dumb criminals, because we want the students to find the evidence we leave behind. The setup of the mock crime actually begins on the outside of the house. We'll walk around the property, making sure we leave good footwear impressions. Hopefully the impressions are found, in which case the class will make casts of them when they arrive on the scene. Then we go around to many of the windows and peer in, leaving the token "karate chop" print on the outside of the glass.

Once we're finished with the exterior of the house, we move on to the interior. But we don't enter the house with a key; that just wouldn't do. Instead, we break into the house in several different ways. We kick open the front door, which should leave a footwear impression—if the students look closely enough. Then we'll pry open another door and a window with a crowbar in order to leave a tool mark. We also throw a brick through a window, and then climb through it, making sure to leave fingerprints and footprints on the glass and on the windowsill. (This is when the neighbors usually start to wonder what's going on.) Once inside the house, we will rebreak the window we climbed through, from the inside out. If the students are really keen, they should be able to figure out from which direction the glass broke by looking at the edges of a piece of glass. Most have never been shown the difference until they come to the NFA. It's a true learning experience when our students collect pieces of glass and are asked to explain why there are some pieces broken from both the outside and the inside.

At this point we begin to walk from room to room, leaving fingerprints on painted surfaces, porous surfaces, smooth surfaces, and in dust. All the while we wipe our foreheads with our hands, absorbing the oil from the skin so we leave really nice prints. We also spray a little blood around to allow the class to use the chemicals they will have prepared and learned about throughout the week. Finally, we handle trash, like pop bottles, soda cans, foam cups, fast-food wrappers, and empty bullet casings, to make sure they have good prints, and then scatter them throughout the scene.

Working the Scene

The following day, after we have set up the scene, the students arrive and work the house as if a real crime has taken place. They are divided up into four teams, with one student in each team being named team leader. Each team is assigned to one of the rooms of the house once they arrive. We give the class a scenario that goes something like the following:

> Some neighborhood kids reported that they entered an abandoned house located at 1234 Mulberry Street, in order to "hang out." Once inside, they claim they saw a lot of trash strewn about and what appeared to be blood on one of the walls. Upon further investigation in one of the adjacent rooms, the kids claim that they saw several bullet casings lying on the floor, articles of torn undergarments, and what looked like a dead person slumped naked over a chair. Your NFA CSI team has been called out to work the crime scene.

This is the first time our students arrive to work one of our mock crime scenes. It looks like a mass response to a tragedy, having all of the disparate police cars with tags from all across the country in one person's yard. Once we convince all of the neighbors that this is just an exercise, the teams prepare to work the scene. On a normal crime scene, a team of CSIs would arrive and work the entire house together. Here, the teams work specific rooms, independent of each other, and are told that the scene has already been secured and protected prior to their arrival. For this particular exercise, they are only responsible for what is in their room.

Following the steps of crime scene management that they have already learned, the students begin to process the scene. They photograph the scene, sketch the scene, search for evidence, and collect the pieces we have left behind. This exercise is a fundamental reinforcement of crime scene management and basic evidence collection. The mock crime scenes will get more complex as the weeks go on.

Processing the Evidence

The day after the mock exercise, the students go to the lab to learn how to process the evidence they have collected. We do not use the university's laboratories because, quite frankly, no one was interested in allowing us access. So we load up our SUV (known as "the Beast") and trailer with all of the necessary equipment, supplies, and chemicals, and drive forty miles east to a local community college to use their state-of-the-art laboratory. We pray no one ever pulls us over, because with all of those chemicals in tow we would seem very suspicious.

We believe it is extremely important for our students to learn chemical processing in a laboratory environment. Teaching CSIs to mix their own chemicals and to process some of their evidence is a new concept, yet it is a very important aspect of the academy, because by mixing their own chemicals the CSIs can save valuable time and money once they return to their own departments. Reality is much different from what is portrayed on *CSI*, where the department has its own lab and can process any piece of evidence that Gil Grissom or any of his colleagues brings in. First of all, most police departments do not have their own lab and must send their evidence to the state crime lab to be processed. Second, these labs usually put a limit on the amount of evi-

Session Nine graduate Jeff Roesler works in the lab processing latent fingerprints.

(Collection of the National Forensic Academy)

dence a CSI can submit for each case. Evidence backlog is a widespread problem all across the United States that is reaching near tragic proportions. Millions of pieces of evidence sit in boxes throughout the country, waiting to be processed. It is so bad that Congress is working on legislation to help alleviate the problem—with very little luck thus far. Because of this limit on the amount of evidence a lab will accept for each case, most of the time CSIs are allowed to submit only five to ten pieces of evidence. Ten items is not very much if you think about it. Clothing, shoes, fingerprints, and a weapon can easily add up to over ten. The CSI who cannot process any of his own evidence must decide which items are more important than the others. Criminals are getting off because evidence either cannot be processed fast enough or won't be processed at all. We're trying to help fix that.

If CSIs learn how to process some evidence themselves, then those pieces of evidence do not need to be sent to a lab. This could make room for other, more difficult-to-process pieces of evidence to be sent. It might take months for a single piece of evidence to come back from the lab, but only a couple of days if the investigator can do it herself. Since we teach them how to mix their own chemicals, instead of buying the expensive name-brand versions, they can also save the department money. And there is no better place to start to teach CSIs how to process their own evidence than with latent fingerprints.

Latent Fingerprints

Latent fingerprints are the key to solving most crimes, ranging anywhere from homicides to home invasions to car theft. There are several things the CSI needs to know about latent fingerprints in order to be able to process them. The first is what they are made of. Most people think of latent fingerprints as merely the impression of the fingerprint ridges left on a surface of some sort, when actually they are simply residue off of the fingers. Latent fingerprints are comprised primarily of three components: sweat, fats, and proteins. This is important to know because it will determine what chemical or process will be used to develop the print, since each chemical reacts with a particular compound.

Second, it is important to determine how long the prints have been left, who left them, and what environmental conditions the prints have been exposed to. For instance, scientists at the Oak Ridge National Laboratory helped determine that prepubescent fingerprints do not last as long as adult fingerprints. This groundbreaking research concluded that until the age of puberty, a child's fingerprint is comprised mostly of water, and therefore will evaporate more quickly than those of adults. Thus, superglue fuming, which is described below, will not (usually) work on a child's print.

Furthermore, research has also shown that fingerprints degrade rapidly when exposed to ultraviolet light. This is especially true with prints left on iron surfaces. For example, if someone wrapped her hand around an iron pipe and left the pipe on the ground outside for a short period of time, only the parts of the fingerprints shielded from the sun

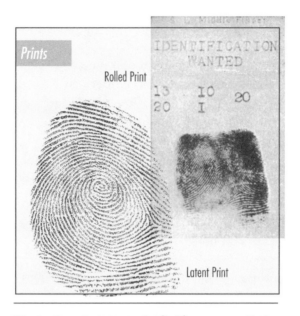

Illustration of a latent print (left) versus a rolled print. (right)

(Illustration by Pamela Johanns of Johanns Design)

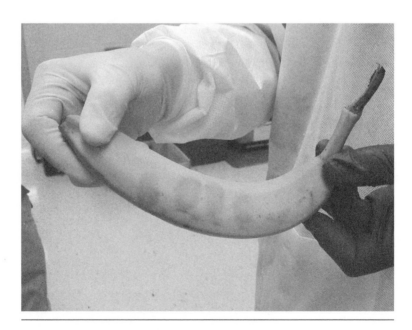

Students develop fingerprints on a banana.

(Collection of the National Forensic Academy)

would develop. What if the person leaving the print is a runner—what then? Runners have much more iron in their sweat than nonrunners (this is why they are prone to anemia), so their prints degrade very fast. So, if you want to become a master criminal, your best chance of not leaving your fingerprints behind is if you are a prepubescent marathoner.

The next thing the CSI needs to know is the type of surface the fingerprint is on. Was it left on a porous or nonporous surface? Does the item have an adhesive backing or was the print left on the smooth side? Or were prints left on both sides of the tape? Were the prints left on a greasy item or on paper? These are all important questions to answer, because each surface brings with it unique challenges in order to develop a latent print. For example, there are several ways to develop prints off of paper, but what if the paper has a waxy surface or has been contaminated by grease, like a fast-food wrapper? This will take two totally different chemicals to develop the print; thus, it is imperative for the CSI to know what processes match what surfaces.

Finally, the last consideration the CSI needs to make is how to protect the print. Will one process interfere with another? Can the print be lifted or does it need to be photographed, or should both be done? For instance, there are multiple ways to process certain pieces of evidence, but one process has to be performed before the other or the print will be destroyed.

INVISIBLE MAN

Sometimes the CSI is sure that the perpetrator touched an object, but for whatever reason no fingerprints can be developed. If that is the case, it is possible to take vinegar and a spray bottle and gently mist over the object where the print is believed to be. The vinegar reacts with the fats and oils in the prints, rehydrating them. Once the surface is dry, the print can be processed.

This is certainly a lot of information for a CSI to know, especially considering there are literally hundreds of ways to develop latent prints. What we teach at the academy are some of the most tried-and-true methods—methods that achieve the best results and are the easiest to use. We will start off with the most basic concept of all—dusting for fingerprints.

Dusting for Fingerprints

Dusting for fingerprints with fingerprint powder is the concept that nearly everyone on Earth is familiar with. From Barney Fife to Columbo, every TV-show cop showed their stuff when it came to using plain old black fingerprint powder. Most of the students that come to the academy are very familiar with fingerprint powders and how they are used. Dusting for prints on such items as doorknobs or pieces of glass is very common for them and very easy to do. But how about developing a print on a brick? Or a piece of Styrofoam? Or a set of window blinds? Maybe even a faint, bloody fingerprint? Almost without fail, many of our students have very little knowledge of other means of processing latent prints on objects or substances that are somewhat out of the ordinary. Time and time again, after spending a week in the laboratory, NFA students talk about cases they have had where "if only they had known how," they might have been able to get a fingerprint and make a case.

For real-world CSIs there are essentially four kinds of fingerprint powders: regular, bichromatic, fluorescent, and magnetic.

REGULAR POWDERS

Regular powders come in various colors, including black, gray, white, and silver, among others. These powders adhere to both water and fat deposits and are used on dry, nonporous surfaces. The color chosen depends on the background on which it will be applied. The powder is applied with a brush, preferably camel hair, using a twisting motion, building up on the ridges as you twist. Once the print has been dusted, it can be lifted with fingerprint tape. Lifted with tape simply means that a piece of tape is placed over the print, and when removed the print is on the adhesive side of the tape. The tape is then adhered to a fingerprint card for evidence.

BICHROMATIC POWDERS

The same is true for bichromatic powders. Bichromatic powder is merely a combination of black and silver fingerprint powder that, when dusted, will show contrast on both light and dark surfaces.

FLUORESCENT POWDERS

Fluorescent powders are essentially the same as regular powders. They are used on "confused" backgrounds, such as pinstriped wallpaper or a watercolor painting. The difference is that they must be viewed with a forensic light source, or FLS, in order to make the fingerprint visible.

In a nutshell, a forensic light source—also known as an alternate light source, argon laser, and a host of other generic terms—is quite simply a high-powered light source that contains the visible ultraviolet and infrared components of the light spectrum. A good FLS has a filter that can be dialed into the individual bands, or wavelengths, of light. If

Fluorescent fingerprint powder and an FLS being used to develop a hidden word written in sebaceous oils.

(Copyright © Jarrett Hallcox, collection of the National Forensic Academy)

used properly, this tool can enhance the visibility of certain types of evidence by either causing them to fluoresce or to absorb the proper wavelength of light. The FLS is primarily used in the detection of latent prints, though it does have several other applications, including the detection of body fluids.

The major drawback of fluorescent powder is that it is very messy and hard to clean up. That might not be of major concern at a murder scene, but when it comes to dusting Grandma's house, it just might be.

MAGNETIC POWDER

Magnetic powder, or "mag" powder, is made up of regular fingerprint powder laced with metal. Magnetic powders are used on nonmagnetic surfaces, such as a table, and are perfect for surfaces that are rough or textured. Mag powder is also good for prints where there is a concern that a fingerprint brush might damage the print. Mag powder is applied with a magnetic wand; therefore, there are no brush fibers to touch and damage the print. A magnetic wand is merely an applicator that has a magnetic end that attracts the powder onto one end, and a touch tip on the other end that releases the powder. Magnetic powders are found in multiple colors and in fluorescent form.

Chemical Processing

Once in the laboratory, we divide the class into groups and set up the various stations for chemical processing. Nearly all of the chemical processes we teach can be purchased premixed, from either a retail store or a forensic supply company. Many of those that come from a forensic supply company are very expensive, however, and are usually not as strong as what we can create in the lab. We have found that it saves a lot of money, and the results are much better, if you buy your own chemicals and make your own working solutions. Because most CSIs are only familiar with the store-bought versions of the various processes we create, we first go through each chemical to familiarize the class with what we are talking about. For instance, a CSI's only knowledge of ninhydrin is what they have seen that comes premixed, in liquid form in a spray bottle. But when we talk about ninhydrin at the NFA, we are talking about the crystal form—the liquid form we create to use for our mock crime scene is what we call the working solution. Here are some of the methods we teach our students.

IODINE FUMING

Iodine fuming is dangerous. It is highly toxic, and some individuals are deathly allergic to the chemical. Yet the process is simple. Iodine particles attach themselves to greases, fats, and oils on porous surfaces. It is especially good for paper and wood surfaces. All that is needed are iodine crystals and a distribution method for the fumes. One way to use iodine with evidence is to place the item, a piece of paper, for example,

Session Nine graduate Ann Marie Ziska uses the iodine fuming method to develop a fingerprint on a coffeepot.

(Collection of the National Forensic Academy)

into a Ziploc bag with iodine crystals, seal the bag, and shake. This allows the iodine to cover the entire piece of paper. The other way is to purchase an iodine fuming kit, which is nothing more than an elongated tube with a place to put iodine at one end. The CSI then blows through the tube, and the iodine fumes exit out the other end onto the area that is being processed. If no one inhales, that is it. It's just that simple.

The problem with iodine fuming is that it is not sensitive to prints that are more than a few days old. Furthermore, the prints often fade very fast after they have been developed and must be sprayed with a fixative solution so they remain visible. That solution is naphthoflavone. It is best to develop the print and photograph it immediately. At the NFA, we process pieces of paper and wood with this method. It is not a great process for use at a crime scene, but it works much better on evidence that can be collected and processed back at the department.

NINHYDRIN

Ninhydrin is one of the more popular chemicals used to develop latent fingerprints. Ninhydrin reacts with the proteins in sweat, turning a purple color when the reaction takes place. Ninhydrin is especially helpful on porous surfaces, like paper, and can be used on other surfaces, like wood. The one drawback of ninhydrin is that it can take as long as seven to ten days to develop—and nobody has the time to wait—but heat and humidity can be used to accelerate the development process. Ninhydrin is not useful on items that have been wet.

We use ninhydrin specifically for developing latent prints off of paper documents that have writing on them. In order to develop the print, the students take a glass Pyrex pan measuring eleven by thirteen inches and fill the bottom up with the working solution of ninhydrin. They then take the document and, with a pair of tweezers, dip the document all the way into the ninhydrin, similar to the process used when developing photographs in a darkroom. The document is removed from the mixture and allowed to dry. Once the ninhydrin has evaporated and the paper is dry, the CSIs take an ordinary clothes iron, place it about an inch above the document, being careful not to burn the paper, and purple fingerprints appear like magic.

5-MTN

Essentially ninhydrin on steroids, 5-MTN (methylthio ninhydrin) re-acts just like ninhydrin when used on paper—it turns the prints a pur-ple color. The real difference comes in the fluorescing.

When there is a document that shows no visible signs of a finger-print after being treated with ninhydrin, there is the option of using zinc chloride. Zinc chloride, if used correctly, can turn the prints a sort of fluorescent orange that can be viewed through an FLS. The problem, however, is that ninhydrin is not reliable when it comes to the zinc chloride process. There are so many variables that impact the fluoresc-ing process of ninhydrin; you just never know what you will get. The good thing about the chemical 5-MTN is that it is very stable and very reliable when it comes to using zinc chloride. It is used in exactly the same way as ninhydrin. Then, if the fluorescence is desired, the CSI will take a working solution of zinc chloride and mist it lightly with a spray bottle over the entire document. Here, the prints turn more pinkish than orange, and jump off the page when viewed under the green spec-trum of light, in conjunction with an orange filter. It has been our ex-perience at the academy that 5-MTN is categorically better than ninhydrin. Regular prints develop better, zinc chloride prints develop better, and clearly, when viewed with an FLS, the prints are much crisper. It has only one flaw—5-MTN comes from somewhere in Hol-land, and the supply never seems to meet the demand. Our advice: Or-der it in bulk.

PHYSICAL DEVELOPER

Physical developer is a less common developing procedure, but one that has a lot of utility. Like ninhydrin, 5-MTN, and iodine, it is most use-ful on porous surfaces, though it can be used on certain nonporous sur-faces as well. Its real claim to fame is that it works very well on currency, reacting with fats, oils, and waxes, while developing older prints and not freshly placed ones. Physical developer, or PD, can be used after the ninhydrin method without any interference. The use of

PD is somewhat laborious in that it is a four-step process. Here is the abbreviated method we teach the students for using PD. First, they dip the evidence in a maleic acid solution for five minutes (until the bubbling ceases). Next, they place redox solution in a stirring device, and then add detergent and silver nitrate (they must be combined in this order). Once the solution is mixed, they will shake it vigorously. The evidence is then put into the solution for a period of anywhere from five to fifteen minutes, and the solution must be shaken the entire time. Finally, the students remove the specimen from the solution and rinse it with water. The item may be air-dried or heat may be applied to speed up the drying process.

CYANOACRYLATE (SUPERGLUE)

Cyanoacrylate fuming is used to develop latent prints off of evidence that is nonporous. It is also used to develop latent prints off of human bodies (we know that a human body is porous; we will talk about that in a later chapter). Superglue reacts with the trace proteins found in sweat and moisture. The only items needed to perform this process are

PIPE SMOKE

One way to create a small superglue fuming device is to take a foam cup and a cheap brand of pipe cleaner. Take the pipe cleaner and poke it through the open side of the cup until it pierces the bottom. The cleaner needs to be cut so that it is shorter than the cup. Next, put a drop or two of superglue on the end of the cleaner that is inside the cup. It will begin a chemical reaction and the glue will begin to fume. Hold the cup over the item in question. The cup acts as the mechanism for trapping the vapors, allowing the glue to come in contact with the object. This trick is great for superglue fuming doorknobs.

common everyday superglue, a small aluminum dish about the size of a half-dollar, a heat source, and an aquarium, Rubbermaid tote, or some object to use as a chamber to trap the fumes. That's it. We teach the students to place the piece of evidence in the chamber, heat the super-glue in the dish from thirty seconds to five minutes, and *presto*, you will have a sticky white material forming along the ridges of the finger-print. The key to the process is cooking the superglue long enough to get it into a gaseous state. This process can be accelerated by heating sodium hydroxide along with the superglue. If you are performing this process and you're a smoker, you're in luck, because cigarette ashes will work just as well. Once the print has been developed, the CSI will photograph it, dust it with fingerprint powder, and lift. A word of cau-tion: When the superglue reaches a temperature of over 495 degrees, it turns from superglue fumes to cyanide gas. Though the process is sim-ple, it is also very dangerous. Do not try this at home.

DYE STAINS

One of the biggest problems with superglue fuming is that it is very hard to see the developed latent prints. They are very faint when they are coated with the superglue fumes and they do not show up under a forensic light source (they don't fluoresce). For several years, the FBI has funded research in an attempt to add some substrate to the chemi-cal composition of superglue so that it automatically fluoresces when it turns into a gas. To date, they have been unable to make this work. Our organization picked up a component of this research, funding a scientist at the Oak Ridge National Laboratory to colorize, not neces-sarily fluoresce, the gaseous state of superglue. Though the scientist was able to turn it into a pale yellowish brown color, funding ran out before any real resolution could be developed. Thus, CSIs must continue with the old methodology of fluorescing superglue through the use of dye stains.

Dye stains are simply different colored stains that fluoresce superglue-fumed prints under various spectrums of UV light. The forensic light source that is shown ad nauseam on *CSI* can be an in-valuable tool for the crime scene investigator. The different spectrums of light that the FLS can be dialed to help to potentially bring out more robust fingerprints, under the right conditions. Note, you must also have the right color of UV goggles on in order to visualize the print. Without getting overly technical, what dye stain is chosen depends upon the surface and background on which the print resides. There are several different dye stains, including Basic Red 28, Basic Yellow 40, Sanfranin O, MBD, and Ardrox, to name just a few. A good forensic light source is very expensive, about $15,000, meaning many departments cannot afford one. Basic yellow and MBD fluoresce with a long-wave ultraviolet light source—a light source that is less expensive to purchase. Depending on the department and how much money it has probably helps determine the process of choice for the CSI.

SUDAN BLACK

Sudan black, though technically a dye stain, is not used to fluoresce a latent print that has been superglue fumed. Instead, this dye stain is used in circumstances where the crime scene has been contaminated with foodstuff, oils, or other greasy substances. It is extraordinarily useful in developing latent prints off of fast-food packages and in fast-food restaurants where crimes have been committed.

Specialized Latent Processes

Criminals love to use tape—all kinds of tape. They use black electrical tape to help make their bombs; they use shipping tape to mail their anthrax; and they use duct tape to tie people up. It would be easy to just discard tape and not think of it as evidence that can be processed. There is a lot of information that can be gleaned from it, but how in the world do you process a wad of tape? We know how.

Think about wrapping Christmas presents for a moment. When you pull that Scotch tape toward the end of the cutter and tear it loose, you end up handling the sticky side of the tape as much as you do the nonsticky side. Good CSIs are not usually as interested in the nonadhesive side of the tape. This is because the adhesive side of tape pulls dead skin cells off of the fingers, making this side of the tape a gold mine, if you know how to process it.

There are several methods for processing tape, but the one process that seems to do the best across all types of tape is known as *Liq-Nox*. The *Liq-Nox* process, also known as the alternate black powder process, was developed by some very innovative scientists at the Michigan State Crime Laboratory. This process consists of twenty drops of tap water, twenty drops of Liquinox soap, and .5 grams of black powder (we have found that Lightning brand works best). All of the ingredients are mixed together until it's the consistency of shaving cream. The substance is then painted on the sticky side of the tape with a camel hair brush. The soapy substance is then carefully rinsed off of the evidence. Once the evidence has been completely rinsed off, it is allowed to thoroughly dry. We have found through experimentation that Dawn dish liquid actually works just as well as Liquinox detergent.

The Liq-Nox process works unbelievably well on tape. It also works very well on another favorite item among criminals—latex gloves. Let's face it, criminals have become very enterprising. They know they had better not leave their prints behind, because NFA graduates will be hot on their tail. Many crime scenes are processed finding few, if any, fingerprints. But, alas, someone working the scene will find a pair of discarded latex gloves in the garbage. Bingo.

Believe it or not, there are a lot of cases made each year by getting fingerprints from the inside of latex gloves. It is simply amazing to think that if you turn a pair of used latex gloves inside out and paint on the soap-powder substance, then rinse, fingerprints will be staring you in the face. So, to paraphrase the late Johnny Cochran, if the gloves fit, you can get a print.

One of the more difficult items to process is cartridge casings or bullets from a gun. Getting a viable print off of a bullet that has been fired is essentially a million-to-one long shot. Yet if the weapon can be recovered, the bullets inside the gun can be very helpful. Developing a print, especially a good thumbprint on the back of a bullet, is possible. At the academy, we teach a trick on how to develop prints off of unfired bullets, and it costs all of $2.49. Gun Blue, a gun-cleaning material that you can purchase at any retail store, and water, are all you

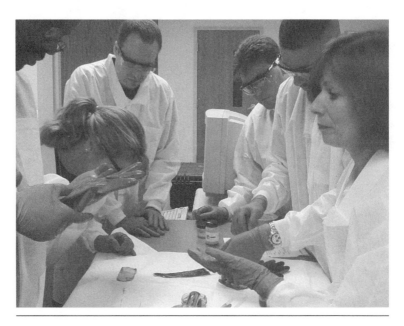

Session Four students, along with NFA instructor Diane Bodie, develop fingerprints on the inside of latex gloves.
(Copyright © Jarrett Hallcox, collection of the National Forensic Academy)

need. The recipe is simply one-half a milliliter of water to twenty milliliters of Gun Blue. All we do is drop the bullet into the solution and watch the print develop. It brings out a beautiful print and it is so simple. This process also works well on coins. We have yet to meet a CSI who knows this process, until they are introduced to it at the NFA.

Bloody Prints

To this point, we have been discussing developing latent prints left behind at a crime scene. These prints are essentially pieces of the perpetrator (dead skin cells, oil, and so on) that are left behind, and with some type of chemical massaging, if you will, the prints are revealed. Bloody prints are different. Instead of developing the print, the CSI is

RED TAPE

Lifting a print on metal can be difficult, especially if the metal is galvanized. One easy way to do this is to use masking tape. Take the masking tape and fold it into something resembling a wick about six to eight inches long. Next, light the end of the tape and hold it underneath the object in question, allowing the sticky smoke to come in contact with the area that the CSI wants to print. After about ninety seconds, the area should become covered in soot. Gently wipe away the excess soot with a paper towel. The print will be revealed. This works great on pipe bombs.

actually using chemicals to visualize the print. Many, many crime scenes are violent, and violence usually means bloodshed. Now, everyone knows that individuals involved in these types of crime scenes try to clean up the mess, and often they do a pretty good job. But there are several chemical ways to bring out or enhance fingerprints, shoe prints, and so forth that paint a very condemning picture for the suspect. One of these chemicals is amido black.

AMIDO BLACK

Amido black is, in its best form, a methanol-based protein rinse that is sprayed on an area where there are believed to be bloody prints. Here's an example of how it is used at a crime scene. A perpetrator flees a crime scene where there is very little blood. The perp steps in a little blood in a carpeted area, walks down the hallway, and exits through a linoleum-covered kitchen floor. The CSI arrives on the scene and realizes that the perp has stepped through the blood on the carpet, but it is smeared and the soles of the shoes cannot be determined. The CSI traces the perp's path and realizes he has fled across the linoleum be-

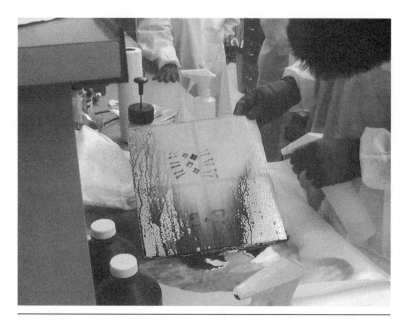

Students spray amido black on a piece of kitchen tile to develop a faint bloody footprint.

(Collection of the National Forensic Academy)

cause he can see faint spots of blood trailing across the kitchen. The CSI grabs the solution of amido black, contained in a spray bottle, and begins to spray across the area where he thinks the perp has walked (remember, the blood must be dry). After about a minute, the CSI washes the amido black with distilled water. And, like magic, the amido attaches itself to the remnants of blood and forms a perfect outline of the soles of the perp's shoes. This process works for latent fingerprints left in blood as well.

Now, amido black is a protein rinse, which means it will react with nearly all proteins, including semen. We only mention this because this question invariably arises: "Will amido black develop semen prints?" The answer is yes. If someone ever steps in enough semen that it covers the bottom of his or her shoe and they walk through a surface where amido can be used, then it is possible, though not plausible, to develop semen footprints.

LEUCOCRYSTAL VIOLET

Leucocrystal violet, or LCV, is another chemical that is used exactly like amido black. LCV's main advantage is that it does not interfere with protein rinses, and therefore can be used after amido to help further enhance prints. Traditionally, the CSI starts with amido and moves to LCV. The two processes normally bring out prints unbelievably well. Since the blood does not have to be dry, however, LCV can be used sooner than amido. It just depends on the situation and how much time the CSI has.

MISCELLANEOUS CHEMICALS USED FOR DETECTING BLOOD

Because of perps cleaning up bloody crime scenes, there are myriad chemicals designed specifically to detect the presence of blood. The most popular of these are luminol, Lightning-Luminol, Hema-Glow, and the new guy on the block, Blue Star. Each of these chemicals was designed to enhance or bring out areas where blood is or has been, without the necessity of a forensic light source.

Luminol is the oldest and most well known of these chemicals, but is fast becoming obsolete. In order for luminol to work, the room must be virtually pitch-black. If luminol is sprayed where blood is thought to have been, it will react with the iron in the blood and faintly illuminate the area.

Lightning-Luminol performs the exact same function but works in rooms that have a little more light. Unfortunately, the shelf life is about half that of regular luminol. Hema-Glow is a product that is no longer produced. It worked much better than either luminol or Lightning-Luminol and had a much more robust reaction in relatively well-lit rooms. Unfortunately, it seems to have worked all too well, and its formula was rumored to have been purchased and eliminated from the competition.

Blue Star is a very new chemical and seems to bring with it the most hope. It will actually brightly fluoresce blood in the daytime, a feat that none of the other products ever achieved. It comes in tablet form (the others all come in a liquid), and it is up to the user to properly create the solution from the directions provided with the product. Without question, this is an academy favorite.

Blood-detecting chemicals are not the be-all and end-all for CSIs. These chemicals, because they attach themselves to the metallic properties in blood, all have the same flaws. One of these flaws is that they will react with areas that contain metal. A good example of this is leaded paint, and there are a lot of old houses and buildings that still have lead paint in them. If you spray any of these chemicals on a wall with leaded paint, the night lights up like fireworks. It would be impossible to tell from merely one of these chemical processes whether the solution was reacting with cleaned-up blood or lead.

The other, more major flaw with these products is that they react with bleach in the same way they react with blood. Now, it does not take a genius to see the inherent problem with this situation. Most people, criminals or not, use bleach to clean up hard-to-remove stains, including blood, and there is no way to tell just from looking at the reaction of the chemicals which is which. Interestingly, we performed a luminol demonstration in the attic of an abandoned house. After spraying the solution against the side of one of the walls, there was an incredibly bright reaction that lit up the very dark room. You have never seen so many seasoned crime scene veterans make their way down a flight of attic stairs without touching a single one. It was a creepy sight to behold. We never did officially find out what happened in that house, but needless to say it graphically illustrated the need to use more than just a chemical process to work a bloody crime scene.

As the week comes to a conclusion, the students present their findings to their peers as the instructors critique their methods and methodologies. By this time, their choices are spot-on, and it is safe to say that we have laid a solid foundation to build the rest of the academy on. This is one of our most important weeks. Sure, it is not full of eye candy, like arson and bombs, but it is practical. In the end, it is this week that our alumni remember, and it is this week that propels our students forward, giving them a new arsenal in their fight against crime.

LATENT FINGERPRINT

Technology is reinventing the world of the crime scene investigator. Digital photographs, microchip laboratories, alternate light sources, lasers, and all the rest are changing the way investigators catch criminals. This world is still unfolding in the courtroom as the court system tries to catch up to the twenty-first-century technological wave. Though they lag far behind, the courts are beginning to accept this new way of catching the bad guy.

In 1997, Ohio police received numerous, consecutive 911 calls in which the anonymous caller stated that he knew the location of a woman's mutilated body in a nearby apartment complex. Upon arrival, the police could not find a body. The caller phoned 911 again and gave better directions for the location of the woman. Upon entering an apartment, the police found her mutilated, naked body on the floor of the bedroom, next to the bed. Her throat had been slit and she had been strangled. The woman had also been stabbed one hundred thirty-eight times. One of her legs was bound to the bedpost by the ankle with a pair of panty hose. A plastic patio chair was resting on her chest. Both of her hands had also been severed. They were not found in the apartment.

Outside of the crime scene a man by the name of Brett Hartman approached one of the detectives securing the scene and began asking questions as to the gruesome condition of the crime scene. He repeatedly asked the officer if he had ever seen such a terrible scene, and said that he had heard the scene was a bad one. Hartman then walked away from the scene, only to return several minutes later. He told the detective that he had known the woman and that she slept around a lot and was a whore. He said he thought the woman got what she deserved. Hartman then told the detective that the crime scene investigators would find his semen and fingerprints in the apartment because he, himself, had sex with the woman on several occasions, including the previous night.

Becoming very suspicious of this strange man, the detective began questioning him about his relationship with the slain woman.

Hartman admitted to having intercourse with the woman, but when she refused to do exactly what he wanted, he became angry and left the apartment. He then said he returned to the apartment, but that the woman was already dead when he arrived. He stated that he tried to lift her off the floor and onto the bed to see if he could save her. Realizing that the woman's hands were missing, he became scared, and realizing that he could get into trouble, he washed her blood off of his hands and wiped his fingerprints off of items he touched.

Because Hartman had admitted to being in the woman's apartment and having sexual intercourse with her on several occasions prior to the murder, the police would need evidence other than semen and fingerprints to help link him to the crime. Lucky for them the crime scene technicians found two key pieces of blood evidence in the bedroom. Evidence that would eventually link Hartman to the crime.

Investigators were able to find a bloody fingerprint on the plastic chair that was found on top of the deceased woman's body. They also found a bloody print on the bedspread. The state called in a fingerprint expert from King County, Washington, to analyze the suspect's fingerprints. Through visual analysis, as well as computer enhancement, the fingerprints were confirmed to be that of Hartman. Hartman was arrested and a search warrant was obtained.

At trial, the enhanced fingerprints were introduced into evidence. It marked only the third time in history that computer-enhanced evidence had been allowed into the courtroom. It was concluded that the use of this technology "was blazing new ground" and was no different from using a microscope or an overhead projector, which have both been traditionally used to enhance images.

Though there were other pieces of evidence, the fingerprint evidence found at the scene clearly established Hartman's presence with the victim, as well as having her blood on his hands. The jury agreed with the courts on the enhanced fingerprint evidence and found the defendant guilty of felony murder, assigning him the death penalty. After several unsuccessful appeal attempts, Hartman is in prison awaiting his execution.

DOWN ON THE FARM
The Body Farm and Time Since Death Research

On the other side of an unassuming wooden gate behind the University of Tennessee Medical Center lies one of the most talked about and least understood research centers in the entire world. Its real name, the Outdoor Anthropological Research Facility, sounds benign. But when you talk to someone about the "Body Farm," its more common and macabre name, your mind conjures up ghoulish images. Some imagine an actual farm that has dead bodies laid out in a field like rows of corn. Others picture a scene right out of *Night of the Living Dead.*

Actually the Facility, as it is more commonly referred to by those who work there, is little more than two acres of rural hillside. There are no cows; there are no barns. There are no markings or signs saying you've arrived. You probably would not even pay attention to the gate if it weren't for the razor wire that guards the entrance—except for the smell. If the temperature is high enough, you might be able to smell what's hidden on the other side. While sometimes it is possible to get right up to the gate and not smell a thing, other times it is possible to smell the aroma from the highway, more than a mile away.

Other universities have desperately tried to start their own facility, but to no avail. Dr. Bass has championed this idea, hoping to research further into the world of death in desert climates, such as in New Mex-

The foreboding, not to mention razor-wire-laden, wooden gate to the Body Farm.

(Copyright © Jarrett Hallcox, collection of the National Forensic Academy)

ico, and in more arctic climates, such as Michigan. But it takes a special kind of person and personality to convince a community to allow them to let people decompose out in full view, and there are few Dr. Basses in the world with that ability. As a tribute to him, one lawyer proposed an ill-conceived name for the Facility, calling it the Bass Anthropological Research Facility, or BARF for short (you can see why they didn't use that name). For now, there's only one Dr. Bass and only one original BARF.

The whole concept of studying how someone decomposes really came about as a fluke. Dr. Bass moved from the University of Kansas to the University of Tennessee to head up the fledgling anthropology department back in 1971. Within months of arriving in Tennessee, he was called out on a case, only to discover his first maggot-covered body. In Kansas, a hotter and more rural environment than east Tennessee, bodies were rarely if ever found covered in maggots—they were found mummified or skeletonized. Dr. Bass realized then and there that no one really knew anything about how a body decomposes.

For more than thirty years, this facility has been the mecca for morbid curiosity, forensic research, countless documentaries, and at least one novel. Patricia Cornwell's book of the same name, *Body Farm*, popularized this facility and made it an indelible part of American pop culture. Though many credit her with giving this facility its more popular name, she did not. In fact, it is not known for certain who first called it the Body Farm, but it is widely accepted that someone with the FBI made a tongue-in-cheek remark about the Knoxville facility upon his return to Quantico. Cornwell did, however, create an image of an awesome place of death—an image that has taken on mythological proportions.

We have heard tales of the Body Farm having so many cadavers that they have to be stacked up like a cord of wood; that if a person dies at the hospital, their body is shipped across the parking lot to the facility; and of bodies being buried underneath the football stadium. Though none of those things is true, they do contain elements of truth. At times, there are a lot of bodies at the facility, sometimes so many that you cannot take more than two steps without being on top of a rotting, writhing corpse. Furthermore, the Body Farm is actually on the same property as the university hospital (all Body Farm residents are there by choice, individuals who have donated their remains to help further the world of forensic science). And, deep within the recesses of the football stadium, the third largest in the country, mind you, resides the largest collection of modern skeletons in the world.

Because of these myths, it has become customary for us to drive the academy students out to the Body Farm on their very first day. You can cut the anticipation with a knife as veteran crime scene investigators from all across the country prepare to enter the holy grail of forensic science. And as that foreboding wooden gate creaks slowly open, it releases one of the secrets like water from a dam. Only this "water" does not wash over you; it just sits there, waiting for you to walk through it so it can stick to your skin, your hair, and your clothes. There are pockets of this "entity" throughout the Body Farm. It is a sickeningly sweet and putrid smell that does not waft over you like perfume or homemade pumpkin pie. That first smell, you will never, ever forget.

When the students walk through that gate for the first time, it takes them a few seconds to believe what they're seeing. Unless, of course, the researchers decide to put the newest resident of the Farm on the ground just inside of the gate; then you only have time to think about not stepping on it—or in it. Many times, there will be a "freshy" churning with maggots not more than twenty feet from the entrance. As your eyes begin to adjust and take in all of the scenery, you become nauseatingly aware of a color spectrum unimaginable even to Crayola—puke greens, vile reds, rotting blacks, and a host of other inexplicable colors. The worst part of it is that after spending time at the Body Farm, pizza is never the same.

Some days, we walk through the gate and immediately notice new bodies lying on the ground that weren't there the day before. The bodies are so new that if you didn't know better, you'd think they were just asleep. They are part of a new research project that aims to document the entire process of natural decomposition through a pocket color atlas for CSIs. These bodies, as if they were going to leave once they awoke, are guarded by a one-foot-tall electric wire fence. The fence is to keep out animals, such as raccoons, squirrels, and other east Tennessee critters that tend to feast on the bodies, altering the natural decomposition process.

All of the bodies at the Facility eventually become part of the Dr. William Bass Skeletal Collection. Some are first used in decomposition research, while others are allowed to simply skeletonize. Through the years, employees of the facility have tried several methods to help the decomp process along. So far, the best method has been to leave a body zipped up inside of a body bag. The bag protects the bugs from sunlight, fooling them into devouring the flesh all the way through the epidermal layer of skin, which they normally leave intact for their protection.

To the left of the new bodies, on the other side of the electric fence, lie eight more cadavers that have been at the facility for a few weeks. Some are in plastic bags, some are not. The bodies not in plas-

Amy and Jarrett examining skeletal remains at the Body Farm.
(Copyright © Nathan Lefebvre, collection of the National Forensic Academy)

tic happen to be in the bloat stage of decomposition. This is by far the worst stage of the decomposition process. A cadaver, especially in the summer, can swell to four or five times its normal size. This is caused by cellular breakdown within the body, which creates a gas that inflates the abdomen. The stomach, face, arms, and legs also swell up like swollen balloons. It is during this stage that the skin begins to slough off and maggots begin to overwhelm the moist areas like the mouth, eyes, and groin. Maggots invade these areas by the thousands, crawling in and around the skin, making the body seem alive to the untrained eye.

The gravel path to the right leads up the hillside to the older part of the facility, where a camper, once used to house experiments, sits rusting away. Near this camper, scattered among the trees, lie several dry and leathery-looking bodies in a latter stage of decomposition known as mummification. A mummified body is one that has been allowed to decompose, uncovered and unburied, in the sun. The bugs will only eat up so far, leaving the skin for protection, which accidentally creates what look like mummies fresh out of Egypt.

Sometimes, though, if the conditions are right, the body will not mummify at all—it will turn to, well, soap. When some bodies are placed where the soil stays moist, their flesh turns into what is called adipocere. Adipocere has essentially the same chemical makeup of lye soap—only you don't want to wash your clothes with it. Adipocere can turn into either a dark blackish gray color, with white, crumbly chunks of flesh marbled throughout the entire body. Or, if you are really unlucky, it can turn into a grotesque paste that smells like the nastiest blue cheese you've ever smelled. We don't eat blue cheese anymore.

The Body Farm is not for the faint of heart—or stomach. Over the last two years, we have seen and smelled just about everything. Believe it or not, there are law enforcement officers in every class who have never seen a dead body, nor worked a case involving one. We are asked all the time if anybody has ever thrown up, and though no one has ever lost their lunch, several have been close. We've been close.

We've seen stuff that most people would never dream of, and wouldn't want to, for that matter. Once, a student reached her hand down into the soil to remove some dirt in a grave and uncovered the most putrid concoction of mud, body juice, and maggots ever imagined. We nearly conked heads running out to get fresh air—the fresh air of a Port-A-John, no less. Later that year, another student tried to exhume a partially unearthed cadaver by pulling on its still fleshy calf. Two tugs into that mistake and all we heard was what sounded like a giant can of Spam sloshing out its contents. As the flesh released itself from the bone and the student went tumbling into more slop, the goo from that leg plastered his face. Several of us gagged.

The show *Fear Factor* has nothing on us—and there's no fifty thousand dollars at the end. You might think you have seen gross stuff on television, but it's nothing like what we see in the flesh—literally. By far the worst experience we ever had was with a cadaver we buried that had maggots pouring out of its heel like a bottomless box of Minute Rice tipped on its side. We drug the cadaver up the hill, tugging on the slimy black plastic it had been buried in, gasping for air. A rotting corpse smells bad enough undisturbed, but when you move one, it

A mummified body at the Facility.

(Collection of the National Forensic Academy)

Students exhuming a grave uncover a white, crumbly substance known as adipocere.

(Collection of the National Forensic Academy)

reactivates the smell tenfold. When we reached the grave, we had to flip the body over off of the plastic and into the hole. Unfortunately, the body had adipocere tissue that spat back out of the grave and onto us as it plopped into place. This is about the time we are very, very glad we have worn all of the proper PPE (personal protective equipment). When you choose not to wear it, and it happens all the time, you end up with little splotches of decomp clinging about your body, particularly the face. There are no OSHA standards for cleanup and no products created that claim to "get even the toughest decomp out." In reality, all you're left with is your own devices. Most people simply squirt whatever antibacterial hand lotion is available onto the spot and wipe clean—and hope they forget it ever happened. We scurried to grab the shovels and finish the task, but before we could even fill in the grave the entire pit filled with maggots. That was the absolute grossest thing we have ever endured during our time at the Farm. Well, at least for now. We never know what will be in store for us behind that fence on our next visit to the Facility.

Time Since Death Research

What happens when you die? Most people have only experienced the cosmetic version, where the mortuary places the body in a virtual state of suspended animation. The process of embalming is merely a slowing down of the decomposition process in order to have enough time to perform the religious ceremonies associated with death (trust us, it does not stop it). Having seen death, death in its purest and most natural form, something we don't wish on the masses, it is very clear why the funeral home industry stays in business.

Unfortunately, we do not turn into ashes when we die. It can be a long and awesomely gross process. Telling just how long someone has been in decay—or in forensic science circles, their time since death— is difficult, to say the least. Being able to pinpoint the time can help CSIs determine when a victim was killed and help immensely with their investigation. But how can you tell how long someone has been dead?

Medical examiners rely on several methods, including sorting through the gastric contents of the deceased. If the deceased had eaten a light meal, it would take approximately one and a half to two hours for the stomach to empty. If the person had eaten a medium-size meal, it will take about three to four hours. A traditional Thanksgiving meal probably takes about four to six hours. All in all, it takes anywhere from six to eight hours for the head of the meal to reach the cecum, or where the small intestine empties stool into the large intestine. Dr. Michael Baden, deputy chief ME in New York City, has made a career of reading stomach contents after he personally conducted over fifteen thousand autopsies, studying the gastric contents of every one. But reading stomach contents is only as reliable as the physiology of how the person's body digested food and how long the person has been dead. If someone had just eaten a pizza and then was murdered, the pizza would look and smell just about like pizza, if an autopsy was performed within several hours. But if it has been more than about forty-eight hours, that pizza will not look like pizza, and you can rest assured it won't smell anything like pizza. Most of the time, though, bodies are not discovered early enough for stomach contents to matter. Therefore, other ways to determine the postmortem interval, time since death, had to be found.

Nearly all of the time since death research has come out of the pioneering works of Dr. Bass and his Body Farm. The Body Farm has provided a rich environment for Dr. Bass and his students to learn and observe. For nearly thirty years, researchers of time since death have been recording every meticulous detail of how a body changes when placed in different environments: in cars, in trailers, underwater, underground, in trees, and through each of the four seasons. From this research, it became clear that it was possible not only to tell visually when a person died; it was also possible to tell by studying the insects.

The study of bugs, known better as entomology, focuses on how insects take over and live within a cadaver during the decomposition process and the rates at which their offspring hatch. There have been all kinds of research conducted with bugs at the Body Farm. As a matter of fact, the first study ever conducted on the effects of bugs on human cadavers was performed at, where else, this one-of-a-kind facility.

In the early eighties, one of Dr. Bass's rising stars in forensic anthropology, Dr. Bill Rodriguez, provided the seminal work with regard to bugs and bodies. Dr. Rodriguez literally sat next to dozens of corpses for a period of two years, studying the cadre of bugs that arrived to consume the human body. His study focused mainly on blowflies and the blowfly hatchlings, also known as maggots. Dr. Rodriguez's studies included the tracking of the fly's arrival, the timing of when it lays its eggs, and when those eggs hatch. In doing so, Dr. Rodriguez helped discover the life cycle of the blowfly, which is approximately fifteen days, depending mainly upon the ambient temperature outside. Basically, eggs are laid on day one. By day two, the eggs hatch and the maggots feed on the corpse for about five days. Around day six, the maggots begin to pupate in the soil underneath and around the body. At day twelve, the flies emerge, only to mate by day fifteen, lay new eggs, and die, beginning the cycle all over again. That is the wonderful world of the blowfly in a nutshell.

One of the more interesting studies Dr. Rodriguez performed was painting the abdomen of several flies orange and releasing them from underneath the stadium to see just how far they would travel to nest in a cadaver (incidentally, it's about seven miles from the stadium to the Body Farm, or one mile as the "fly flies," and within hours, the orange flies arrived). Five were released and three were captured. Flies are unbelievably persistent and overwhelmingly numerous. They arrive by the hundreds, they lay eggs by the thousands, and if conditions are right, their wonderfully writhing offspring can hatch in as little as four hours. They are so pervasive that if we are not careful in the summer, flies will swarm even the moist areas of our living bodies, attempting to lay their eggs in our ears, eyes, mouth, or whatever area fits their needs. Dr. Rodriguez found this out the hard way. We're glad he paved the way and we don't have to learn through trial and error. Blowflies, suffice to say, are the nastiest creatures at the Body Farm.

After blowflies, wasps, beetles, and a host of other insects arrive to set up house, with carpet beetles usually the last to arrive. It is commonly thought that the blowfly is the main fly when it comes to corpses. Mummified bodies will also attract the common housefly, however, which lays a much smaller egg that turns into a larva known

SHOO FLY

Blowflies will not fly once the temperature falls below fifty degrees Fahrenheit. This means that if a relatively fresh body is found covered in maggots, the individual was more than likely killed in warm weather and not in cold. This might give the investigator at least a starting point in discovering time since death.

as the cheese skipper maggot. The cheese skipper maggot, if the season is right, will go through a migratory process where they literally skip in droves from one corpse to another, like tiny white Mexican jumping beans. This is rarely seen in real life, but it is relatively common at the Body Farm. It is a sight to behold and one that is guaranteed to make you itch.

The Body Farm is a constant source of research and discovery into all things gross. It is this unparalleled, twenty-four-hours-a-day, seven-days-a-week experience with the dead that has given Dr. Bass the credential of being one of the world's foremost authorities on time since death. But even the best make mistakes. With all of Dr. Bass's brilliance and expertise, even he once miscalculated in a time since death case. He was called out to examine an exhumed corpse in an effort to find out when the person had died. After examining the body, finding it still full of flesh and very pliable, he determined that the person had been dead for only a few weeks. In reality, the person had been dead for more than one hundred years! Looks can be deceiving. There are so many factors that can impact the rate of decomposition, from the soil in which a person is buried all the way down to a person's diet, that it is impossible to calculate with any degree of certainty. Visible indicators and insects are good, but they are not precise. As a direct result of this error, new methodologies have been pioneered to help better determine and understand the process of decomposition.

Oak Ridge National Laboratory

Crammed beneath a concrete bunker, deep in the bowels of the Oak Ridge National Laboratory, the same laboratory that's famous for creating the atomic bomb, sits a brilliant and unassuming young scientist, poring over thousands of bits of data. This scientist, Dr. Arpad Vass, with Dr. Bass's encouragement, has set out to find a better and more scientific method for determining the time since death interval.

Oak Ridge National Laboratory, more commonly known as ORNL, is host to some of the world's most important and one-of-a-kind research. You can walk around any corner and see scientists working on relatively simple projects, like perfecting RF transmitters used to track shipments of medicine, to more complex concepts, such as the creation of biological, self-healing skin for airplane wings. It's never a dull moment at ORNL. It takes a certain kind of brain to come up with some of the wild ideas that come out of the lab, and Dr. Vass's brain is no exception, being one of the true pioneers in the field of forensic biology—a field essentially created by him.

Visiting Dr. Vass out at the lab is a surreal experience, to say the least. Walking through his small laboratory, stepping over bags labeled "radioactive waste," we reach the part of the lab where he conducts his research. There are several "refrigerators from hell," as we like to call them, scattered throughout the laboratory. These fridges are just like the ones we have at home. Except for the contents. Some hold decomposing human remains (that is, body goo) collected for research, while others, and the ones we initially leaned against on our first visit, hold live vials of anthrax and other even more deadly viruses that we were told would make our brains melt out through our ears. That didn't sound all that fun to us, so, needless to say, we no longer lean, sit, or touch anything while visiting Dr. Vass.

The main focus of Dr. Vass's research revolves around the volatile fatty acids (VFAs) that leach out of the body during decay. These fluids begin to seep out of a corpse, mainly through the anus, sometime after the process of putrefaction begins. Putrefaction, the process that gave rise to the wonderful word *putrid*, is where the bacteria within the body begin to liquefy the organs and soft tissue. In other words, all of the bacteria that live in our bodies, helping with digestion, digest us when we die. Pleasant dreams.

Dr. Vass figured out through his research that it was possible to analyze the contents of the soil from underneath a decomposing corpse and determine the time since death with a high degree of accuracy. In order to make this determination, he took the average temperatures during the decomposition process of his test subjects, as well as the amount of time it took his corpses to go from the fresh stage to the pseudo-skeletonized stage, and came up with a number for accumulated degree days (ADDs). That magic number is 1285. If a CSI finds a decomposing body, a rough "guesstimate" of time since death could be taken on the spot simply by taking the average historical temperature for that day and dividing it into 1285. On the other hand, if a CSI takes a sample to Dr. Vass, something that is beginning to happen more and more, he can estimate time since death with a degree of accuracy of plus or minus two days for every month of decomposition. That is unprecedented accuracy.

Dr. Vass and other researchers have continued to fine-tune this research to better pinpoint what is now more commonly known in anthropological circles as the *postmortem interval* (instead of time since death). New studies involve the analysis of the organs (heart, kidneys, and brain) of a decaying corpse to determine their chemical makeup at the various stages of decomposition. They have concluded that accumulated degree days are no longer accurate enough to predict the postmortem interval. What is more accurate are cumulative degree hours (CDHs). This research has begun to redefine the study of decomposition.

Determining when someone died is crucial for an investigator. Knowing how long a body has been decomposing in the woods gives the CSI a good starting place from which to work. But human remains are not always found even when there is information that the person in question is probably dead. Often, the bodies are buried, or, as the tragedy of the collapse of the World Trade Center illustrated, they are simply impossible to pinpoint. This is where cadaver dogs are usually brought into a case.

Cadaver Dogs

Cadaver dogs can be a useful tool in locating hidden human remains, but they are not as accurate or as reliable as they are portrayed to be. There are a few dogs in the United States that have proven their worth, but the vast majority of cadaver dogs never find the first body. It is not known exactly what the dogs smell, and therefore, it is nearly impossible to train them and standardize their abilities. It is believed that they pick up on one of five historically known gases produced during the decomposition process: methanol, ammonia, carbon dioxide, hydrogen sulfide, or organic acids.

Commissioned by the Federal Bureau of Investigation, Dr. Vass was challenged to lay the groundwork to ultimately develop a mechanical cadaver dog—so to speak. The initial goal of the project was to first document what gases actually are released from a corpse as it decays, in the hopes of one day creating a portable machine capable of

Dr. Vass, using his decompositional gas-catching invention.
(Collection of the National Forensic Academy)

"smelling" clandestine graves. Though the research is still in its infancy, Dr. Vass has detected no less than 104 different gases—99 more than previously thought. Needless to say, his research will once again revolutionize the science behind decompositional analysis.

It's clear that, in only a little more than thirty-five years, we have come a long way toward understanding how we are ultimately returned to the earth. The process is so very complicated—and the more that is discovered about it, the more complicated it becomes. Death has been such a scary subject, and one that very few people have ever wanted to broach. The country and the world owe a great deal of gratitude to Dr. Bass and to all of those who have followed, and continue to follow, in his footsteps.

TIME SINCE DEATH

One of the most notorious murder cases in the country occurred right in our backyard. In October of 2002, a severed head was found floating in Boone Lake, located in Washington County, Tennessee. A couple of days later, a pair of hands washed ashore on the beach of that very same lake. An investigation into the dismembered body led the police to a rented storage facility, where two bodies were found stuffed into fifty-gallon Rubbermaid containers. The two individuals were identified as a recently married couple from Georgia who had been seen with a known felon by the name of Howard Hawk Willis.

Mr. Willis was indicted on two counts of murder and currently sits in a Washington County jail awaiting trial. He is also the prime suspect in the murder and dismemberment of his stepfather.

We were contacted by investigators from Washington County about funding Dr. Vass to perform a time since death study on the two bodies found at the storage facility. It was important for their case to establish whether the bodies in question were killed on the same day or there was an interval between the slayings. This information would either help to corroborate or refute the defendant's testimony.

In June of 2004, investigators arrived at our office with notebooks filled with information regarding the case. We could only stomach about one page of the crime scene photographs that depicted one of the most appalling murders ever imagined. We got to work right away in funding Dr. Vass's work.

The investigators transported to the Oak Ridge National Laboratory a sample of the volatile fatty acids from the remains of both of the decedents. Their remains had essentially turned to nothing but fluid, not counting the skeleton. But there was enough left for Dr. Vass to work with.

Ultimately, Dr. Vass concluded that there was about a three-day interval between the deaths of the two young people, refuting the defendant's testimony. Dr. Vass determined this by grinding up tissue samples of the decedents and comparing the ratios between the amino acids and the other biomarkers in the tissue. He then took the results and correlated historical temperature data to determine the postmortem interval of the victims. The district attorney general sent a letter to our office thanking us for our assistance and letting us know that Dr. Vass's incredible work "was of great benefit to the office and strengthened the case immensely."

Dr. Vass's research has already begun to make a tremendous impact on the field of crime scene investigation—an impact that has only scratched the surface.

5

DIGGIN' UP BONES
Burial Recovery

"The leg bone's connected to the ankle bone, the ankle bone's connected to the foot bone, the foot bone's connected to the . . ." You
know the old childhood song. And it's relatively true if you find a body
completely intact. But that doesn't happen very often in real life, and
it's especially rare at the Body Farm. Years of decaying bodies have
provided at least one change to the ecosystem behind the university
hospital: extra-large "critters." Animals growing up around the Body
Farm have become accustomed to a never-ending bounty provided by
the anthropologists doing their research. Birds, rats, possums, and raccoons feast daily and nightly, tearing flesh from limbs and limbs from
flesh. When it comes time for the anthropologists to collect the bones
left after a body has decomposed, it is a veritable scavenger hunt, looking for where the animals have dragged the pieces. That's part of what
each class is taught. Rarely does anyone stumble across human remains; it's only after a dog brings in a bone or a skull that the search
really begins. But first you need to know whom, or in some cases what,
you are looking for.

We cannot tell you how many times we get a call from someone
who has found bones in their yard. We are inundated by overzealous
people desperately wanting to be part of the forensic wave. Too bad

they can't remember they had KFC for dinner and dumped their chicken bones outside of their house.

Bones play a critical role in the art of crime scene investigation. Most people understand the concept that the bigger the bone, the bigger the animal. But that's about all you can really tell—that is, until you come through the Forensic Academy.

One hundred six thousand. That's how many people traverse the steps up to the University of Tennessee stadium on Saturdays during football season. All of these people, walking around in a sea of orange, unknowingly pass right by the doors of the forensic osteology lab. Any forensic case that needs an anthropologist, regardless of whether it is a missing person case, makes its way through the dingy brown doors. With an eerie creak, the doors swing open to reveal boxes upon boxes of skeletal remains, tables full of skulls and other disparate bones, and bags and bags of teeth. These hundreds of boxes are complete skeletons from Dr. Bass's early endeavors working with Native American remains in the plains of South Dakota. It is as if hundreds of Humpty Dumpties have fallen down and all of the university's anthropologists are trying to put them back together again. Most of the loose bones and teeth are from active cases, but there are several that represent cases that are unsolved. The anthropology department has no fewer than eighty unidentified human remains from nearly five thousand cases nationwide.

Down the hall from the osteology lab lie the remains of those who have donated their afterlifes to scientific study, numbering just over five hundred strong. These relics of the Body Farm lie in state, as part of the largest skeletal collection in the world. The repository for these remains is actually an old dorm room that has been turned into some kind of bizarre tomb—minus the ornate ossuaries. Instead, these bones have come to rest in oversized cardboard containers stacked in order by date of donation on shelves like shoeboxes in a shoe store. Only here, you do not ask for a size seven. Dr. Bass's Necropolis is complete, down to the parishioner who comes by once a year to bless the remains, as well as the crypt that houses them. It is a strange place that transcends time, hanging somewhere between the modern world and the Middle Ages.

Boxes of skeletal remains—part of the Dr. Bass Skeletal Collection.

(Collection of the National Forensic Academy)

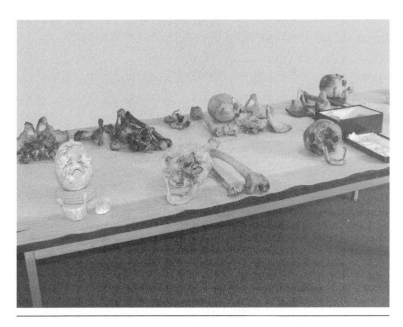

A table full of human remains placed out in the hallway at the academy.

(Collection of the National Forensic Academy)

As we march down the corridor toward the collection, it reminds us of the Overlook Hotel, made famous by the movie *The Shining*. We even half expect a set of resurrected twins to meet us at the door to the collection. Anyone who enters the hallway of the dead immediately notices the smell. It is not decomp, per se. The ancients had a term for all of the rotting bones entombed beneath their places of worship—they called it effluvia. Effluvia will emanate for a millennia as the bones continue to break down. Ask anyone who has undertaken a tour of the catacombs of the Crusades. A wave of effluvia hits your nostrils the moment you enter the corridor, and it sticks to the back of your tongue, where the taste buds for anything putrid exist.

The remains in this collection are studied, measured, and cataloged, providing the world's most complete data on the ever-changing population that is the modern *Homo sapiens*. Statistically speaking, the skeletons of modern people, regardless of ancestry, are becoming taller, less dense, and most important, more homogenous—the latter fact providing the biggest challenge for anthropologists and CSIs alike.

When the class arrives at the forensic lab, they are introduced to tables upon tables of bones, including skulls, femurs, knees, and pelvises, not all of which are human. Academy students are taught how to differentiate between human bones and commonly found nonhuman bones, such as those from dogs and deer. This can be done easily if long bones like the femur are found. The joints in humans are obviously different from a deer's, particularly in their roundness, as well as size. Students are also taught how to determine the sex, age, and ancestry just by looking at certain bones. There is no better place in the world to study human bones than at the Anthropology Osteology Laboratory. Dr. Bass wrote the definitive book on bones, titled simply *Human Osteology: A Laboratory and Field Manual*. This groundbreaking guide can be found on the shelves of virtually every forensic anthropologist and medical examiner across the country. It is a perfect manual for a CSI to have at his or her disposal at all times, and we send our students home with it when they graduate. It can be an invaluable guide for when bones are discovered at a crime scene.

Forensic anthropologists, unlike medical examiners, cannot actually determine cause of death because they are not medical doctors. In a forensic case, it is the forensic anthropologist's job to determine what Dr. Bass calls the Big Four: race, ancestry, sex, and age. Through their examination of human remains, if there are definitive markers that seem to contribute to a person's death, like bullet fragments embedded in bone, then they can determine what is typically called the "manner of death." Some would argue that *manner* and *cause* are one and the same.

Dr. Bass's protégés give the students a brief lecture on how they can determine, if they have enough evidence, the Big Four. If, for example, a hip bone or pelvis is found in the woods, both age and sex can be determined. Age can be determined by looking at what is called the pubic symphysis, and sex can be determined by the size. Here's how. A man's pelvis is narrower than a woman's. This is because of the metamorphosis a female goes through as she reaches adolescence. The female pelvis begins to broaden, allowing for the future possibility of childbirth. This is also why women are more flexible than men. Second, the pelvis behaves similarly to the skull, in that it has sutures where the bones eventually fuse together as we age. This suturelike feature, called the pubic symphysis, is bumpy in a female's teens, smooth in her twenties, and spongy by her forties. Since these differences are easily observed, if you know what to look for, it is of paramount importance for the class to actually hold the bones, observing them up close, and determining for themselves what is what and who is who.

In order to figure out the stature or size of a person, the anthropologist ideally needs some of the long bones, like those found in the arms (radius, ulna, humerus) and legs (tibia, fibula, femur). But of all of these, the femur represents size the best. For years, anthropologists at the Body Farm have been measuring and cataloging the skeletal remains of those who decompose at their facility. This has allowed the creation of a database called FORDISC. FORDISC, an acronym for forensic discrimination software, is the world's leading database with regard to information on modern human skeletons. An anthropologist with this software can simply measure one of the long bones and plug the results into the program, and it will immediately produce an approximation of size. This software was instrumental in helping one poor family after the tragic events of 9/11. The living relatives of this decimated family sent some pieces of bone to the Anthropology Department to try to determine whose they were. DNA tests had proven a familial relationship, but two daughters were lost in the Pennsylvania plane crash tragedy. One was in her early teens, while the other was five years old. The anthropologists were able to use FORDISC to determine that the bones came from the older sibling, shedding a little light on the human remains the family was desperately trying to identify. FORDISC is one of the research projects that our Forensic Academy is currently funding to help put it online. This would allow other anthropologists from around the world to catalog their data as well.

Ancestry is commonly determined by studying the morphological (form and structure) traits of the skull, though the patella (kneecap) can be used to a lesser extent. Typically, skulls have a specific look if you're of Asian descent, African descent, European descent, and so on. The comingling of ethnicities over time, however, has made the morphology of skulls quite similar. This has made it more difficult to determine ancestry just by the skull—a fact that becomes readily apparent to the class. In reality, it is experience with human remains that makes all of the difference, and Dr. Bass has more than most.

Back in the classroom, our students wait anxiously for one of the more anticipated parts of the entire academy. Dr. Bass, wearing his trademark Snoopy necktie and carrying several boxes of bones and gross slides, arrives to lecture for the first time. It is truly a sight to behold, Dr. Bass, in his element, feverishly going from case to case as he tries to give just a glimpse into what he has learned over the past forty years. He is a showman, augmenting his humorous lecturing style with items like prosthetic hips, artificial knees, and sternums wired together, fresh from a heart bypass surgery that did not take. As the items are passed around from student to student, most of them looking down at the object and cringing, Dr. Bass makes the point to the class that it is not enough just to recognize various bones—it is just as important to recognize how they are augmented through various surgeries. The inexperienced crime scene investigator, searching the woods for human remains, might discount a metallic-looking object sticking out from under some brush, not realizing that it is the tip of a femur with a re-

Dr. Bass wearing his traditional Snoopy necktie.
(Collection of the National Forensic Academy)

constructed knee. Dr. Bass also always brings in an entire spine, held together by fishing line. The discs of the spine look very jagged, and if you did not know better you would assume that it was the spine of a very old individual. You would have assumed wrong. The jaggedness of the disks is caused by what is called osteoarthritic lipping—a process that begins at age thirty. Invariably, someone asks Dr. Bass if there is a way to prevent this from happening, and in traditional fashion he answers as if it has been choreographed, "Die young!" After a lot of laughing, Dr. Bass finishes his lecture by giving the students the first scenario for their upcoming work at the Body Farm:

A hunter, passing through the woods, saw what appeared to be a bone, lying among the leaves, at the top of a hillside where he was hunting. About two years ago, a young female, twenty-six years of age, went missing, last seen at the entrance of these very woods.

Your CSI unit has been called to the scene where the hunter spotted the bone in order to find out if it is human and if it could be that of the lost female.

The next day, the class arrives at the Body Farm. Once they settle down and their nervous anticipation wanes a bit, they suit up for their upcoming experience. At a minimum, each student must wear a complete Tyvek suit and gloves before they will even be allowed to dig. Face shields, masks, and hair protection are all provided, but not required and rarely worn. In fact, no one has ever worn a face shield or the hair protection, and very few have even worn a mask, as these are deemed signs of weakness.

If it is warm and bugs are prevalent, industrial-strength bug spray is liberally applied on everyone to prevent the transfer of fluids via insects. Hepatitis B is the major concern, and a vaccination for it is required to participate in the class. Though all bodies are screened

Session Nine graduates suit up for their journey into the Body Farm.

(Collection of the National Forensic Academy)

thoroughly (no one with HIV, AIDS, hepatitis, and/or tuberculosis is accepted as a donation at the Body Farm), you just never know what might be out there. Besides, insects at the Body Farm are just nasty. There is a very old saying in the South about flies, "First on the cat's ass, then on the butter." Trust us, you do not even want to think about that analogy while at the Body Farm.

The first task the students must accomplish at the Facility is what we refer to as the scatter search. When human skeletal remains are discovered, they have usually been scattered about by many things. Weather clearly plays a role, but animals are the main culprits. Researchers at the facility have discovered many interesting things about how animals participate in the decomposition process. For instance, raccoons will arrive at a decomposing body and pick at the fleshy, fatty parts of the body, particularly the thighs. They are interested in the meat that lies underneath the epidermis. They reach their bounty through a hole that they have bitten into the skin. Many anthropologists had theorized that these holes found in decomposing bodies were simply an anomaly with regard to the decomposition process. It wasn't until recently that it was discovered that raccoons invariably caused these holes.

Furthermore, animals are attracted to a decomposing body in succession, much as insects are. Larger carnivores (raccoons, possums) arrive first, devouring most of the flesh. When most of the meat is gone, along come the smaller animals, like rats, whose interest lies solely with the joints of the cadaver. This is where the fattiest nutrients reside within the marrow. Next come the herbivores, such as squirrels. Squirrels nibble away at the small bones, like those in the ribs, searching for calcium and other minerals.

For a long time, it was readily believed that when the body was turned into nothing more than bones, all of the animal kingdom continued to return in an attempt to pick the bones clean of any remaining flesh, thus causing the remains to be scattered. This hypothesis is not entirely true. Most of the time, when the body is in this stage of the decomposition process, animals will scatter the bones about rather wildly, not in search of flesh but in search of maggots. Maggots burrow themselves in the ground underneath and around a body in a radius of five or six feet. Animals know this and go looking for these juicy bits of protein. Hence, this is the reason they scatter the bones about. It is imperative for the CSI to understand these processes so they will be able to recover as many of the bones as possible, because they never know which one might hold that all-important clue. This is why we teach the students scattered remains recovery.

In three separate areas a precise number of bones and pieces of evidence have been scattered among the leaves, branches, and vines, and the students must find each and every item. We, along with the instructors, do this several months before the class arrives. We map each item, marking its coordinates with a GPS so that we will know precisely where each piece of evidence is. This is done three times, trying to stage as closely as possible the same crime scene in each area. The class will be divided into three teams, with each team using the same scenario that Dr. Bass gave them back in the classroom. The team leader of each team will be led to the place where the hunter spotted what appeared to be a bone.

The first thing each group must decide is how to work the scene. Unfortunately, they do not know that they have been tricked. By finding a bone at the top of a hill, most CSIs will make that the point at which to begin the search, as in the case involving the remains of Chandra Levy.

Chandra Levy was a Capitol Hill intern who mysteriously disappeared in 2001. It wasn't until a year later, in May 2002, that her remains were found in a park that the police had already searched on numerous occasions. The police had committed a major error in their search.

As the class has learned, when human remains are found in an advanced stage of decomposition, it is probable that the elements like wind, rain, and snow, along with various animals, have scattered the remains over time. Therefore, in all probability, the bones will have been scattered down the hill—not up. This is especially true for a round, heavy object like a skull. By searching from the top, a lot of evidence is missed or destroyed. We allow each team to decide how they will work the scene, and if they choose to work it incorrectly, which

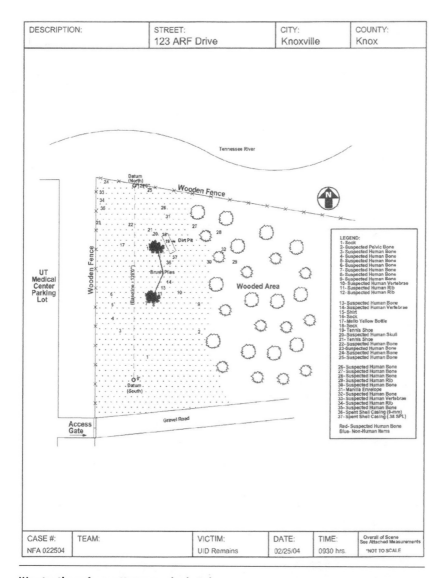

| DESCRIPTION: | STREET: 123 ARF Drive | CITY: Knoxville | COUNTY: Knox |

Tennessee River

Datum (North)

Wooden Fence

UT Medical Center Parking Lot

Wooden Fence

Dirt Pit

Brush Piles

Wooded Area

Datum (South)

Gravel Road

Access Gate

LEGEND:
1- Sock
2- Suspected Pelvic Bone
3- Suspected Human Bone
4- Suspected Human Bone
5- Suspected Human Bone
6- Suspected Human Bone
7- Suspected Human Bone
8- Suspected Human Bone
9- Suspected Human Bone
10- Suspected Human Vertebrae
11- Suspected Human Rib
12- Suspected Human Rib

13- Suspected Human Bone
14- Suspected Human Vertebrae
15- Shirt
16- Sock
17- Mello Yellow Bottle
18- Sock
19- Tennis Shoe
20- Suspected Human Skull
21- Tennis Shoe
22- Suspected Human Bone
23- Suspected Human Bone
24- Suspected Human Bone
25- Suspected Human Bone

26- Suspected Human Bone
27- Suspected Human Bone
28- Suspected Human Bone
29- Suspected Human Rib
30- Suspected Human Bone
31- Manilla Envelope
32- Suspected Human Bone
33- Suspected Human Vertebrae
34- Suspected Human Rib
35- Suspected Human Bone
36- Spent Shell Casing (9-mm)
37- Spent Shell Casing (.38 SPL)

Red- Suspected Human Bone
Blue- Non-Human Items

| CASE #: NFA 022504 | TEAM: | VICTIM: UID Remains | DATE: 02/25/04 | TIME: 0930 hrs. | Overall of Scene See Attached Measurements *NOT TO SCALE |

Illustration of a scatter search sketch.

(Collection of the National Forensic Academy)

usually happens, the instructors step in and tell them why they should work the scene from the bottom up. By making this error in practice, they should always remember to do it right when back in the real world.

Working the bone scatter is very laborious. The students search leaf by leaf, on their hands and knees, while moving across the landscape in a straight, horizontal line. They look for anything that looks like it could be either a bone or a piece of evidence. When a piece of evidence is found, it is marked with a flag and recorded in the evidence log. Once they believe they have exhausted the search and all of the items are found, each piece is photographed, labeled, and placed in a brown evidence bag. Each object's location within the crime scene is also recorded. This data will be used to make a crime scene sketch after they get back in the classroom.

We usually place about thirty or so bones, three or four shell cas-

Session Eight graduates search on their hands and knees for human remains and evidence during an aboveground scatter search.

(Collection of the National Forensic Academy)

ings, and maybe a piece of clothing. Once the teams have finished the search, we go over their results. Usually, the teams end up with about thirty-two or thirty-three bones because they have collected what we novices call sticks (sometimes it's hard to tell). Occasionally they will be short a bone because it just looked too good for one of the critters, usually a squirrel, to pass up. The fun of chasing a squirrel around the Body Farm for a bone has worn on us.

It takes about eight hours, give or take, to complete the bone scatter search. Some classes finish earlier than others, and when that happens, they're in for a real treat. Recently Dr. Vass, the same Dr. Vass responsible for developing some of the most extraordinary capabilities used to discover human remains, has fallen in love with the prospect of "divining for bodies."

In order to do this, he takes a metal coat hanger like you would get from the dry cleaner, the kind with the cardboard tube, and cuts it in half, discarding the hook portion. Using the cardboard pieces as handles, he ends up with two L-shaped divining instruments that can move independently of the cardboard. He then holds his hands at his waist; with the metal portion of the hangers pointing straight out, he walks toward where he thinks a body might be decomposing. As he gets close, the metal pieces will point inward. It is unbelievable, to say the least, but we have both done this and it feels as if a force is acting upon the metal. Dr. Vass is convinced that the gasses that are released from the body create a magnetic charge that is opposite of the earth's magnetic field, which interacts with the divining hangers. Can you say new research? This is something the class will try on the following day during their burial recovery exercise.

It has become a running joke among NFA students that as soon as they graduate from the academy, they will undoubtedly go back to their departments and within weeks end up with a burial recovery case. That has happened at least seven times over the past two years, in cities such as Detroit, Philadelphia, and Seattle. Though it has become more common for graduates of the NFA to have cases involving buried bodies, across the country it is not as widespread as you might think. Because of TV shows like *CSI* and the media's tendency to overhype crimes, people are under the impression that finding buried bodies happens almost every day. Yet there are over 18,000 different law enforcement agencies in the United States, many of which have never even responded to a homicide, let alone recovered a buried body. Furthermore, unless they are members of the FBI's Evidence Response Team or graduates of the NFA, they haven't been trained on how to properly recover human remains.

Most departments, when confronted with a buried body case, simply rely on the expertise of a backhoe operator to perform the excavation in one "scoop," destroying any chance of actually processing the scene. To further illustrate how widespread that technique is, each and every class has asked for a backhoe during burial recovery week at the academy. Though we do not provide the students with any motorized earthmoving equipment, we do provide them with good old-fashioned know-how—not to mention many, many shovels and buckets.

After everyone is suited up, sprayed down, and ready to go, the class is once again divided into three teams, with each team being assigned one grave to find and exhume. The teams are each given a scenario about why they have been called to the scene, such as:

A convicted serial killer has decided to tell where he has buried some of his victims, in exchange for leniency. He does not remember exactly where he buried the bodies because it was so long ago. Officers have learned over the years not to trust him. They are at their wits' end. They want to put these cases to rest, but they are afraid to take him out of his cell. They have no place else to turn. They've decided to take that chance.

Driving down a winding gravel road that leads to a deserted wooded lot, he yells, "Over there!" They stop at the edge of a hill that leads down to the banks of the Tennessee River. Handcuffed and shackled, he is led out of the car. They know the killer might get pleasure out of reliving his crime, so they are hesitant to take him down the hill. But at the same time they have no choice, so they do. He leads them to the northwest corner of the lot where he believes three bodies are buried. Your team has been called in to discover and, if found, exhume the bodies.

Each team is then led to approximately one acre of land, where they have to find a body or bodies that were buried by a previous NFA class. They do this through a tedious process called probing. Probing is more of an art than a science. Essentially, students each push a large metal "T" through the ground, feeling for soft areas that might indicate a disturbance in the soil. The entire team probes, with each person walking in a straight line, moving forward one step at a time. If someone feels a "soft spot," the entire team moves to that particular area and tries to determine if it is an anomaly or a grave. Once a grave has been identified, flags are placed to mark the edges. Four stakes are strategically driven into the ground outside of the grave area and twine is stretched from each point, forming a giant plus sign, dividing the grave into four sections, or quadrants. Line levels are attached to each piece of twine. These lines will be the measuring point for gauging depth when evidence is uncovered and recorded.

The exhumation of the grave begins with one student digging in each quadrant, while the fifth member of the team removes the buckets of dirt and sifts them through a mesh screen. In this way, each of the four quadrants is dug meticulously by hand with a trowel, and measurements are taken at regular intervals from the original lines to ensure the uniformity of the dig. While it is not imperative to keep the dig uniform, the students are taught to do so because it is easier to control the speed and thoroughness in which the scene is processed. The exhumation continues until a piece of evidence is unearthed.

The evidence, be it a bone or penny or some other "foreign" object, is photographed with sizing scales and directional markings. Then a measurement is taken from the original line to the object, cataloging the depth and quadrant where the item was discovered. If by chance there is evidence found by the team member sifting the soil (finger and toe bones usually make their way here), the item is photographed in the screen where it was found and cataloged using only the quadrant it was discovered in as information, and not the depth or direction. The item is then removed and bagged to be processed later. This is done for every piece of evidence, and since each NFA class buries the bodies for the next, you can bet that there is a lot of evidence in the grave (stu-

Session Three graduates quadrant off two adjacent graves.

(Collection of the National Forensic Academy)

Session Two graduates Brent Murphy and J. R. Wallace sift dirt from a burial site.

(Copyright © Jarrett Hallcox, collection of the National Forensic Academy)

dents have planted everything from Old Bastard Ale bottles to pink bunny ears to packets of KY Jelly).

Most of the graves we dig for the class are relatively shallow—not more than four feet deep—to simulate the typical real-life situation. Murderers are usually in a big hurry, for obvious reasons, and do not dig deep holes to place their victims in. It is ironic that those who do take the time to dig deep—especially in areas like east Tennessee, where the topsoil turns to cool, moist clay at about three feet—end up preserving the body, the evidence, and their chances of getting caught.

It usually takes one full day of digging before each team reaches its

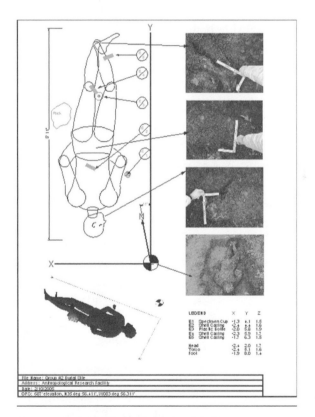

A computerized sketch of the burial site crime scene, created by Session Eleven graduate Danny Mouttet.

(Collection of the National Forensic Academy)

MAGGOT MIGRATION

If a CSI does not have a compass, there is a way to determine directionality. Typically, maggots will migrate about five or six feet from a body, moving due north, and burrow down in the ground until they hatch. If the CSI finds the burrowed maggots, he will be facing due north.

body, with the next day being the day the body is actually exhumed. When the team reaches the body, they carefully remove the dirt from all sides using trowels and small paintbrushes. The body is then removed gently, pulling the flesh and bone away from the soil. These remains, every single piece, are placed in red biohazard bags to be taken to the forensic center. The final resting place for the remains is the Dr. William Bass Skeletal Collection. But before they can be added to the collection, they must be processed. Flesh not attached to bone will be incinerated, while all other remains will be literally cooked in large military-style metal pots in order to remove the still-attached flesh—another smell not soon forgotten.

If this were a real-life situation, officers would go by the old rule, "If it's wet, it's a good bet. If it's dry, let it lie." This simply means that if the body is wet, meaning it is relatively fresh, it is more likely that there will still be evidence, such as wound patterns, that a medical examiner could interpret. If the body is dry, meaning it is more mummified or skeletal, then a forensic anthropologist should be called in to examine the remains.

Once the body has been fully recovered and all visible evidence photographed and collected, team members continue processing the grave and learn how to carefully identify all of the edges of the grave, including the bottom. This is a skill that is perfected the more it is performed, and is important for a couple of reasons. First, if the grave was dug with a tool that has a definitive mark on it, such as a shovel with a broken blade, it is possible to match that tool with its corresponding pattern along the grave wall. Second, and most important, the students learn to dig even after the body is removed, until they reach the very bottom of the grave. Often after digging a hole, perpetrators throw a cigarette butt or a condom pack (both common) or other debris into the hole before dumping the body. These can be extremely important pieces of evidence that might be missed. A cigarette butt and yes, even a condom pack, could yield a possible DNA hit. Now, most people think that the condom pack might yield a fingerprint, which is highly unlikely in those conditions, and rarely think about DNA. It has been shown, however, that more often than not the perpetrator will actually hold the victim down with one hand and use his other hand and his teeth to tear open the pack, thus leaving behind possible DNA evidence.

With the grave completely exhumed and all of the evidence col-

Jarrett and Amy begin digging a grave for an upcoming session of the academy.

(Copyright © Nathan Lefebvre, collection of the National Forensic Academy)

lected, the teams take a collective sigh of relief. Work at the Body Farm is hard, tedious, nauseating, and emotional. The experience is once in a lifetime, but it is also a test of one's mettle. Excitement and anticipation run high. Nearly every class exhibits the kind of anxiety that leads to nervous laughter at some point.

When the exhumation is complete, it's time for us to bury bodies for another NFA class. We use the freshly exhumed graves to bury the bodies in. There have been a few instances where the exhumed grave had been used so many times we needed to dig a new one. The bodies that are buried are normally already partially decomposed and have been used as part of decomposition research. Once the bodies have been selected, the students move the bodies, via a gurney used for snow recovery (like a sled), to their graves, careful to take every piece—both natural and man-made. The last body we buried had been placed face-down and allowed to decompose naturally. When we went to collect the body, turning it over gently, we noticed two odd-looking round, brown objects lying underneath, in near perfect symmetry. Discolored, but still very pliable, the two breast implants lay where the newly de-composed breasts had been. They, along with the rest of the body, made it to the grave.

As we place the bodies into the graves, the students toss in any evidence they have brought with them. Most teams leave some sort of note, either as merely a greeting or a way to throw off the next class. Some have left their pictures, while others have gone so far as to leave taped "confessions." The bodies are then covered with dirt, not to be exhumed until four months later. Then, as one last event—a group picture with the infamous Body Farm sign is taken, a final memento of an experience of a lifetime.

Session Eight graduates pose for a picture after our first-ever snow exhumation.

(Copyright © Amy Welch, collection of the National Forensic Academy)

FORENSIC ANTHROPOLOGY

Hunters are notorious for stumbling across bones, especially in largely rural areas like Tennessee. Law enforcement officials all across the state are inundated with all kinds of bones. But, unless it is a skull, they cannot tell one bone from another. For that, you need either a graduate from the NFA or, better yet, an anthropologist. Around here, we're fortunate to have a "decent" one right in our backyard.

Almost thirty years ago, a young woman (the victim), her sister, and a family friend left home one Friday evening to go to the county fair. Instead of going to the fair, the sister had the bright idea of going to a local "juke joint" called the Rainbow Club. At the club, they met several friends, including an old boyfriend of the sister. The victim, too young to get into the dive, was helped by the ex-boyfriend to get into the bar. Once inside, they all began drinking liquor and smoking pot. After a while, the ex asked the victim to go outside to smoke a joint. The victim told her sister where she was going. Thirty minutes after the victim went outside, her sister went to look for her, only to find that she was nowhere in sight. The sister eventually went home early Saturday morning to still-awake parents, waiting for their daughters to come home. Though they were worried that the one sister had not made it home yet, it was not all that uncommon, seeing as she had "run away" several times before, only to return the next day. But by Sunday they had not seen or heard from the girl and decided to go to the police to file a missing persons report.

Several weeks later, the sister went back to the club and confronted her ex, demanding to know what had happened to her sister. The ex simply ignored her, never saying a word. The parents of the victim posted a substantial reward and traveled all across the United States over the next couple of years, following leads to no avail. Police interrogated the ex-boyfriend, several of his relatives, and a couple of his friends, but turned up nothing concrete.

Three years later, on Thanksgiving Day, some hunters came across a skull, missing a jaw bone, not more than two feet from the road. They took the skull to the local authorities. A group of law enforcement officials and local citizens went to the scene to perform a "grid pattern search" of the area. Their efforts turned up a large mass of bones, approximately forty feet from where the skull was found. The police sent the bones to Dr. Bass to analyze. Immediately, Dr. Bass concluded that, except for the skull, the bones were nothing more than animal bones—bones from a pig, two dogs, and a goat.

Though the find was odd, it was not a crime and it was definitely not the victim. Five days later, the police returned to search the scene more thoroughly, expanding the perimeter of their search. Nearly 110 feet from the spot where they began their search, a piece of a blouse, a ring, and more bones were found. Only this time they were not animal bones.

Dr. Bass, once again analyzing the bones, concluded that this time the bones were from a white female, between the ages of fourteen and seventeen. Dental records confirmed that the skull and jaw found were that of the victim (the mother of the victim confirmed that the ring was her daughter's). Furthermore, Dr. Bass stated that the bones had been lying in the woods at least four months and less than four years. Dr. Bass concluded that the time of year the bones were found meant that flesh could have been on the bones four months previous to their discovery. Once a body is down to bone, however, there is little change to this extraordinarily durable human remain for five to ten years, when they begin to change color, become more brittle, and split on the ends. Therefore, since there was no flesh on the bones and the bones were not splitting, Dr. Bass gave investigators a time frame from which to work. A week after the second bones were found, the ex-boyfriend, now the primary suspect, was picked up and taken into custody.

The only physical evidence that was presented was the bones that Dr. Bass had examined. That evidence, along with a witness testifying about overhearing a conversation the suspect had where he bragged about raping and killing a girl, were the only items entered into court. Though Dr. Bass could not determine cause of death, he could determine her death was a direct result of criminal activity. The victim's remains were found in a desolate, backwoods area, littered with tremendous overgrowth and marked by a physically challenging terrain more than thirty miles from where she was last seen alive (only three miles from where the suspect lived). The victim did not own a vehicle, which meant that she would have had to have been transported to the area. All of these things, coupled with the suspect's admission that he had been in the car with the victim that night and that he had been to the exact spot in the woods where she was found (though he claimed he was searching for her body), led to his conviction. He is currently serving a life sentence without the possibility of parole.

6

IT'S A RIGOROUS JOB, BUT SOMEBODY'S GOT TO DO IT
Postmortem Printing

Nine out of ten times, the bodies used by the academy are either indigent or unwanted, or both. Most of the bodies are old—very old nursing home patients who have gone on to their great reward with no one left on this side to give a damn. Bodies that are so thin, frail, contorted; bodies with pale, translucent skin pulled so tightly as to reveal the numbers on their pacemakers. These people could be someone's mother or father, but for us, they are practice.

If you've ever cracked your knuckles or played the childhood game "mercy," bending your opponent's hands backward until the point of breaking, then you are familiar with what it's like to break the rigor. Most people cringe at either activity, stretching the human body beyond the point it appears it should be stretched. But, as in most cases, the world of forensic science challenges most of what we, the living, have come to hold as acceptable.

Most people understand what rigor mortis is, hence the slang term for the dead, *stiff*. What most people don't know is that rigor mortis is a temporary effect that lessens after about twelve hours into the decomposition process (though the body never, ever regains full pliability). That being said, the crime scene investigator must use whatever means necessary to accomplish the fingerprinting. The means used depend on what stage of decomposition the body is in when it is found, and each stage brings with it a new set of challenges.

A cadaver found in the early stages of decay, better know as the "freshy" stage, will be intact with only the earliest signs of decomposition visible. There will be some degree of rigor mortis (stiffness) as well as livor mortis (the pooling and settling of blood), and even possibly some blistering caused by cellular breakdown in the body. But, all in all, the cadaver is in relatively good shape. In order to take a viable fingerprint, regardless of whether the person is living or dead, the CSI must be able to take the fingers and flex and roll them, one by one, in order to capture the detail of the fingerprint ridges. Rigor mortis, whether or not it is full blown, impedes flexibility. When that's the case, there are a couple of options.

Fingerprinting the Dead

One trick of the trade is to take common plumber's putty, roll it up into a ball about the size of a golf ball, and put the fingerprint paper on top of the rolled-up putty. Then the fingerprinter, in this case the student, takes the finger of the fingerprintee, the deceased, and forms the ball of putty around the finger. Thus, instead of making the finger conform to the device, you make the device conform to the finger. To date, no one who has come through the academy had ever seen this trick.

Another option, the one that gives most people the chills, is to break the rigor. In other words, loosen up the joints until they're pliable enough to print. Breaking the rigor is done by taking the joint and moving it up and down, as fast and as vigorously as possible, for several seconds. The students must pry, twist, and contort the joint and, on occasion, break it in order to get a good print. This is very hard to watch, especially if it is performed on an elderly lady. We have seen twenty-year-veteran crime scene investigators cringe at this very activity.

The last option, and the least favored, is to take a pair of bolt cutters or whatever tool necessary and cut the appendage off. Sometimes the body is just not in a good position to print or time is of the essence,

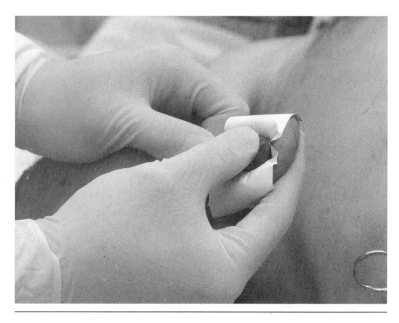

Students use plumber's putty to fingerprint a cadaver.
(Collection of the National Forensic Academy)

and therefore the printing must be done back at the office. We must confess, there is nothing more disconcerting to a janitor than Mason jars filled with hands and fingers, and this is one of the reasons why the academy no longer receives janitorial service.

Now, if a body is found a little less "fresh," getting a viable print becomes a little more interesting. Around the time of the bloat stage of decomposition, and if conditions are right, the skin begins to slip off. Skin literally sloughs off in large sheets, especially around the hands and feet. This process is eerily similar to a snake shedding its skin. Sloughed-off skin from a body keeps little if any of its original look, making it hardly noticeable to the untrained eye.

Unfortunately, little is known about the viability of this sloughed-off skin. It has been theorized by forensic anthropologists that a large number of scenes where skeletal remains are found contain this skin. But most crime scenes where bones are found are not worked properly. Most CSIs are not trained in the art of recovering skeletal remains, and fewer still are taught to look for dried skin. So many things happen to a body as it decomposes in the wild, such as animal scavenging, it makes it hard to establish the perimeters of the crime scene unless you have been trained in what to do. Again, in the Chandra Levy case, the crime scene perimeter was established at least three different times, and who knows what evidence was trampled into the ground. Yet even if the scene is worked properly and skin is found, no one knows how long the ridge detail will last over long periods of time. Dr. Bass has wanted some of his researchers to do work in this field, but to date no one has taken it on. Thus, in the end, the skin is rarely looked for or collected.

If the sloughed-off skin from the hand is still moist (which is highly unlikely), it is possible to simply take the skin and put it on like a glove—a glove made out of human skin. Once on, you just take prints like you normally would. More often than not, though, the skin is too dry to put on like a glove. In that case, the sloughed-off skin can be placed into a pan of Downy fabric softener. (It can be any brand, but Downy has been proven to work better.) That's right, common every-day fabric softener makes more than clothes soft. Once the skin has been immersed for several minutes, it can be removed and put on like a glove and printed.

On the most rare of occasions, the CSI might have to take the prints off of a body that has been exhumed. Exhumations are extraordinarily uncommon, but as technology advances forensic science even further, they are becoming more commonplace. If a body has to be exhumed in order to simply confirm or to make a positive ID, someone will probably lose their job for incompetence. But that won't be the worst part. An exhumed body is different from a body that is decomposing naturally, in that the exhumed body is partially preserved by chemicals. Taking the prints off of a slowly rotting, embalmed cadaver is nearly impossible. One of our graduates told us about having to perform this malodorous task at a local mortuary. She said it was like taking prints off of a waxy, green Vienna sausage, where the fingers were very slick and very mushy. After trying nearly all of the fingers, she was finally able to get a good print and make a positive ID.

But what if you find just a hand? One morning during an academy class, we heard on the news that a woman's dog had found a severed

DRY SKIN

Bodies or floaters that are found in water are difficult to take major case prints of. One way to dry out the skin without damaging the epidermis is to lay the hands and feet on warm concrete. The porous concrete pulls the moisture from the skin, safely drying the skin so it can be printed.

hand near some railroad tracks. We didn't think anything else about it until "it" showed up. The police brought the hand to the morgue and asked us if we could print the hand and help identify whose it was. When the hand was pulled out of the sealed brown evidence bag, we could tell by the horrible smell that is was badly decomposed. It looked like someone had overcooked it on a charcoal grill. The skin looked the way a hot dog does when you burn it over an open fire—crispy and black. Downy would be of no use. There were only two fingers that remained on the hand. The others had been severed by who knows what—or whom. The students made several attempts to take the prints off of one of the fingers, but they were in just too bad a shape. Eventually they were able to get a partial palm print by using magnetic powder and good old plumber's putty. Though the print turned out beautiful, it did not help identify whose hand it was.

Up until this point the students have been working with several different aspects of latent fingerprints. Processing prints, lifting prints, taking prints of cadavers, among other things. They have learned almost everything they need to know about latent fingerprints. Almost.

Fingerprints on the Dead

Taking the prints of a corpse is one thing; lifting prints off of a corpse is another. This is one of the most argued and disputed forensic processes in the entire field. There is no one tried-and-true method, and a CSI may try to perform this task hundreds of times without one single success. Developing prints on human skin is still considered an "experimental" process. Skin is an extraordinarily difficult surface to lift a print off of. It's oily, it sweats, it's pliable, it has ridges, it's hot—it even sheds and renews. In fact, it has no good characteristic when it comes to lifting prints. With all of the crime scenes that have ever been worked, there are less than a dozen known successful lifts of prints off of skin outside of an experimental setting. Unfortunately, the key piece of evidence that links the perp to the scene of the crime rarely reveals its secrets.

Conditions must be just perfect in order to even have a shot at lifting a print. For instance, if the perp kills someone and dumps the body immediately, there is approximately an hour to an hour-and-a-half window when the print might be lifted. That's because the prints were left on the body while the victim was alive. Prints placed on live victims are very, very volatile. Think of leaving a fingerprint in Vaseline and then heating up the surface to nearly one hundred degrees—the print will melt and wash away in conjunction with the heat and perspiration. That is essentially what happens when a print is left on a living person.

WRAP IT UP

Strangulation is a very common assault. Lifting a fingerprint off of a living human or someone who has very recently died is nearly impossible. One way to attempt to lift a print off of a warm body is to take common plastic wrap and press it to the victim's neck, or wherever contact with the assailant took place. Then, peel the wrap off of the skin and superglue fume it. This process must be tried within thirty minutes of contact. If it works, the print will appear white on the transparent background.

Now, as luck would have it, violent crimes are rarely planned out. People who are enraged or insane do not prepare a course of action for if and when their victim is murdered. Therefore, they wait a while before they move their victim, trying to come up with some sort of scheme to hide the body. Traditionally, the perp places the partially clothed or naked victim into the trunk of a car and drives to a secluded area, where the body is dumped. Unfortunately, by the time the body is found, it is already in an advanced state of decomposition, or the weather has wreaked havoc on the body's condition. But, in cases where the body is found still "fresh," not more than three days after death, and if conditions are just right, it is possible to get a fingerprint off of a cadaver.

There are several methods for attempting to develop prints on skin, ranging from simply using mag powder and dusting the body like you would any other surface, to the newly devised and more complex process of iodine fuming a body and then spraying a-napthoflavone on the area, turning the fingerprints left on the cadaver blue. The most success has been achieved by using superglue to fume the body and dusting for fingerprints. This is the process we teach at the academy.

When heated, cyanoacrylate, or superglue, produces a fume that will react with the traces of amino acids, fatty acids, and proteins that are found in a latent print. The reaction produces a visible, white sticky material that forms along the ridges of the print. After fuming, the CSI can do one of three things: photograph the print as it is; enhance the print with a powder, preferably magnetic, and then lift the print with tape; or apply a dye stain to the print to further enhance the print and then photograph it. This last technique is used primarily when the print is on a problem background, such as a light-colored surface. This is a relatively simple process, unless you leave the glue on the heat source for too long. At approximately 485 to 490 degrees, the cyanoacrylate fumes convert into deadly cyanide gas. Proper ventilation while performing this procedure is a must.

The night before the class arrives to practice the superglue technique, we go to the morgue to prepare the bodies that will be printed. The morgue is essentially a visual obituary—a running tally of the previous night's tragic events. All of the deceased are placed in the cooler.

Most people don't know that unidentified bodies do not remain indefinitely at the morgue. If no one comes to claim them very soon, they will be cremated. Depending on the morgue and the morgue's facilities, the bodies could remain at the morgue for up to six months. More often than not, however, most morgues do not have enough room for any more than one or two bodies. Therefore, they might cremate an unknown within as little as three weeks. Sometimes even less. Case in point: Michael Jordan's dad. When Michael Jordan's dad was murdered and dumped into a South Carolina swamp, his body washed ashore in a very small town with a very small morgue. Though it was not known exactly how long he had been dead, he was cremated ten days after his body was found.

Think about how many people go missing every day. The only way positive IDs can be made once the bodies are cremated depends upon the protocol of the morgue. One, the morgue might take an X-ray of the deceased's head to possibly match to existing dental records at a later date. Or, they may actually cut the hands off of the deceased and cremate the rest. Hands are easier to store and provide not only the possibility of fingerprints, but DNA as well. Fortunately for us, the morgue we use has plenty of storage space and keeps John Does for at least six months. That means at any given time there may be several bodies to choose from, and we get the pleasure of picking a couple out.

The bodies we pick have to be removed from the cooler and allowed to stay out at room temperature. In the real world, the bodies would be superglue fumed before they were ever put into the cooler because moisture tends to destroy prints. For our purposes, we put the prints on the bodies after they have warmed up a bit and been patted dry of condensation. Once the bodies have reached room temperature, we handle them, leaving behind our prints. Basically what this means is that we leave thirty or so sets of our own fingerprints on the dead person in order for the students to have prints to process the next day. For us, this is more disturbing than the Body Farm. Even though the Facility is gross, we don't have to actually touch any of the bodies with our bare hands.

Have you ever touched a dead body? Maybe you have, maybe you haven't, but we guarantee you have never had to feel all over a corpse, leaving fingerprints and palm prints on the arms, legs, feet, and torso. There are few things worse in life than touching dead skin, fresh from the morgue cooler. And it's more than just touching and feeling the skin; it's handling the arms and legs as if you are trying to move the body. Raising their arms and then letting them go, watching them eerily move slowly back down into place, as if the body was trying to hold the arm up. But if there is anything worse, it is touching a body you expect it to be cold and it turns out to be warm. Imagine touching the skin of a cadaver, feeling the warmth of life instead of the coldness of death. It's like touching someone who is still asleep. At times, we find ourselves being careful not to wake the cadaver up. We have used a few bodies that came straight from the hospital, still warm, just hours after death, and on rare occasions, *still moving*. This is by far the most chilling thing we ever experience—going to put prints on a body as it begins to twitch and jerk and even gurgle. Two people, alone, in a morgue, handling dead bodies as they continue to move and make sounds—that's the stuff horror movies are made of!

We continue to set up the body, placing strips of masking tape on the arms and legs. In the real world, this would not be done prior to fuming. But for educational purposes these strips will be used as "test spots." If the print shows up on the tape when the body is fumed, then it means the conditions are right and the prints should show up on the body as well. After we have left enough prints on the corpse, we make sure to place a towel over the face and genital region out of respect for the deceased. With the bodies finally prepared, we go back to the hotel to relax and have horrible, horrible nightmares.

The next morning the students arrive at the morgue to process fingerprints on cadavers—most of them for the very first time. Many of the students are skeptical. They know how hard it is to get a print off of skin even in a controlled environment like ours, much less at a real crime scene. Learning how to do it from a pioneer in the field, however, helps change their minds.

Art Bohanan, a quirky, retired investigator with the Knoxville Police Department, worked with members of the FBI's Latent Fingerprint Section in the 1990s, performing some of the most cutting-edge research with regard to superglue fuming bodies. Their research showed that su-

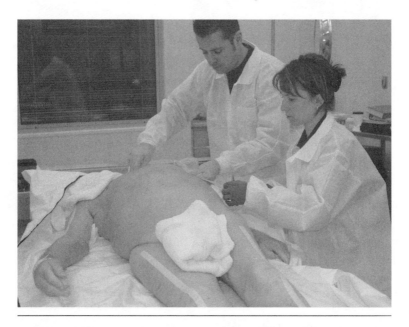

Jarrett and Amy tape off a cadaver in preparation for lifting finger-prints.

(Copyright © Kerri McClary, collection of the National Forensic Academy)

perglue provided the most consistent results when developing prints on human skin. Initially, the group used makeshift tents with battery-operated fans inside to contain and blow the fumes across the test cadavers. This proved to be cumbersome, however, and did not contain all of the superglue fumes very well. Eventually, Art created a portable machine (Cyanoacrylate Blowing Contraption, CBC) that is now used in many departments, including the FBI and the NFA.

Art's machine is a self-contained unit with a heating chamber, a fan, and a long tube. Art first demonstrates how to use the machine by placing a few drops of superglue into a small aluminum pan, about the size of a silver dollar, and inserting the pan in the fuming chamber. The machine heats the glue to produce fumes. Inside the machine is a small fan that blows the fumes through the long tube and into a boxlike attachment that is placed on the section of the body where the print is believed to be. After a few seconds (ten to fifteen is sufficient) the

The Cyanoacrylate Blowing Contraption, or CBC, invented by
Art Bohanan.

(Collection of the National Forensic Academy)

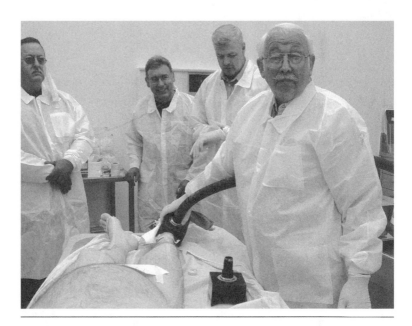

NFA instructor Art Bohanan cyanoacrylate fumes a cadaver.

(Collection of the National Forensic Academy)

machine is removed from the body. So far, we have never failed to develop prints, and the students are amazed by the opportunity to try something so few people ever have success in.

The students then try their hands at superglue fuming, first gulping in a cloud of fumes and almost passing out before getting used to operating the machine. It's very important not to inhale the fumes or to let them get into your eyes, especially if you wear contacts. Though in a gaseous state, it is still superglue. The fumes can stick to contact lenses, coating them with a nonremovable film. Furthermore, it has been recently reported that the fumes, if inhaled, will forever coat the lining of the lungs, causing permanent damage. It is extremely important to be careful. Once the students have finished developing the prints, they each break out their magnetic powder to dust the prints, photograph the results, and then lift them with tape.

Fingerprint lifting tape is not the only way to lift developed finger-

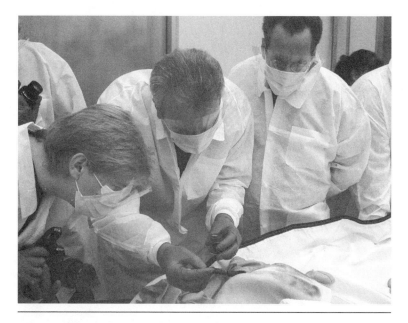

Session Five graduates Joy Smith, Steve Lewis, and Chris Guthrie mag powder a cadaver that has been cyanoacrylate fumed.
(Collection of the National Forensic Academy)

SILLY PUTTY

There are several expensive tapes that are sold expressly for the purpose of lifting fingerprints. We have found through our work that when dealing with fingerprints, especially those left on cadavers, Silly Putty lifts them perfectly. Silly Putty will, unlike most tapes, conform into any position and fill in every imperfection on a body, making it easier to lift prints off of areas that are not smooth and flat. We've also found that Play-Doh is great for taking an impression. Leave it to us to use childhood toys as forensic supplies.

prints off of a body. Many choose to use the old hinge lifters or even the newer gelatin lifters to remove the prints. But we have found that the best way to actually lift the print is to use Elmer's Blue School Glue. The students take the glue and slowly pour it over the entire print. Once the glue dries it is carefully peeled from the skin. Its tacky consistency pulls the print off fantastically well, and because it goes on as a liquid, it covers every single detail on the skin—something that tape just does not do.

The students continue to experiment, trying every powder known to man to see which one develops the best possible print. Once the students are finished and gone for the day, we are again left alone with the cadavers to wash all of the glues and powders off of the bodies so we can put them back in the cooler. By now, twenty-four hours out of the fridge have taken their toll on the bodies, accelerating the decomposition process. Sometimes the bodies begin to marbleize, weaving a putrid yellow and green tapestry just underneath the skin. Other times, giant, watery blisters emerge that rupture under the tiniest movement. As we roll the bodies across the tiled floor, one or two of those blisters invariably begin to ooze. Putting the corpse back in the cooler will not stop the process, but it will slow it down.

It is always at this point that we wonder if this part of the class is worth it. The odds of any of our students ever superglue fuming a body, much less getting a viable print from the process, is probably a million to one. Then we remember the old adage used by our fingerprint experts that goes something like this:

> "There are only three surfaces that you cannot develop a latent print on: running water, air, and the ones you don't try."

We teach a lot of different techniques and ideas at the academy, knowing full well that many of them will never be used by any of our students. But it is that off chance that one day one of our graduates will be confronted with a unique situation and he or she will know exactly what to do to get that key piece of evidence that puts the guilty away. It is those thoughts that keep us sane, and it is those thoughts that keep us going.

POSTMORTEM PRINTING

The first time that postmortem fingerprint evidence was introduced into court was in the summer of 1978. The murder of three people, called the "Spa Murders," occurred in North Miami Beach, Florida, in a local health spa. When police arrived on the scene they found one male and two female victims. One of the young female victims was found nude. Her clothing was thrown around the room, and based upon the position of her body she appeared to have been sexually assaulted. Using black magnetic powder, crime scene investigators were able to lift a fingerprint off of her left ankle. The print was examined and matched to the fingerprints of a known suspect, Stephen William Beattie.

Based on the fingerprint evidence, Beattie was found guilty of three counts of murder and shortly thereafter was sentenced to three death sentences to be served consecutively. Three years after the trial, while Beattie was in prison awaiting his execution, he committed suicide. To date, postmortem fingerprint evidence has led to the conviction of over forty criminals.

In order to lift fingerprints from skin, the conditions must be just right. It is nearly impossible to lift a print off of living skin, because the temperature of the body is warm enough to melt the oils and sweat that make up a latent print. Fingerprints that are on a dead body, however, whose temperature has dropped significantly without getting too cold, are much easier to lift.

Aside from applying magnetic fingerprint powder to the skin, one effective method is to superglue fume the body. Art Bohanan, a retired investigator with the Knoxville Police Department, has perfected this method with his invention called the Cyanoacrylate Blowing Contraption, or CBC. The machine uses a small fan that blows the superglue fumes through a tube, which can then be directed onto the body in places where fingerprints are suspected to be. The superglue fumes adhere to the print, turning them white in color. Once fumed, the prints are then dusted with powder and lifted with tape.

Another case in 1993 sent Art Bohanan on a new quest for research. While working the kidnapping and murder case of a three-year-old girl in Knoxville, Tennessee, his fingerprint evidence disappeared. It wasn't stolen or lost. The fingerprints had vanished into thin air. The young child had been kidnapped from her neighborhood by a family friend, who sexually molested her before killing her.

Because the man was insistent that he had no involvement in the murder, Art was determined to link him to the crime. Finding the little girl's fingerprints in the suspect's car would do just that. Witnesses in the neighborhood said they had seen the child in the man's car. When Art processed the inside of the car for fingerprint evidence, however, the only prints he could find were that of the suspect. The reason was later found out to be that fingerprints of children evaporate in only a few hours.

This case began the research into the length of time a child's fingerprint will last. Armed with two cases of Coke bottles, Art Bohanan began an experiment. He had his grandchildren touch the glass bottles, and then he stored one case in his cool basement and the other in the back of his police car. Every day for the next month, Art would remove a bottle from each case and dust it for prints. What he found was that the children's prints had disappeared almost immediately.

With additional help from Oak Ridge National Laboratory, it was concluded that the reason children's prints don't last very long is because their sweat glands have not fully developed. Currently, research is continuing into trying to develop methods to enhance the capabilities of lifting children's fingerprints.

7

VINYL RESTING PLACE

Autopsy

Have you ever slapped an uncooked turkey on the fat part of the breast? If you have, then you are familiar with the wet smacking sound a two-day-old cadaver makes when it is flipped on its back onto a cold, steel gurney. That's what you become at death—meat. Nothing more, nothing less. The first cut into a turkey on Thanksgiving is eerily similar to the first cut in an autopsy—except that you're probably more careful with that prized bird.

The word *autopsy* comes from the Latin word *autopsia*, meaning "seeing for one's self." We're not talking about the *CSI* version of a dark, poorly lit autopsy suite with squeaky-clean labs, shelves of chemicals arranged in neat rows, and doctors running around in crisp blue or white attire, using brand-new steel instruments on Claymation dummies that don't bleed when they're cut into. What we're talking about is a real, honest-to-goodness autopsy. The one that you'll get; the one that most of us will get, when our time finally comes. Here's what happens when the cameras are turned off.

The cooler door is swung wide open, and the assistant wheels the patient, still locked inside his vinyl resting place, into the autopsy room. Autopsy suites have anywhere between one and four stations. That largely depends on the average number of deaths that occur in the area. At each station, there is a steel sink with a cutting board, an au-topsy table, an instrument tray, and a hanging meat scale, like the scales used in supermarkets. Each station will also have either a clip-board or a dry erase board that is used to record the weight of the ma-jor organs when they are hoisted into the metal container. Above the autopsy table is a sprayer hose that will be used to clean off the area for the next victim.

The medical examiner (ME), donning the, shall we say *less* tradi-tional, SpongeBob SquarePants scrubs, prepares his instruments for the work at hand. A few of the tools at his disposal are similar to what is seen on *CSI*, like scalpels. But that is where the similarities end. The rest of the tools used can be found in anyone's garage. Wal-Mart prun-ing sheers, Black & Decker razor knives, Craftsman limb pruners, and, of course, Kmart hammers. As far as we have come in modern medical science, the autopsy suite contains the last remaining vestiges of me-dieval medicine.

The gurney and its patient's journey ends near the instrument tray. Its wheels are locked, making sure it will not roll away as the body bag is unzipped. The patient may or may not be fully clothed upon his ar-rival, though most arrive in their underclothes. This does not become evident until the bag is turned over and its contents are dumped onto the table, like dirty laundry into a washing machine. If the clothing is deemed to be evidence, such as a bloody shirt, then the clothes are hung in a closet to avoid further contamination. Otherwise, the clothes will be returned to the family, provided there is a family to return them to. The temperature change from the cooler to the autopsy room causes the body to go through condensation, or "death sweats," as it is more commonly called. As the body is dumped from the bag, the condensa-tion tends to splash on those nearest the body. When you are covered from head to toe in body fluid and other unknown substances, you are glad you put on a face shield. A body block, which resembles a small anvil, is placed under the upper back, elevating the body so the ME can get a better angle with the blades.

With the patient out of the bag and in full view, it becomes readily apparent why mothers want you to put on clean underwear. Very few people say to themselves when they get out of bed, "Hey, I'm gonna die today, better change my drawers." Take it from us: Always change your drawers.

The initial examination of the now nude patient is a sobering event. Every crack, crevice, wrinkle, and fold is scrutinized as the doctor looks for abnormalities and visible signs of death, recording his voice into those tape recorders that doctors for the living use. Every square inch of the cadaver is photographed from all possible angles—top, bottom, left, right, above, below, and sideways. Depending on the amount of trauma inflicted upon the individual, the number of pictures taken can be in the hundreds.

Then it hits you—the awful realization that the underclothes you have on right now house the last remaining shreds of dignity you have both in life and in death. Once removed, your most personal secrets are unveiled for all to see. Every infirmity and every scar become obvious—both those left from repair and those created in the name of vanity. Most people deny it when asked if they have ever had any type of "augmenting" surgery. There is no denying it here; the evidence of this type of surgery is up close and personal.

How would you react at an autopsy seeing a cadaver, unclothed, lying in a pool of "death sweat," with (and there is just no other way to say it) a fully erect penis? Follow that visual with these words from the medical examiner as he fumbled around the scrotum area: "Get a glove on and come feel this." (Remember, forensic people love to shock non-forensic people.) We're not sure what you would do, but we took a rain check on that glove thing. The medical examiner then proceeded to push the skin of the scrotum upward to reveal a small protuberance—a penis pump. In twenty years of performing autopsies, the ME said he had never seen anything like this before, and then proceeded to grab his tools and begin the autopsy.

It is a common misconception that the autopsy begins with the infamous and aptly named "Y" incision. Not true. Instead, the first procedure is the collection of body fluid to help determine (or corroborate) time of death. This is performed by two different means. The most common is to collect the vitreous fluid of the eye. This is done by opening the eyelid to reveal the eyeball, plunging a needle across the length of the eye, perpendicular to the face, and using the attached syringe to

suck out the eyeball fluid. For the vast majority of those who have witnessed an autopsy, they claim this procedure is the worst part of the entire process.

The other, less common way of collecting fluid, in this case blood,
is to plunge a syringe—and might we add, a syringe the size of a gutter
spike—deep into the femoral artery, at the groin area of the leg, collecting any residual blood that might still remain. Depending on how
long the patient has been deceased, this "plunging" might be done multiple times to get enough blood to send to the lab. Neither procedure is
for the faint of heart, especially if your heart is faint of needles.

Once enough fluid has been collected, the real autopsy begins. The
Y incision consists of two diagonal, intersecting cuts, starting from
each shoulder and going across the chest, followed by one straight cut
down the center, beginning where the first two cuts intersect and ending at the waist. There is almost no bleeding since the body no longer
has a blood pressure. The skin, muscle, and soft tissues of the chest are

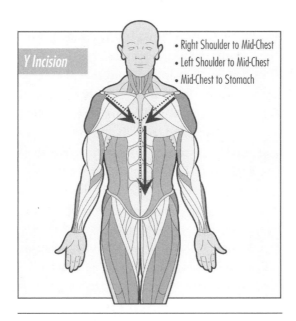

Illustration of a Y incision.

(Illustration by Pamela Johanns of Johanns Design)

then sheared away and reflected back from the body using a scalpel in the same way a hunter would skin a deer.

This is immediately followed by the cutting through of the rib cage. This can be done with pruning sheers, cutting each rib like small twigs on a tree, or with a linoleum knife, digging into the collarbone with the hook part of the knife and ripping downward with great force. Once all of the ribs have been cut through, the breastplate is removed, revealing the internal organs of the torso.

One by one the organs are removed. Each is cut and detached from the membrane and tossed onto the edge of the sink for later examination. With all of the organs in the torso removed, the now empty chest cavity is nothing more than a large puddle of blood and blood clots. These remaining fluids are ladled out and poured into a plastic juice pitcher to measure the amount of blood in the cavity. What's left of the cadaver unfortunately resembles a hollowed-out human canoe with genitalia and a brain. Those are left for last.

The genitalia, in this case the male genitalia, are next to be removed. The medical examiner runs his hand through the initial waist-high cut and down toward the scrotum, forcing his hand downward, submerging his arm up to his elbow. It's like watching someone struggle to reach their wedding band in a grease trap, his face edging closer and closer to the edge of the trap, or, as in this case, an erect penis and its pump. The pump device crowds an already confined space, making it even more difficult for the medical examiner to reach the testes. So to free up space, the pump is pulled from its resting place. For reasons neither of us understands, the inner workings of the testicles are quite strong—like a bungee cord. During an autopsy, the testicles are pulled, cord and all, out of the scrotum, through the waist-high opening—though still connected by the cord, mind you. One last tug, a stretch and a snap, and the testicles, along with the cord, are removed. With all of the tugging and pulling and jerking, the extremity continued to flip and flop around the entire time, making us, as well as the doctor, just a little uncomfortable.

While the medical examiner places the testicles on a table with the other organs, the assistant begins the process of removing the brain. The body block is removed from the underside of the patient and is placed under the back of the head. The assistant grabs the scalpel and, beginning at the top of one ear, cuts all the way around the back of the head to the other ear. Then the hair cap and face are pulled forward over the back of the head and then downward, turning the face inside out across the front of the skull, where the face used to be. The click of the bone saw signals the beginning of the cutting of the entire circumference of the skull. No matter how many times we've heard the buzzing of this small handsaw, it still sends a chill down our spines. Of course, just like using a saw in any wood shop, cutting with a saw during an autopsy is an imperfect science. So, with an imperfect science, not to mention an imperfect cut, force must be used to finish the job. A Kmart hammer and chisel do that nicely.

Two or three swings of the hammer, then a pop, and the skullcap is removed to reveal the brain. The brain is remarkably easy to pull from the body, as compared to the other organs, and it is one of the few organs Hollywood has perfected (the movie *Young Frankenstein* comes to mind). The brain is merely lifted out from the base of the skull and weighed, then tossed onto the table with its fellow organs. With the brain removed, the membrane is torn loose from the skull with a pair of pliers, not unlike pulling the slimy skin off of a chicken before cooking. With this complete, all that is left to remove is the pituitary.

The pea-sized pituitary gland resides at the base of the brain, at the top of the brain stem. This gland is not always removed, but many morgues harvest this gland for growth hormone. A common misconception about the human body is that you have to be kept on life support to have useable parts. Not so. The body is a veritable cornucopia of viable components; ligaments, corneas, bone, and yes, the pituitary, are just some of the pieces gathered from the dead to keep the living running smoothly. With one strike of the hammer and chisel, the pituitary pops out like a gumball from a gumball machine. The autopsy is almost complete.

It is a truly awesome sight staring at what now resembles a creature right out of *Alien*—chest open like a canoe, face pulled inside out, and skull cut in half with its contents dumped. By now the autopsy table is swimming in old, black, coagulated blood that has flung off of the organs as they were tossed onto the cutting board. The hanging scale used to weigh each organ is dotted with bits of flesh and dripping with the ever-blackening mixture. Blood is also smeared all over the dry erase board, as well as the markers that have been used to record the findings. It is almost like watching someone keep score in hell, hands dripping with blood as the numbers are jotted down and tallied. Sometimes the felt tip of the marker hits a rough spot on the board, a dried reminder of the previous patient's postmortem score (there is no time-out to wash hands). It's a very disconcerting scene. With all of the organs lying on the bloodstained steel sinks, the assistant gathers a five-gallon bucket and several plastic grocery bags that will be used to finish the autopsy.

After lining one of the buckets with a bag and placing the bucket between the ankles of the cadaver, the examiner begins processing the organs. Anyone who has ever worked at a butcher shop is very familiar with the next steps: Organs are sliced, diced, and quartered with a butcher knife, not unlike what you might see on an infomercial. Small sample pieces are sent to the lab for tests, and the remaining parts of the organs are tossed into the bucket. Samples may remain at the ME's office indefinitely.

The same process is repeated for each organ with such speed that it is unbelievable that cause of death could ever be determined. Now, as part of the autopsy team, we chart numbers called out to us by the ME as fast as an auctioneer, and the assistant removes the bag from the bucket and places it into the gaping chest of the patient. Pieces left on the sink are raked into palms and flipped into the bag until there are no more to flip. By law, all organs (as much as possible) must go with the body to the funeral home, though unfortunately that does not always happen. With bits of human flesh, blood, bone, and other unknown morsels of gelatinous material hanging from all of our gowns, the autopsy is declared complete.

The assistant then prepares the body to be picked up by the funeral home. The section of the rib cage that was removed is placed back in the chest like the last piece in a puzzle. The plastic bag containing the organs and other remnants is folded down into the abdomen. The body is sewn back up with thick twine, making the "Y" even more pronounced. The top of the skullcap is then placed back onto its base, and the face is pulled right-side out, making a sound like hitting a tennis ball. The head is stitched closed, without the brain, leaving a wound that goes around the back of the head. Another grocery bag is tied around the head to catch anything that might dislodge—the funeral home will fix him up from there. The assistant then takes the spray hose from above and washes all of the blood off of the body with water, a sponge, and store-bought antibacterial dish soap. The body is removed from the autopsy table, placed into a bag, and wheeled back into the cooler. Here it will await its final journey to the funeral home.

As the cooler door closed one time around Christmas, we were brought back to reality with the sounds of Elvis's version of "Silent Night." It was playing faintly in the background, piped through the music system at the ME's office. Christmas carols seemed eerily inappropriate for what we had just witnessed. It was a sobering thought to remember that it was the holidays and we would be going home to our families and friends, celebrating the most wonderful time of the year. Yet, somewhere, this person's family would not be having a merry little Christmas. This particular deceased died of an apparent heart attack caused by the tiniest sliver of calcium being trapped sideways in one of the smaller arteries. It couldn't have been much bigger than a flea. If it had passed straight through the artery, it would not have caused the blood to stop flowing. "One in a million," the ME said. The fragility of life is so unbelievable. Enjoy every moment you can because you just never know which Christmas will be your last.

AUTOPSY

Nashville, Tennessee, is the country music capital of the world. Every single day, people arrive in droves on busses with the aspiration of being the next Shania Twain or Garth Brooks. Only a very select few ever make it in this cutthroat industry. More often than not, within a few months these aspiring musicians have been spit out the other side of the country music scene, joining legions of others who have preceded them, moving on to their next big gig as food servers.

Nashville restaurants, bars, and other establishments are the reposi-tories for many of country music's "once weres" or wannabees. Some move on and get over their dreams of being country music stars. Oth-ers simply can't handle failure and lose control.

Back in 1999, a former *Star Search* winner came to the Music City in order to make it big. By month's end, he was going nowhere, work-ing as a server at a local Denny's restaurant. And then, one day, some-thing set him off.

He began his tirade at an Econo Lodge, attempting to assault the front desk clerk. Luckily, someone spooked the assailant and he fled. The clerk called the police. The assailant moved on down the road, hiding from the sirens, eventually moving on to a small house occu-pied by two elderly women, one of whom had been handicapped by a stroke. One of the residents of the house, while out watering flowers in the yard, recognized the man from the restaurant and offered him a cup of coffee. Tragically, it would be her last kind gesture.

The man brutally assaulted both women with scissors, killing them both, but only after he strangled and raped the kind woman who had offered him coffee. After he washed himself of the woman's blood, he stole some items from the house and fled in the ladies' pickup truck, fleeing back to his home in Branson, Missouri.

CSIs investigating the crime were able to lift fingerprints off of the coffee mug the perpetrator had held and recovered DNA evidence from a vaginal swab of the woman he raped. Luckily for the police, he had prior convictions, and the fingerprints they lifted matched a set that was in the AFIS database. They alerted the Branson police, who ultimately picked up the killer from a local tavern, where he was once again attempting to resurrect his music career. When he was arrested, he claimed that "something just snapped."

There was little doubt that the police had their man. But making a strong case was important. That's where the medical examiner came in. The ME who performed the autopsies on both of the deceased ladies painted a picture for the jury that was incredibly heinous and brutal. He walked the jurors through the entire set of events, events that were emblazoned throughout the victims' bodies. Through his evaluation, it was determined that both ladies died as a result of strangulation. The handicapped lady had been dragged by a ligature that had been placed around her neck into the bedroom, where the assailant sat on her chest as he tightened the noose. This was concluded by the ME during the autopsy, which revealed severe congestion in the woman's upper chest and face, indicative of heavy pressure on the woman's body. Furthermore, she had been hit at least twice, enough to cause bleeding in her brain.

Both ladies had been stabbed, and the wounds matched those usually associated with scissors. The other woman had severe injuries to her head, a broken nose, a broken breast bone, and three broken ribs. Tragically, she had bruising on her ankles and vaginal tearing, both signatures of a horrible rape. The ME concluded she died during the sexual assault.

The court allowed not only the testimony of the ME into evidence, but also pictures of the autopsy itself in an effort to prove the Tennessee statutory burden of "heinous, atrocious, or cruel"—activities that render the death penalty. A jury found the defendant guilty and he was sentenced to death for his crimes. He is out of appeals and currently sits on death row.

8

HEART STRINGS
Death Investigation

Well-trained CSIs work each and every crime scene the same. To them, a crime scene that has a dead body is no different from any other crime scene, except that it has another organic piece of evidence. To us, they are crimes that make us question the foundations we believe in. To them, it's just another scene—unless that scene involves some sort of unusual circumstance. Then, working the crime scene is a little different.

Let's face it, the world is chock-full of weirdos. We are all too aware of the Mansons and Gacys and Dahmers, who breathe the same oxygen we do on a daily basis. These people committed crimes so heinous that it is truly hard to comprehend what a person is capable of doing to another. Yet not every death scene is a murder scene. There is a whole group of people out there, doing things to themselves inside their homes under the cloak of night, that go virtually unnoticed. When they do these things to themselves to death, however, their acts come into the light.

No matter where our students come from, their stories often have a similar theme—human waste. The number of crime scenes that involve death and feces is truly incredible. Some of our students have worked scenes where people are found dead in their homes after having used their unflushed commode as a playground. Others climb down into portable toilets to masturbate and ultimately end up drowning. (These are not, we repeat, not crime scenes that the NFA recreates.)

There are many, many ways people can die and many more that we have yet to think of. Death comes in all shapes and sizes, quite literally. Statistics show, and it has been true for bodies arriving at the Body Farm, that Americans are getting, and dying, fatter. Now, that may seem trivial to the layperson. "What does it matter if the dead person is thin or fat? They are still dead," one might say. Well, there is a big difference.

The bigger you are, the more of you there is to decompose. At least every other session of the academy has had the fortune or misfortune of witnessing a morbidly obese, decomposing body arrive at the medical examiner's office. These bodies have to undergo the same autopsy as others who have died of unknown causes. In Tennessee, the medical examiner has a state-of-the-art facility that was built with a special room to handle a badly decomposing body. This room is simply called "the decomp room." This room has a ventilation system that pumps fresh air in, while forcing the "bad" air out. It also has a special autopsy table that has a downdraft ventilation built into it as well. But the most interesting item found in a decomp room are the ambient, buzzing, violet lights. These lights, more commonly known as bug zappers, get a tremendous workout, especially after an exhumation. The life cycle of the fly is so short, it is possible for them to hatch by the hundreds during the autopsy and bounce off of the ME before their lives become even shorter when they visit the zapper. This is another reason why the doctor performing the procedure will wear a face mask and protective gear like one might find at a nuclear facility.

Many believe that the worst part of a decomp case is not performing the autopsy; it is finding the body and working the scene—a point that CSIs and MEs regularly debate. Invariably, students at the academy get into a friendly discussion of who has had the smelliest crime scene. It's hard to say who has won this debate over the years, but the stories that involve finding a dead person locked inside an un-air-conditioned house for weeks all win honorable mention.

There was one story, though, that always stuck with us. It is every CSI's worst nightmare, and of anyone in forensic science, for that matter, to have a body in the bloat stage pop. It's not a pop in the traditional sense; it is more of a rupture, where the gases and fluids have built up so much that they have to go somewhere. The technical term for this rupture is *purging*. Usually, this buildup seeps out through the anus and other orifices, but sometimes it gushes. Then there are other times when the natural process is sped up.

One of our students was dispatched out on a call one sweltering July day, and the only information he had was that the caller said she "smelled something funny next door." A funny smell almost always spells trouble. He and his newly assigned CSI partner arrived on the scene to find a small house, with no one answering the door. After kicking the door down, they followed the smells to a back bedroom that seemed unusually dark for the middle of the afternoon. The bedroom windows were covered with flies and other bugs so completely that it actually darkened the room. These bugs had been feasting on a very large and very dead man lying on a bed in an advanced stage of bloat. After surveying the scene, the two CSIs began to work the room.

The rookie CSI began to take pictures of the scene, walking into the room and then turning his back to the bed to get a shot in the opposite direction. Nervous, the rookie made a misstep and bumped into the bed, setting off a chain reaction. Imagine a runny Jell-O mold sitting on top of a picnic table in the middle of July and someone runs into the table. That Jell-O mold will wiggle and jiggle and maybe, just maybe, the force will be sufficient enough to push through the opposite side of where the initial bump came from. This is the same for a large cadaver in the bloat stage. You think that the human skin would prevent such an occurrence, and in life that would be correct. In death, however, after a couple of weeks of maggots and bacteria eating away from the inside, the skin becomes paper-thin, just like the skin on our guy lying on the bed. The bump from the rookie CSI caused the juice to slosh around and rupture through the cadaver's side and send gallons of decomposing, bacteria-ridden fluid cascading down the side of the bed and onto the floor. Both CSIs ran outside to get some air just in time for the rookie to lose his lunch.

Regardless of who sees or smells the worst dead bodies, it is the role of the medical examiner to try to figure out what caused that person to die. Historically, the ME performed the autopsy part of the investigation without the CSI present. Nowadays, it is common practice for the CSI to be present during the autopsy, to help assist in answering questions about how the scene looked and the conditions the body was found in. This will help assist the ME in answering several questions as the investigation continues. But knowing the crime scene is only half the battle. Finding out how and why someone died is not an easy task, to say the least. Sometimes there is not a crime; the individual just died of natural causes. But it is still a death investigation. By the way, the phrase "died of natural causes" is a misnomer. If something caused you to die, it is unnatural—you continue to live because of natural causes. It is just another way for the living to feel better about dying.

The world of the medical examiner is a strange one—a very strange world indeed. One day, the ME might perform an autopsy on an adolescent who has overdosed on OxyContin, and the next day extract a gourd from the rectum of a cross-dressing traveling salesman who has accidentally strangled himself while masturbating with a Bic pen jammed in his penis (we kid you not). You just never know.

The medical examiner's role in forensic science is to be the physician who ultimately determines the cause of death in cases where the person dies unexpectedly, dies violently, dies suspiciously, or dies due to some type of substance like drugs, alcohol, or poisons like carbon monoxide. Though these categories are not universal by any means, they do represent the vast majority of cases worked by the medical examiner.

The ME traditionally works with fresh bodies, meaning persons that have died within approximately a seventy-two-hour span (though at times the ME will work on a badly decomposed body). Unlike the forensic anthropologist, who studies and evaluates decomposed human remains, the forensic pathologist studies the changes or markers that occur during the initial stages of death. These markers are the first things observed and noted during the initial stages of death investigation.

Stages of Death

It is obvious that the earliest signs of death are the cessation of breathing and the circulation of blood. This is almost always accompanied by what is called pallor, or extreme paleness of the skin. All of the muscles relax, including the sphincter, which unfortunately means that the urban legend is true—you usually crap yourself when you die. All of this happens within the first hour after death. (We have come to realize that the only good thing about death is that you are dead and not aware of all the embarrassing things that are going on, because if you were aware, you'd probably just wish you were dead anyway.)

Next come the three Ms of forensic pathology: rigor mortis, algor mortis, and livor mortis. Rigor mortis, the contracting of the muscles, is the most famous of all death indicators. It takes roughly two or three hours for rigor to begin, and it usually ends by hour forty-eight. Rigor can assist the ME in recognizing whether the body has been moved at a crime scene. For example, let's say that a person dies while sitting upright on the couch. After the rigor has set in, if that person were to be pushed off of the couch, she would still be "stuck" in a sitting position. But rigor is not a good indicator of how long a person has been dead, because it is impacted by several factors, including disease and, especially, temperature. Heat will speed up the process, while cold will slow it down. Algor mortis, or the cooling down of the body after death, is another classic death measurement. Though several things can impact the body temperature after death, a good heuristic to use is to take 98.6 degrees and subtract the number of the measured rectal temperature of the deceased and then divide that number by 1.5. The resulting number is the approximate hours since death. Finally, livor mortis is the pooling or collecting of blood within the body. Livor mortis, sometimes referred to as lividity, begins immediately at death, though it is not "fixed" until about five or six hours after death. Livor refers to the pooling of the blood in the lowest points in the body. Think about someone who dies in their sleep on their back and is not discovered until the morning. That person will have a purplish collection of blood on the backside of the body. Where the body is not in contact with the bed (the lowest point), however, such as an arm resting on a pillow, lividity will not be present. The blood always pools in the direction of gravity.

Livor mortis can play a critical role in death investigation. For instance, lividity will not form where there is pressure from clothing or objects. This can help determine whether a person was clothed for a period of time after death and quite possibly where someone died. Take the commode, for example. The commode is a common place for even the best of us to die (remember the king dying on his throne). If the person dies and remains on the toilet for some time, this person will form the most ungodly and unbelievably pale ring in the shape of the toilet seat—the rest of the undercarriage will be purple. Finding this person outside, with clothes on, in the car, would tell a lot to the death investigator.

The pathologist also looks for several other telltale signs that occur in the body right after death that can be confused or misconstrued as foul play. Take Tardieu spots, for example. Tardieu spots are brownish black, round spots that occur in areas of the body where large amounts of lividity has collected. These spots are caused by capillaries rupturing within the body. This is a normal process, not to be confused with petechial hemorrhaging. Petechial hemorrhages are smaller spots also caused by the rupturing of capillaries; however, these hemorrhages are usually indicative of asphyxiation. This is especially true if they are found in the facial areas, and particularly the eyes. On the other hand, petechial hemorrhages in the eyes are not to be confused with tache noire, which is simply a drying of the cornea when someone has died with their eyes open, turning the cornea a shade of black.

Death can even mimic life. We've already told about our experiences with the dead continuing to move. But how about *cutis anserine*, the Latin phrase for "gooseflesh," or, in layman's terms, goose bumps. The dead can get goose bumps, too! Actually, rigor mortis causes muscles in the epidermis to constrict, causing these so-called goose bumps in the deceased. Many an investigator has mistaken these bumps for the person to have been cold or excited at death.

How about fingernails and hair continuing to grow after death? We've all heard about this supposedly happening. Several cultures tell of their beloved kings continuing to grow hair and fingernails even after death, making divine rituals around the trimming of these out-growths. This has been passed down into our lore as well. We're sorry to burst everyone's bubble; they don't. They only *appear* to grow on certain individuals during the early stages of a slow decomposition. What actually happens is that the skin begins to recede, giving the impression that the fingernails, toenails, and even hair are still growing. But it is merely an illusion. That doesn't mean, however, that it too hasn't fooled even the most seasoned investigator.

Manner of Death

Death can occur for many reasons and in absolutely any situation. Yet, pathologically speaking, death falls into seven main causes: blunt force trauma, sharp force trauma, asphyxiation, gunshot, fire fatalities, drowning, and substance-related. Within these categories there are sub-categories referred to as the manner of death: homicide, suicide, acci-dental, sex-related death, and the ever-boring death by natural causes. These are not "causes" in and of themselves, but situations where death occurs. For the medical examiner, it is important not only to de-scribe what caused the person to die, but also the manner in which he died. By the way, in real life—meaning anything other than what's on *CSI*—homicides comprise less than 1 percent of all cases.

BLUNT FORCE TRAUMA

Blunt force trauma encapsulates the vast majority of death in the United States. This category is the broadest of all of the causes of death and covers everything from baseball bat attacks to falling off of build-ings. Blunt force trauma is also the category where most of the inter-personal violence between people occurs. People will kill each other with anything and everything. Take a look around your house. There are things that you would never consider being used as a weapon, but in the heat of violence, everything is fair game. That is why the medical examiner must be able to differentiate between different types of wound patterns.

A photo of blunt force trauma to the skull. The injury was the result of a hammer blow and the pieces of the skull have been placed back together.
(Collection of the National Forensic Academy)

Wound pattern interpretation in forensic science is the skill of being able to match up the shape of a wound on a body with a particular object. Common, everyday items used in violent attacks will leave their signatures behind on the person, and serve as crucial evidence if the pathologist is adept in determining wound patterns. Belt buckles, Phillips-head screwdrivers, baseball bats, and hammers all leave very distinctive patterns on a victim. That's why it is important during a death investigation to examine the body thoroughly and not mistake an elongated bruise for a fall instead of contact by a Louisville Slugger.

When most people think of blunt force trauma, they think of hitting someone with an object, using their hands. Yet the most common form of blunt force trauma occurs in car fatalities. We have seen the most unfathomable fatalities as a result of accidents involving cars. Nothing can compare to an SUV hitting a pedestrian in the middle of the interstate at full speed, pulverizing the victim into an unrecognizable mass. Individuals killed in this manner are hit so hard that they leave impressions of their *clothing* embedded on the vehicle. Many an ornate belt buckle, and the button on the fronts of Levi's jeans, have been pressed into the hood or quarter-panel of the killing machine. That also means that those vehicles leave their marks on their victims as well, literally branding reverse images of the makes of the perpetrator's car.

We once walked into the autopsy suite only to be confronted with what looked like a disassembled mannequin lying on one of the tables. As we got closer we noticed it wasn't a mannequin at all, but a man who had been hit by three different cars going at least seventy miles an hour as he tried to cross an interstate highway. There was blood and tar smeared on parts of his skin. His left leg was twisted and contorted upward, resting on its own thigh, while the right leg was nowhere in sight. The right arm was attached to the shoulder by only a thread of tendons, allowing it to dangle off the edge of the autopsy table and nearly touch the floor. The torso showed classic signs of road burn, evidence that the body had been dragged by at least one of the cars. But the head of the cadaver was in the worst shape of all. All of the bones had been crushed, making his face look like a Halloween mask that someone had stepped on, caving in the nose, mouth, and eye sockets. This was an example of blunt force trauma personified.

SHARP FORCE TRAUMA

Sharp force trauma consists of cut, or incised, wounds and stab wounds. The difference between the two is simple: A cut in the skin is wider than it is deep, whereas a stab wound is deeper than it is wide. For the medical examiner, recognizing the difference can tell a lot about the manner of death. For instance, multiple cuts and stabs on the neck, face, and arms are typical defensive wounds, whereas several incised wounds on the wrists can suggest a suicide. At a crime scene, sharp force trauma can be very bloody. Once the body is at the ME's office and has been rinsed of the blood, however, the incised and/or stab wounds can just look like small incisions in the skin.

These cases do not typically result in death. But when they do, the wounds may look no worse than small cuts. Dying from stab wounds and cuts is a matter of luck—bad luck. If arteries are severed or organs punctured, then death is imminent. But someone can be stabbed all the way through, and as long as the object misses the vital areas, then the person will have little problem recovering from the wound.

Death resulting from sharp force trauma is often associated with sexual homicides. The reason—the assailant does not want to kill the victim immediately, so a knife is a good threat as well as a torture device. Fear and a little pain will usually be enough to subdue someone until the perp is ready to kill them. That's why victims are stabbed so many times when they are killed in this manner. Multiple stabbings in a fit of rage is sometimes called *overkill*. We were privy to one case in which the assailant stabbed his victim through the skull, all the way through the bone, burying the blade deep into the brain. It takes great strength to push a knife through bone, much less a skull. It was certainly an unnerving sight, and one violent stab wound was all it took.

ASPHYXIATION

Asphyxiation is the manner of death most often portrayed in the movies. Everybody is familiar with the scene of someone smothering a person with a pillow or strangling a person with their bare hands. There are several other manners in which a person can suffocate: They can choke; they can have their oxygen depleted in an enclosed space; they could have their oxygen replaced, such as asphyxia related to carbon monoxide poisoning; or they could be hanged.

Asphyxia can be difficult to diagnose. There are a couple of classic markers to look at when investigating an asphyxiation death. Take strangulation, for example. Cases of manual strangulation occur all too often in the supposedly civilized world. The astute medical examiner, during the examination of a body, would recognize the petechial hemorrhaging in the eyes, indicative of asphyxiation, but not necessarily strangulation. If violence or foul play is suspected, the ME would then, during autopsy, perform a tracheotomy-like incision into the neck of the deceased, digging deep within the area of the trachea to find the hyoid bone. The hyoid bone is a horseshoe-shaped, very flimsy bone that helps support the larynx during speech. It is unique because it is the only bone in the body that does not articulate, or join, with another bone. The hyoid bone is of particular forensic interest, especially in cases where bodies are found badly decomposed, with little or no flesh evidence left to support a neck injury. A broken or fractured hyoid bone found scattered among skeletal remains or deep within the tissue of a recent victim is nearly always indicative of strangulation. This little tiny bone has put more than its share of criminals away.

Asphyxiation can also occur through nonphysical means. Individuals who die as a result of carbon monoxide poisoning (usually by accident or suicide) will have a cherry-red coloration all over their bodies. They do not have the pale color of death, but the rosy-colored cheeks of life. If someone dies of cyanide poisoning (usually a homicide), they, too, will have the same skin coloration as those who died as a result of carbon monoxide. Physically speaking, it is virtually impossible to tell the difference. Except for one small catch—almonds. If someone has died from cyanide poisoning, there is a strong and distinct smell of almonds almost immediately emanating from the deceased. Recognizing this is important not only in establishing the possibility of murder, but also in protecting those involved in the examination of the body and the crime scene.

Finally, there is one other difficult asphyxiation case to investigate—autoerotic asphyxiation. Autoerotic asphyxiation is self-strangulation in an effort to cut off the blood supply to the brain while engaged in masturbation. The hope is that the oxygen-deprived brain will allow the feeling of supreme euphoria when orgasm takes place. This sexual deviation occurs mainly in heterosexual, middle-class white males (though there is an ever-growing number of women doing this), with above-average intelligence. Adolescent males, "experimenting" with sex, will simply use some type of ligature around the neck to cut off the blood flow during masturbation. If they continue the practice into adulthood, however, the autoerotic asphyxiation becomes more complex.

These adult men, oftentimes married with children, will create unbelievable scenarios involving mirrors, fulcrum release mechanisms, and pornographic paraphernalia. They wait until they are alone, some-times actually checking into a hotel with all of their "stuff," and begin their ritual. The intricate nature of the devices created to strangle these individuals would be envied by some of the best engineering schools in the world. The contraptions conceived usually involve rope, which is strung through various pulleys and then attached to various levers. The purpose is to allow control over the amount of strangulation and to ul-timately have a safety release mechanism in case things go wrong. The safety release mechanism is invariably as simple as merely sitting up, which takes the pressure off the neck. The individual then sets out his most prized erotic fantasies in the form of a ton of various kinds of pornography (sometimes a mirror is used to watch the "goings-on"). Finally, the individual begins masturbation, though sometimes penile mutilation happens first.

Unfortunately, what usually happens is that the victim passes out before he can release the device. Thus, he strangles himself to death. Then, with the apparatus and pornography still in place, the family re-turns to the horror, finding their loved one dead amidst a very weird and masochistic backdrop. Often times, the first reaction the family has is to clean up the scene before calling for help, making the classifi-cation of autoerotic death versus suicide more difficult for the investi-gator. Though there are approximately one thousand cases of autoerotic asphyxia reported each year, the number might be substan-tially higher if they were not characterized as suicides.

GUNSHOT DEATHS

Gunshot deaths are relatively straightforward when compared to other deaths that can be easily masked. The challenge in these fatalities is de-termining whether the one-shot deaths are suicides, and even those can be difficult because there have been cases of people firing multiple shots into themselves (if at first you don't succeed . . .). There are two com-mon characteristics to look for in gunshot wound cases: close contact between the muzzle and the skin will produce a scorching effect, de-positing soot around the wound; and the entry wound will be smaller and more rounded than the exit wound, which will be much larger and jagged. That's generally true, and that's what the literature will tell you is *always* true—but there are exceptions to every rule.

We have witnessed firsthand the destruction of gunshot fatalities. During one session of the academy, we participated in the investigation of a murder-suicide between two lovers—a thirty-year-old man and his sixty-year-old sugar mamma. In this part of town, murder is uncommon; suicide is unheard of; and a woman being behind it all is out of the question. The sixty-year-old woman, who, by the way, looked no older than thirty thanks to the wonderful world of plastic surgery, picked up a .38 caliber pistol and shot her boyfriend in the chest at close range. In his case, he looked just like the books say he should— small entrance, large exit, and so on. Then the woman put the gun underneath her neck at an angle and shot herself.

Years and years of plastic surgery have an impact on gunshot fatalities, a fact that is not discussed in the literature. So when she pulled the trigger on her extremely taut face, it ruptured like the *Hindenburg*, creating a massive entry wound. As far as the exit wound goes, there wasn't any. The taught skin around where the bullet would have exited trapped the bullet between the skin and the skull. No one had ever witnessed such a sight.

Gunshots, though very common, are not the only method of suicide that people choose. Many people jump from buildings or bridges in the hope of ending their lives. Personally, we can't think of anything more stupid, because there is no guarantee that death will result from such a fall. There are much more successful ways a person can end his or her life. But no matter how stupid, it doesn't keep people from trying, and, unfortunately, succeeding. We'll never forget the time we watched the autopsy of a man who had jumped off of a building, killing himself at the ripe old age of thirty-nine. On the autopsy table, the corpse looked relatively normal, from the waist up. We wouldn't have been able to tell he had jumped from a building just by looking at his face and torso. His legs, however, were a different story. They were a tangled mess of crumbled flesh and bone. There wasn't much blood. It just looked like he had stuck both of his legs into a compression machine, crushing the bone on the inside, but leaving the skin virtually intact. The investigation into his death led us to find out that all of the men in this person's family suffered from some type of mental illness, not living past forty years of age. The man, seemingly in good spirits, killed himself out of the sheer anxiety of turning forty.

When they got to his heart during the autopsy and pulled it from the chest cavity, it looked like a gob of bloody kite string. His heart had beat at the same time he made contact with the ground, causing his heart to explode, stretching apart into angel hair pasta. Cause of death—heart attack. Most people who choose this method of suicide never live to the end; they die of a heart attack en route to the ground.

FIRE FATALITIES

Fire deaths are always a gruesome sight. Depending on the severity of the fire, the entire body may be charred black. An odd thing happens when a body burns that makes it look distorted as it lies on the autopsy table. The large joints and muscles of the body contract, causing the arms and legs to curl inward up toward the chest. This is called the pugilistic, or boxerlike, pose. Sometimes the hands will also curl into a fistlike position.

The smell is unparalleled as well. It is like barbecued meat, and as odd as it sounds, it will make your stomach growl with anticipation and then churn with nausea (hunger is our most primal instinct and one we have no control over). We've only experienced this once, and it was during the burning of a car in which animal remains had been placed.

Most people who die in a fire die early on from carbon monoxide poisoning. Others tragically die by rising up in bed when their fire alarm goes off, only to have their lungs explode due to the inhalation of extremely hot gas. That's something they don't tell you when they tell you to change the battery in smoke detectors.

A fire will not and cannot consume a person completely. There will always be pieces of bone, at least as big as a quarter, no matter how hot the fire gets. Typical house fires rarely if ever get above two thousand degrees and never remain that hot for very long. In contrast, a typical crematorium reaches sustained temperatures of nearly twenty-two hundred degrees, and the remains still must be pulverized into dust by an industrial-strength blender. As a matter of fact, there are enough recognizable pieces left that a forensic anthropologist can determine race, age, sex, and even stature if some of the long bones survive.

The fire deaths we have witnessed are those who have died at the hospital, succumbing to the effects of the fire. A fire victim is flushed with lots and lots of fluid in an effort to treat the patient. When the person does not make it through the ordeal, the fluid remains in the body, swelling the victim up like one of the *Five Chinese Brothers*. Between the overhydrated tissue and the heat, the body almost appears to be in the bloat stage of decomposition. In yet another one of Mother Nature's embarrassing death moments, a man's scrotum will bulge in size enough to make Spalding himself jealous. Of all the ways to die, fire is probably the worst.

DROWNING DEATHS

Drowning is not a common method of homicide, no matter how many Mafia movies illustrate the contrary. Drowning is the fourth leading cause of accidental death, killing nearly eight thousand people a year. One would assume that drowning is simply asphyxiation by water and that people who drown suffocate to death. That could not be further from the truth. Only 10 percent of people who die by drowning actually suffocate to death. Recently, it was discovered that when people drown in fresh water, the water that is swallowed and absorbed by the victim dilutes the blood within the body. This diluted blood causes a rapid increase in the volume of blood in the body, which in turn overburdens the heart, sending it into rapid tachycardia. The victim dies of a heart attack within three to five minutes. In salt water, the reverse is true. The water that is absorbed actually draws blood into the lungs, again causing the heart to be overburdened. Oddly enough, people who drown in salt water have a better chance of being resuscitated because it takes longer for the osmosis process to occur in the lungs. Though there are several things that occur within the body that are peculiar to drowning, none is glaringly indicative of a homicide. Because of this, all information from the scene must be gathered in order to get a complete picture.

Bodies that have been found in water are called "floaters." These floaters are always in an advanced state of decay—their bodies fill with gas. This is actually why they float, and it normally takes one to two weeks for this to happen. We have seen floaters at the Body Farm. Their skin is very green and translucent at the same time. They are also always massively swollen. They look like something out of the movie *Seven*. We're not sure why, but birds love floaters even more than they love other bodies. When one arrives, it becomes the main course for the birds, who dip their beaks deep into the eye sockets. For medical examiners, drowning victims are the most difficult cases to investigate. If there are no visible signs of struggle or no signs of the victim being bound, then it is virtually impossible to prove someone died by homicidal drowning. Ninety-nine times out of a hundred, these cases, regardless of the circumstance, will be classified as accidental.

SUBSTANCE-RELATED DEATHS

Substance-related deaths can involve recreational drugs, like alcohol or crack cocaine, prescription drugs, like OxyContin, or poisonous agents, such as arsenic. Someone being poisoned is one of the rarest occurrences of all homicides. Yet, when it happens, it explodes all over the media, creating fervor across the country. Think of Jim Jones and the infamous cyanide-laced grape Kool-Aid. Though in actuality it was Flavor Aid, sales of grape Kool-Aid plummeted for nearly two years, and the event spurred the phrase "I Drank the Kool-Aid," meaning a person has given up his or her personal integrity to go along with the crowd. Cases of poisoning clearly leave an indelible mark on the American psyche.

It's important for the death investigator to know that certain poisons, like cyanide, have a distinctive aroma, though they may be clear and tasteless. For instance, arsenic smells like garlic, ethyl nitrite smells like rum, and diphosgene smells like newly mown hay. Aside from an investigator being able to smell the poison, the investigation into a poisoning death is extremely difficult because there is no crime scene. Furthermore, the victim is usually diagnosed as being merely sick or dying from a disease. If there is no suspicion on the part of the doctor, then, more than likely, the perpetrator will get away with the murder.

Most deaths associated with substances are accidental, however, occurring only after a period of abuse or because of an overdose. These are the traditional drug deaths that most medical examiners come in contact with on a regular basis. We have seen the effects of years of drug abuse on a body. People who look so old and ragged that you would bet they're in their late eighties, when in reality they have not even reached the age of forty-five. Illicit drugs do wonders not only for the outsides of the body, but for the insides as well. The liver, the organ that takes the brunt of the abuse, no longer looks nice and purple, maintaining a nice, spongy feel. No, the liver now looks pale in comparison, a reddish gray, with fatty marbling lines and weird spots coursing throughout, turning it the consistency of oatmeal or mush. Depending on the type of drugs abused, various organs will have become "mushy" or distended or grainy, with black splotches and yellow mucuslike patches clinging to the underlying membranes within the body cavity. Many will have the markings of intravenous drug use, better known as "tracks," stitched up one arm, down the other, even reaching into the legs and torso if no other veins can be found. Clinically speaking, the vast majority of these individuals will have died of a heart attack or a liver disorder, like cirrhosis. But in reality they committed suicide—choosing to die a long, arduous chemical death.

Someone once wrote "life's a bitch and then you die." Well, death's a bitch, too. It's complicated, it's smelly, and it's gross. But most important, it's sad. We see so many types of death in a year, happening to people from eight to eighty, that it makes us scared to even drive home at night. We are so anxious to find out how the people died when we're at the morgue, hoping that they have done something stupid that we would never do. "Whew! He died while jumping rope on a balance beam between two buildings while juggling running chain saws. That's a relief." But that rarely happens. It really brings home just how fragile life truly is and the absurdity of why anyone would want to end it. Suicidal patients ought to spend time with us as treatment; they might think twice about killing themselves.

DEATH INVESTIGATION

What is it about duct tape that everyone loves so much? There are even books and calendars written on its uses, selling millions of copies. Criminals love duct tape, too. We figure it produces some sort of Siren song; a tune that only the deranged can hear. Everybody has a roll of duct tape. It's strong. It's extremely tacky. It works great on just about anything. It's a funny thing that if you are pulled over and the police find a baseball bat in your car and it does not appear you are coming from a game, you can be arrested for carrying a deadly weapon. But if you are pulled over and have a giant-size roll of duct tape sitting on the passenger seat, the cop will just smile, thinking to himself all of the great things he could use that duct tape for. Well, my friends, duct tape has been involved in way more homicides than the Louisville Slugger. Trust us, in crazy hands, duct tape is a deadly weapon.

About ten years ago, a young woman hired a local man to work on her car. Her sister saw her talking to the man and everything seemed to be okay. At ten o'clock that night, they were supposed to talk on the phone, but the conversation never took place.

Twelve days later, local police found a woman's body floating in a nearby creek, her feet and hands bound behind her back with duct tape. When they brought the victim in from the water, they found her head to be completely encased by duct tape, as if someone was wrapping up a mummy. Though the body was in an advanced state of decomposition, the woman was identified by her fingerprints, which were taken postmortem.

The doctor who performed the death investigation and autopsy of the victim concluded that she died of asphyxiation caused by the duct tape covering her mouth and nostrils, wrapped so tight it constricted her breathing.

The sister, knowing the man who had worked on her sister's car, told the police what she knew of her sister's last day. The investigation led to an abandoned house owned by a friend of the suspect, where investigators found the victim's prescription glasses and an earring that matched the one found on her body. Further investigation by the police led them to discover that there were several conspirators involved in the kidnapping and murder of the victim. They had kept her bound for days, some using her off and on as a sex toy during their sicko cookouts.

The police questioned one of the brothers of one of the suspects, asking him if he had any duct tape in his possession. He willingly handed over a half-used roll that was stashed under the front seat of his car. The roll was sent to the crime lab for analysis.

At the crime lab, the roll of tape was compared to the tape found on the victim. The trace evidence specialist found that the two tapes were identical. Further investigation also found that the tape was produced by a company in England that did not market or sell its tape in the United States and exported only 1 percent of its tape to other European countries.

During the trial, the jury was presented with the evidence, including the only substantial evidence that linked the men to the killing, the duct tape. In the end, seven men were charged in part with this crime: five were convicted of murder and sentenced to life, one was convicted of conspiracy to commit murder, and the last one—the repairman who instigated the whole event—sits on death row, determined to be mentally incompetent to stand trial for a period of five years. He is still awaiting this trial.

WOUND PATTERN INTERPRETATION

Drug addicts will do absolutely anything to get more drugs once they run out. They have an incessant itch that they can never scratch no matter how hard they try. They become some sort of perversion of humanity, as they spiral down toward their demise. Lord help those who are unfortunate enough to get in their way.

In July of 1999, a couple, boyfriend and girlfriend at the time, went on a crack-smoking spree of unheralded proportions. The two began the day by smoking $150 worth of crack they already had, then buying $50 more and smoking that as well. When they were finished with that, they pawned a ring for $20, bought more crack with their newfound wealth, and smoked all of it up.

After the lot of crack was gone, they moved on over to a friend's house, where they asked to borrow some more money to buy more crack. The enterprising girlfriend cut a deal with the friend, performing oral sex in exchange for $125.

They spent the $125 on more crack, and guess what, they smoked it all up, too. The duo went on to another friend's house to beg or work for more money, but he was not interested. So they went back to the original friend's house to try to get more money. As the girlfriend lured the man back for "more of the same," the boyfriend pounced on him, killing him with a hammer. They took his wallet, containing $165, and fled the scene, throwing the hammer out the window of the car somewhere down the road. They stopped after a while to—you guessed it—buy more crack cocaine.

All hopped-up on crack and getting braver by the puff, the duo, once again out of crack, decided they knew how to get more money, but they would have to kill a couple of old people. En route to the old couple's house, they stopped at a Shell gas station to borrow a hammer, reportedly to fix their car.

By now, it's obvious what happened next. The dynamic duo got to the old couple's house, killed them both with a hammer, took the old man's wallet that contained $500, and fled the scene, throwing the hammer out the window. Continuing on with the insanity, they bought and smoked up $500 more crack. By now, the paranoia associated with drug overdose began to kick in and the two got scared. They decided to flee the state, stopping to get gas just across the state line. By now, the girlfriend was really freaking out and she called 911, eventually cutting a deal with the police for life imprisonment for her story.

She led the police to the only piece of physical evidence they would need, the hammer that was used to kill the old couple. Upon investigation into the cause of death, the medical examiner observed several lacerations and fractures in both of the victims' skulls. It was concluded that their deaths were the result of blunt force trauma. The man had injuries consistent with a flat, rounded object, the nailing part of the hammer, while the woman had injuries consistent with the claw end of a hammer.

The ME went on to conclude that parts of the skull had "distinguishable indentations." Upon receiving the supposed murder weapon, the ME made an impression of the nail end of the hammer in clay, comparing the mold to the injury on the skull. At the trial, the ME fit the hammer into the skull and then the clay impression, showing that it indeed was a hammer that made the indentations in the skull. After seeing this evidence, the jury convicted the accused, charging him with the murders of all three victims.

9

SPATTER UP!
Bloodstain Pattern Analysis

Bloodspatter, the most popular forensic discipline in the world today, sounds more like a bad Van Damme movie than a training subject. Blood that is shed and thrown about during a violent crime is no longer called bloodspatter, like all of those so-called experts espouse on TV. After thirty years, the technical name was changed to bloodstain, simply because not all of the blood found at a crime scene is spatter. Bloodstain training is the most talked about and most misunderstood forensic field. Everyone thinks that they are experts in this field, and the more blood they can throw or spit out from between their cheeks in court (literally), the better. Bloodstain experts are second only to anthropologists in their bitter rivalry to outdo one another. Most are true prima donnas, who sincerely think they are the best when it comes to reading the blood at a crime scene, and who jump at the chance to flamboyantly challenge one of their colleagues in court. The antagonism has become so intense that many have begun a ranking system that is worse than that found in the world of boxing.

The study of bloodstain lay dormant for years until Herb McDonnell, considered by most to be the godfather of bloodspatter, resurrected the science back in the 1970s. McDonnell truly pioneered the study, training many of the experts that are around today. The fervor for his methodology is so great that his protégés are actually known as disciples of his training. Recently, however, a new generation of blood-stain analysts has emerged and begun to challenge some of the "old school" ways, even forcing the change from calling it "bloodspatter" to "bloodstain." This bloody war is playing itself out once a month at the FBI academy as a collection of both old and new school experts partic-ipate in what is called SWG-STAIN, a scientific working group that meets regularly to discuss the leading theories and practices in the field of bloodstain pattern analysis. SWG-STAIN is forging the standardiza-tion of bloodstain pattern analysis not only for the country, but for the world.

Bloodstain pattern analysis is the study of the shapes, locations, and distribution patterns of what happens when blood is set in motion. When applicable, bloodstain analysis might be the most important as-pect of crime scene investigation. The proper interpretation of the bloodstains can tell a CSI several things, such as where the attack oc-curred, where the victim was in relation to the suspect, how the victim was injured or killed, and what type of weapon was used. This is all critical in solving a case, and if worked properly, a bloody crime scene can provide most, if not all, of the information.

At its core, bloodstain training is a complex process, not for the mathematically challenged. It uses an advanced trigonometry that places the victim in three-dimensional space, while only calculating bloodstains that exist in two. It is a daunting task for the crime scene investigator when they first begin the study of bloodstain pattern analy-sis. The complexity of the class, coupled with the apprehension of the students, makes it difficult to teach this discipline. It takes a very expe-rienced instructor who really understands the discipline and is willing to leave his or her ego at the door. Needless to say, it is hard to find a good one.

We worked relentlessly, trying out various instructors over a couple of years. We found that the best bloodstain instructors are the ones who do not have to tell you how great they are—their body of work speaks for itself. After two years, we found a couple of instructors that the class really learned from and enjoyed. This fast became our best and most popular course. We have become so well known for our

A unit of human blood is used to create fingerprints on pieces of kitchen linoleum.

(Collection of the National Forensic Academy)

bloodstain training that we have been asked to take it on the road, bringing the course to Seattle, Cape Canaveral, Duluth, Savannah, Columbia, Cincinnati, and Austin—to name just a few places.

It is imperative that our students practice with human blood in order to be able to understand what is being taught; therefore, the number-one item for this week's supply list is blood. Lots of blood. Six pints, to be exact. Some bloodstain courses around the country teach bloodstain analysis using a mixture of red food coloring and Karo syrup, even cherry-flavored Kool-Aid. Though all of these concoctions taste inherently better than blood, they do not adequately represent the real stuff. These other substances also make it very, very hard to perform accurate calculations.

When the academy first began, we had to use animal blood for our class because it was very difficult to obtain human blood. And getting even animal blood was no easy task. It took us months to find a source willing to give us blood to use. "What are you, vampires?" was one question we heard several times during our quest. But after about a hundred phone calls, we, along with one of our colleagues, finally found a place to get animal blood. Too bad for us that their blood was straight from the tap.

Back deep in the woods, at a place that makes scenes from *Deliverance* look like settings right off of Broadway, we found a family-run slaughterhouse. We had no idea what to expect the first time we went to this establishment. Forty-five minutes later, after we drove up a winding dirt road that made us dizzy, we arrived. When we approached the side of a garagelike structure that we assumed was the entrance, we began to feel a little out of our element. With a lot of trepidation, we knocked on the door. It swung open to the tune of tobacco spit splattering the concrete driveway and the question, "Here for the blood?" We answered "yes" in meek unison and received a crooked glare. The gentleman then asked us, "What're y'all puttin' the blood in?" We had just assumed they would put it in something we could transport, but they had no type of receptacle to speak of. Luckily, we had passed a real mom-and-pop store on our way up the winding mountain road. We drove back to the store, but the only thing we could find was a forty-four-ounce plastic soda cup. After we arrived back at the slaughterhouse, we knocked, the spit happened, and we handed the guy the plastic cup to a loud chuckle. "It'll be a minute," he yelled back as the spring-hinged door slammed shut. Within thirty seconds, we heard the worst sound in the history of sounds. It was a cow, bellowing its last sound on Earth. Another thirty seconds passed and the door swung open to reveal an outstretched hand with a plastic cup full of dripping blood. As we grabbed the cup, steam rose up from the liquid like a cup of hot coffee on a cold morning. Needless to say, the drive back was not much fun, especially since a forty-four-ounce cup won't even fit in a regular size cup holder, and there was no lid.

The first time we went to the slaughterhouse, we realized about midway back that the blood was changing. By the time we made it back to the academy, we had one big blood clot to work with. For the entire week, we had to squeeze the clot like a sponge to get enough blood for the class to use in their exercises. Since then, we keep EDTA, an anti-

coagulating agent, in the vehicle at all times, just in case we are working with animal blood. Nowadays, we mainly use expired human
blood from Medic, a local blood donation center. Our academy has become so popular that we get regular e-mails from people wanting to do-
nate not only their bodies to us, but also their blood. Of course we
don't accept it, because we only use blood that has been thoroughly
screened and irradiated. On any given day during the academy, you
could find three or four pints of human blood in our refrigerator,
among other things. That's hard enough to explain to someone. But
imagine trying to explain to a patrol officer why you're three thousand
miles away from home with a cooler full of human blood in the backseat.

Characteristics of a Blood Drop

Before the students begin to practice reading the signs left in blood,
they must first learn a few characteristics of the blood drop. First they
are taught that a blood drop is formed by gravity. When in motion,
blood maintains a spherical shape, falling in a perfect sphere. A blood
drop will not break apart, unless acted upon by an outside force, or
when it ultimately hits a surface. The bigger the drop, the farther it will
travel. This is due to the mass of the drop and not necessarily the size.
Imagine throwing a golf ball versus a Ping-Pong ball. The size of the
two spherical objects is relatively the same, but the mass is totally different. Blood drops can range in size from a few millimeters to a few
centimeters. The volume of a blood drop is in direct proportion to
whatever the blood is dropping off of. For example, the drops formed
at the end of a baseball bat will be much larger than those that fall off
of a screwdriver. Furthermore, blood drops will impact a surface at an
angle of ninety degrees (perpendicular) or at less than ninety degrees.
Finally, blood drops always fly in a parabolic, or arcing, path. If you
can picture throwing a football down the field, it is easier to visualize
how blood flies. The blood, or football, takes flight due to the force
that has acted upon it, propelling it in an upward trajectory. Then, as
gravity begins to act on the blood, it begins to level off, reaching its

apex at the top of the arc, before it ultimately begins falling back to Earth. In most crime scenes, however, walls, ceilings, and furniture get in the way of blood as it flies. Blood still follows the same flight pattern, but some blood will hit the wall on the way up, some will hit the wall at its zenith, and some will hit the wall on the way down. In bloodstain analysis, we only measure those bloodstains that hit on the way up. They produce the best and most accurate measurements because they are the least impacted by gravity.

After the students scratch their heads in confusion as the initial lecture ends, we take them outside to do a little practice, where we have set up several experiments to illustrate what they have just learned. The students are divided up into five groups, each receiving a bloodstain kit with the tools necessary for bloodstain analysis. Each kit contains string, a magnifying loupe, a protractor, and a ruler. We also set up a table with all of the other supplies they will need to perform the activities: latex gloves, plastic cups, pipettes, poster board, twenty-five-foot tape measures, metal yardsticks, and most important, blood. We also provide a six-foot stepladder from our supply closet. The first experiment they must perform is dropping blood from various heights at a ninety-degree angle. The students take their pipettes, draw approximately 5 ccs of blood out of the cup, and drop it at twelve inches—and then at one-foot increments up to nine feet—onto pieces of poster board, using the yardstick and twenty-five-foot tape measure as a guide. This illustrates how blood drops fall and the diameter of the stain that results. The students learn that the farther the blood drops fall, the larger the diameter of the stain left on the target. This is only true, however, to a certain point. If volume remains constant, a blood drop, as it reaches terminal velocity, cannot be any wider in diameter no matter the height from which it is dropped.

Measurement of Bloodstains

After the students have had plenty of time to drop all of the blood that they want to drop for this exercise, we take their dried targets back into the classroom to learn the next step in bloodstain pattern

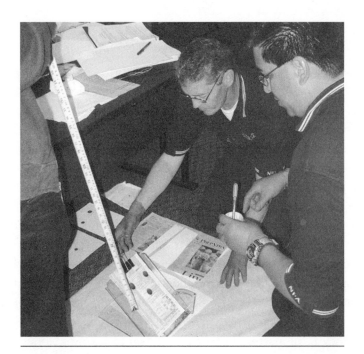

Session Seven graduates Lanny Cox and Mike Velez conducting a bloodstain experiment.

(Collection of the National Forensic Academy)

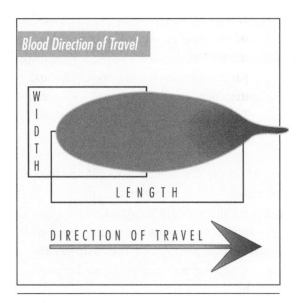

Illustration of a blood drop.

(Illustration by Pamela Johanns of Johanns Design)

analysis—the measurement of stains. Measuring bloodstains is the underlying concept in bloodstain analysis, and it is of paramount importance. The students practice measuring the stains they have created to determine precisely the length and width of each stain. Using advanced trigonometry, the students are taught how to calculate the angle of impact of a blood drop. To do this, the students use the following formula: sine a = W/L. That is, the sine of the angle is equal to the width of the stain divided by the length of the stain. (Each student has a scientific calculator that automatically calculates the sine.) At a bloody crime scene, it is of extreme importance that one person performs the measuring of the stains—and to not include the scalloped edges, just the stain itself—so the measurements will be consistent. This is step one in being able to reconstruct the events at the crime scene. The students continue to practice measuring stains and calculating angles. Once they have mastered that task, it's on to learning about the types of bloodstains that are found at a crime scene.

Types of Bloodstain Patterns

There are essentially ten basic types of bloodstain patterns: drip, flow, splashed, projected, satellite, cast-off, wipe, swipe, transfer, and impact. Students must learn what each type looks like and how to recognize them at a crime scene.

DRIP AND FLOW

Drip and flow patterns are the infamous O. J. Simpson patterns that became known worldwide. A drip pattern occurs when a drop of blood drips into another liquid, usually more blood. If a person is bleeding and the drops are hitting an already formed puddle on the floor, a drip pattern will result. A flow pattern is blood that has dropped in a trail. Though these types of patterns can be caused by other occurrences, they are traditionally represented by someone bleeding and on the move, fleeing the scene of a crime.

SPLASHED

Splashed stains are similar to drip stains, though usually a little larger. They result from blood being projected with little force exerted on them and they usually disperse in a radial pattern. Think of splashing in terms of a mud puddle. If you jump in the puddle, the mud splashes in a radial pattern away from itself. These patterns are not in and of themselves indicative of a violent act, because there is little or no force associated with it. These patterns are extremely rare in crime scenes and are the easiest patterns to stage. CSIs should be cautious when encountering these types of patterns.

PROJECTED

Projected patterns are associated with a larger volume of blood that is acted upon with a significant amount of force. One of the classic examples of this pattern is an arterial spurt, seen in violent crimes when there is sharp force trauma or, in other words, a stabbing or slashing. If the all-too-familiar jugular vein is slashed, it will most certainly create this pattern.

SATELLITE

Satellite patterns are created when blood that was originally part of a bigger stain leaves that stain through some type of force. A drop of blood that is flying through the air will not separate without another force acting upon it. Think of it in terms of dropping blood at a significant height. When the drop hits a surface, it goes through four actions: contact, dispersion, displacement, and collapse. When blood contacts a surface, it flattens out. If there is enough volume and force to break the surface tension of the blood drop when it hits, it will disperse, sending blood out in all directions. If the force is great enough, it will displace. This displaced blood leaves the original parent stain, causing what is called satellite spatter. Satellite spatter is merely small stains leaving a larger stain. Finally, the blood drop will collapse back on itself, with the vast majority of the blood collecting back together. Of course, all of that happens in less than a blink of the eye.

CAST-OFF

Cast-off patterns are patterns that are created by blood being slung off of an object, such as a bloody baseball bat, that is in motion or when the object suddenly stops. The latter is sometimes referred to as a cessation pattern. When a victim is bludgeoned to death with an object like a hammer, the object, once it is covered in blood, will cast off the blood that has accumulated on it when swung. These patterns are traditionally found in a linear fashion, representing a swinging or chopping motion, and can help define where a person was when the pattern was created. In order for there to be a cast-off pattern, a person has to be hit more than once, unless they are already suffering from a bloody wound. It takes at least one blow to bring the blood to the surface and to cover the weapon. Therefore, the second hit or swing will actually be where the first cast-off will occur. These patterns are one of the three patterns that have caused the most debate among the bloodstain experts. The old methodology teaches that you can calculate precisely the number of cast-offs an item makes, which in turn represents a number of times a victim was hit. New school proponents teach that it is impossible to discern from cast-off patterns how many times a victim was hit, and that the only way to do so with any certainty is to actually witness the crime. Their belief is that there are just too many variables involved to calculate this with any degree of accuracy.

WIPES AND SWIPES

Wipe and swipe patterns are the actual reason for the name change from bloodspatter analysis to bloodstain pattern analysis. This is because not all blood found at a scene is bloodspatter, though all blood found at a crime scene is a bloodstain. Wipes and swipes are not spatters at all and have nothing to do with force acting on a blood source, causing it to be propelled through the air in one direction or another. A wipe pattern is simply a stain created by an object coming across a bloodstain that already exists on another object. This type of pattern would occur if, for instance, someone were to "wipe" a nonbloody hand through a bloodstain. In contrast, a swipe is a stain created when an object that is already stained with blood comes into contact with an object that is not stained. This could occur if a person's bloody hand was "swiped" across a nonbloody wall.

These stains can be a little confusing and they are difficult to tell apart. This is especially true if there happens to be a wipe on top of a swipe. The best way to tell the difference between the two patterns is that in a wipe there will be skeletonization of the original bloodstain. In other words, at the point where the original blood resides, there will be at least a few seconds of drying before the other object comes into contact with the blood, thus creating a skeleton image or outline of where the blood was. As soon as a drop hits a surface it begins to dry. Blood drops dry from the outside in, so immediately a semidry ring forms around the drop. If a person were to wipe his hand through the drop, skeletonization of the original drop would occur. Directionality is also key when studying either of these types of patterns. The best way to tell in what direction the event happened is to discern where the most volume of blood has pooled in relation to the wipe or swipe. When the object moves across, the blood will collect the most where the wipe or swipe ends. Think of this in terms of a wet windshield and a squeegee. Whatever direction the squeegee is pulled across the wet windshield will be the direction in which the majority of the water collects. The same is true for wipes and swipes.

TRANSFER

A transfer pattern is created when a bloody object, such as a knife, comes into contact with a nonbloody object, such as a floor. For instance, if a bloodstained knife were dropped onto clean carpet, then it would leave a transfer pattern. Bloody footprints left behind at the scene of a crime are also transfer patterns. These patterns are especially important in matching objects to the scene.

IMPACT

Impact patterns are another pattern of contention. For over thirty years, these patterns have been famous for representing gunshot wounds, better known as high-velocity and medium-velocity impact spatters. More often than not, patterns of this type are created by gunshots. The object that is indicative of creating this pattern, however, like a handgun, is not what should be used to classify all patterns that resemble these types. This is especially true when something other than a gun could be used to create them. For example, if someone is hit violently with a baseball bat in an area that already has blood pooling or collecting, then the spatter created will appear to be the old school "high- or medium-velocity" type of spatter. Therefore, we teach that it is important to recognize the spatters as impact spatters, where the blood has reacted under high force and not as a result of a specific object.

Regardless of the velocity, impact spatters result in a very fine, almost mistlike pattern. The greater the force that is applied to the stain, the finer the spatter will be. And, in cases where there is a gunshot, there are two types of spatter that can be found—forward and back. Forward spatter occurs only if there is an exit wound in the victim. This spatter will travel in the relative direction of the bullet. Back spatter, on the other hand, always occurs. This spatter will occur at or near the entrance wound of the victim and fly back toward where the shot came from, in the opposite direction of the bullet. When someone is shot at very close range, the victim's blood will almost always be on the assailant's gun, as well as on the assailant, such as on his clothes, wristwatch, and skin.

Angle of Impact

With the lectures finished, we again take the class outside for more practice. Next, the students drop blood again from varying heights, but this time at various angles. This also demonstrates the correlation between the angle of impact and the shape of the bloodstain. These drops

NFA instructor Jeff Gurvis demonstrates impact spatter.
(Copyright © Nathan Lefebvre, collection of the National Forensic Academy)

of blood that hit at an angle leave elliptical stains on the target, with a trailing line called a tail. The tail points to the direction of travel of the blood drop. The angle the blood is dropped from directly affects the elliptical shape. In other words, the lower the angle, the longer and skinnier the ellipse. The poster board is then set aside in order for the blood to dry. The students will measure these more challenging elliptical stains later. Next, the students then drop blood from various objects, again at the same height, onto various target surfaces. The students learn how the different objects (knives, hammers, baseball bats, screwdrivers, wrenches, even staplers) and different targets (carpet, wood, glass, tile, sandpaper) can affect the size and shape of the blood drops. These are also set aside and allowed to dry.

Once they have seemingly mastered that task, we take the students outside again to practice with the blood. For this particular exercise, we take regular four-foot rolls of butcher paper, cut ten-foot-long sections, and lay them on the ground. The students will take syringes and

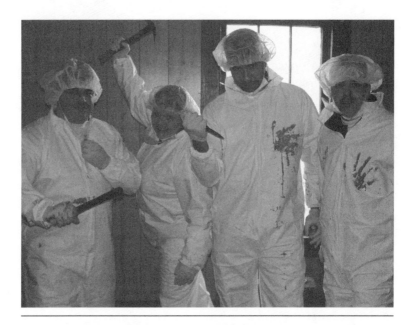

Session Eleven graduates (*left to right*) Mike Manna, Gracie Jones, Steve Wiertel, and Tony Lima pose for a picture after a bloody battle with various murder weapons.
(Copyright © Jarrett Hallcox, collection of the National Forensic Academy)

fill them with blood. The object of the exercise is to walk, trot, and run the length of the butcher paper, letting the blood drip out of the syringe. The toughest part of this exercise is keeping the syringe at a consistent height down the entire length of the paper. The students learn to recognize the different patterns that are made from blood dropped at various speeds. Once this is done, the paper is set aside and allowed to dry. The students then take various "weapons," like hammers and knives, dip them in blood, and walk or run down the length of the butcher paper again, but this time observing how blood flows off of different surface areas at various speeds.

The students then get dressed in full Tyvek suits, head coverings, and face shields, to practice cast-off patterns. We get a classroom and line the room from floor to ceiling in thick plastic sheeting. This is always fun for the class, and for us, dipping items in blood and swinging them around, replicating a beating. Each object that we swing leaves its own distinct pattern. The trick is seeing the cast-off of enough items to be able to differentiate one object's pattern from another's. One of the more interesting things that the class learns during this exercise is how much, or how little, blood is actually cast off of the object. It is very possible to dip an item into blood and swing it overhead in a chopping motion and get little to no blood on yourself. That is always a defense team's best argument—"he would have been covered in blood if he had beat her to death, right?" Not necessarily. Television shows have over-dramatized how much blood is projected on a killer during a violent crime. The perpetrator may not have a visible drop on him, though there might be a lot of bloodshed on the victim.

Area of Convergence

After the students take off their PPE (personal protective equipment), we go back into the classroom for one more lecture, the coup de grâce of bloodstain pattern analysis—the area of convergence. The area of convergence is the actual calculation or reconstruction of what happened at the crime scene. This re-creation is done by first selecting four or five elliptical bloodstains that represent the predominant size of all of the stains from the area where the blood is found. These stains are not necessarily the largest stains, or the smallest stains, or even the average-size stains. They are simply the size stains, selected from the same general area, that are most prevalent and have tails so directionality can be determined. Once the stains are selected and circled (all documentation of the crime scene, including photographing of the scene and DNA swabbing, must be completed before beginning reconstruction), the CSI will take a piece of masking tape several feet long and place it on one of the stains, stretching out the tape in the direction of travel. This is done for all of the selected stains. Where the tape intersects is what is called the area of convergence (there is a plus or minus factor of about two inches). As a checkpoint, the CSI should take a straight edge to several of the other stains that show directionality to see if they generally point toward the same direction. Note, each stain will not point in the exact same direction.

NFA students use a metal ruler to determine the area of convergence at a crime scene.

(Collection of the National Forensic Academy)

The source of bloodshed in three-dimensional space can now be calculated. The CSI calculates the angle of impact using the stains selected to determine the area of convergence. Once this angle is determined, it can be plugged into the formula tan a = H/D. In other words, the tangent of the angle of impact is equal to the height above the point of convergence divided by the distance between the stain and the point of convergence. This calculation will tell the investigator the area where the victim or victims were in space at the time of the violence.

There is also another method, the one that has been depicted on almost all of the crime scene shows. This method is called "stringing." Stringing is another old school methodology that takes different, brightly colored strings that are stretched out from a number of stains in the direction from where they originated. This creates a very nice visual representation of where the bloodshed occurred, but not necessarily an accurate one. Stringing should be used in areas where convergence cannot be readily found, like on a curved surface. We teach both methodologies at the NFA and stress that it is important to perform the mathematical calculations to achieve the best and most accurate results. Then, if the CSI so chooses, he or she can go back with the information and perform the stringing of the stains using accurate calculations. The visualization of the strings is nice for jurors to see; it can really have an impact on testimonies during a trial. Once the class seems to have mastered these calculations, they go home to study for their crime scene practical, and we go to the house to set up the scenes they will work.

Setting up the Bloody Scene

Bloodstain is our favorite crime scene to set up. It is the only time we get to suit up in Tyvek and express ourselves. We have become the Jackson Pollocks of forensic science, except our medium is blood. And we throw the hell out of it. Some who have seen our work just assume that we randomly throw blood all over the room, but that is not the case. Before we begin, we convene with the instructors on how we will set up the crime scenes. We start out by emptying our truck of all of our weapons, including the lawn mower blade, which has fast become a favorite among killers since the movie *Sling Blade*. Few things we do are constant from class to class: We set up four scenes and we use blood. That's about as constant as we get. The rest of the time, we're left to use our imaginations.

Some instructors bring with them a toolkit of various "props" they want to use in the crime scene. Fake money, plastic knifes, a deck of cards, a curly black wig—it's like a Halloween costume gone terribly wrong. Invariably, one of the scenes will have a poker game that has turned violent. Cards will be scattered about, blood will be dropped, and hair from the black wig will be left in clumps. Our running joke is that there seems to be an inordinate amount of card games where someone slits another guy's throat and, before he flees the scene with all of the winnings, pulls out a handful of his pubic hair to leave behind. Damn, we hate that wig.

A bloody Amy poses for a picture in our re-created murder crime scene.

(Copyright © Jarrett Hallcox, collection of the National Forensic Academy)

Other scenes are more "normal." We first determine who will kill whom. Then we choreograph where the assault will begin, where it will go to, and where it will end. Dressed in our Tyvek suits, we begin the assault on one another. In order for the students to be able to accurately reconstruct the crime scene, we try to be very precise with our wounds. The wounds we intend to inflict determine how we will artificially replicate them. Arterial spurts are created with a syringe full of blood, shot out at the appropriate angle. Water guns are awesome for this, too. One way we make impact spatter is to dip the bristles of a scrub brush in some blood and run our hands across them, flicking the blood onto the surface. Or, if we want to create a real fine mist, simulating aspirated blood, we put blood in a spray bottle and spray it very lightly into the air and let it cascade down to the floor. Here's an example of how we would set up a scene:

Jarrett is the perpetrator and Amy is the victim. We have scripted the scene so we know that he is going to cut her arm with a knife, then chase her around the room. Once she reaches the hallway, he stabs her to death. To do this Jarrett has a knife and a small bowl filled with blood. Amy is holding a syringe filled with blood and has blood on her gloves. As the chase begins, Jarrett simulates stabbing Amy by dipping the knife in the blood bowl and making a stabbing motion. This creates a cast-off pattern that we hope the students will recognize. Amy falls on the floor, leaving bloody handprints. We chase each other around the room until we reach the hallway. Jarrett simulates more stabbing motions while Amy squirts blood from the syringe onto the wall. The knife is then either hidden in the scene, so the students can find it later, or we keep it with us, so the students have to guess based on the patterns they find what type of weapon was used.

No matter the scene, we are careful to recreate the wounds at the appropriate height so that the students can calculate the point of convergence. If the scene were a beating, originating where someone was sitting in a chair, we would take a chair and turn a garbage can upside down and place it on the seat of the chair. Then we pool blood on the garbage can and hit it with something to propel the blood. This would simulate someone's head being bludgeoned. When we are finished with the scenes, we end up with a beating, a stabbing, a shooting, and a miscellaneous scene that is either a suicide or a sexual homicide. How we create the latter remains our little secret.

The scenarios we have set up, on occasion, have been weird. But some of the places we have set them up in have been even weirder. In Seattle, we were given access to the entire downtown public safety building, where the old police headquarters was located. The building had been condemned because it had been built on a major fault line. We used several floors, including one of the courtrooms that we're sure had already seen its share of crime. We bloodied the hell out of that place and finished the day with a rousing game of duct tape baseball, playing with the sergeant of the crime scene unit.

In Savannah, we had access to an old set of buildings where the state pest control used to be located. Each and every room in the place was covered in at least three-quarters of an inch of mold from the leaky roofs. Half the class got sick from all of the mold.

In Columbia, we were led to an old abandoned school building in the middle of nowhere. The classrooms were filled top to bottom with old desks and chairs. The officer that took us to the building, well, he scared us, lurking in and out of the shadows of this decrepit building. One time he even commented on the brakes on our vehicle, telling us he had crawled under it to take a look. As pieces of the roof collapsed in around us, we entertained a writer from *Popular Science*, who was doing a story on our "traveling road show." We set up the scenes in the dust-filled rooms, serving "blood cocktails" to the instructors on a tray, mimicking the Cigarette Girls of old. We have found that asbestos really makes you giddy.

Cincinnati welcomed us with, what else, a toilet smack dab in the living room. Unfortunately, the toilet was not hooked up to plumbing and it wasn't sitting right-side up. It was tipped on its side and half full of a gross brown liquid.

In Duluth we created the scene one night as the ceiling dripped rainwater down on our backs. The next day, we were on the radio, two television stations, and made the headlines in the city newspaper. We doubt we would have gotten that much publicity if we had really killed somebody.

Back at home, we have to find another house or building that has at least four or five rooms we can spatter blood in. Nothing has been too out of the ordinary, except for the occasional homeless person who decides to use our crime scene as his own personal toilet, defecating in the corners. Once we deal with the toiletry problems, we give the students directions on how we want them to work their various scenes. We randomly number the groups, assigning them one room to work. Then, we turn them loose, providing support only when it is requested.

The students work the scene as they have been taught over the past seven weeks. On average, the students work the scene for about one full day, taking pictures, recording their findings, and reconstructing the scene. Each group prepares their findings for moot court that will be held in class the next day. We have started filming how we set up these crazy scenes to show to the class on their last day of bloodstain training. It never ceases to amaze us how accurately the class re-creates exactly what we did, even down to the fine details, minus the bawdy dialogue.

This is by far the most underutilized of all the forensic tools and it overwhelms us to see the results. Several of our graduates have gotten confessions from suspects just by telling them that their story had to be a lie because the blood tells a different tale.

As the class draws to an end, the instructors conclude the day with a slide show presentation of some of the more gruesome cases they have worked. These slides are examples of bloodstains the students will invariably find at crime scenes. These pictures are pulled from a homemade book that is lovingly called the *Disgusting Book of Pictures*. This book contains just a microscopic amount of the blood and gore that actually goes on each and every day throughout our country. And yet it is overwhelmingly powerful. The slides are spectacularly gruesome and so hard to look at straight on we always peer at them sideways with one eye. If someone wasn't telling you what you were looking at, you wouldn't even be able to recognize it. Heads shot completely in two, projecting brains halfway across the room. Faces broken apart with sledgehammers, leaving eyeballs dangling from the shoulders. It is shocking and unimaginable.

We feel as if we have fallen through some sort of vortex, into a land where we do not belong and were never meant to see. We no longer look at people the same way and trusting them has become difficult. How can someone do this to someone else? Unfortunately, murder is real, it is horrible, and it is why we had to create a Forensic Academy. We, you, everybody are merely living timekeepers, hourglasses counting down the time until the end. We just hope for everyone that end comes naturally.

BLOODSTAIN PATTERN ANALYSIS

"Chicken bones." That is a phrase that has been used by some in the forensic community with regard to bloodstain pattern analysis. They believe that many analysts can tell the CSI just about as much as a voodoo priest who tells the future by reading chicken bones. The reason is that bloodstains cannot tell everything that happened at a scene, as some experts in the field erroneously claim. Blood evidence is just one of the pieces that the CSI needs, along with photographs, DNA, fingerprints, or whatever else might be collected. But, seasoned bloodstain experts can discern a lot by looking at the clues left in blood. As a matter of fact, there is no better forensic discipline that can tell the CSI what didn't happen when confronted with a suspect's testimony.

Five years ago, a Korean man, in a burst of anger, decided to end his marriage the hard way—by murdering his wife. It wasn't a planned killing. It just occurred, the end result of an argument. He beat her bloody until she was no longer breathing. Then the realization of what had transpired rushed through his mind. "What do I do now?"

The man ultimately decided to seek the help of the Korean Mafia to cover up his trail. The head mafioso wanted no part of the situation, but guided the killer to do a couple of things to help throw the police off the trail. The first thing he told the husband to do was to bind his wife's hands and feet. Next, he told him to go home and strangle his dead wife. These two things would help establish foul play. Finally, he was instructed to wrap his wife up in sheets and move her to a closet, shut the door, and call the police. The man, grateful for the advice, carried out the instructions to a "tee."

When the police arrived, they found the apartment immaculate, with very few traces of blood anywhere—that is, except for some on the killer's sock and and jeans. The police worked the crime scene, amazingly never using any chemical enhancements to bring out possible traces of cleaned-up blood. The only real evidence the police collected were the perp's bloodstained clothes. It would be their best move.

Of course, being the husband of a dead wife made the killer the prime suspect. He was ultimately arrested and charged with his wife's murder, though he vehemently professed his innocence. His story was very believable. He claimed that he arrived home and found his wife beaten, bound, and strangled. This discovery supposedly set him into an emotional breakdown, where he claimed to have knelt beside her, crying in agony, before eventually calling the police. If only that had been true.

The police called in a bloodstain expert who reviewed the evidence in the case, paying particular attention to the photographs and the clothes. Without ever actually setting foot into the crime scene itself, the expert was immediately able to conclude that the husband was, at the very least, lying about what he had told the police. The proof was in the socks.

The front portion of the socks, the part that rests at or near the shinbone, had bloodstains on them. This meant a couple of things. One, if he was kneeling, as he had shown the police, his shins would have been hidden from the blood. But that, in and of itself, is not conclusive of murder. Second, and most important, the socks contained several elliptical stains. Elliptical stains are indicative of blood in flight. Blood in flight means that something had set the blood in motion. And the only way for the husband to have elliptical stains on the socks was to have, at the very least, been there when the beating took place. Someone beat the poor woman to death and the evidence pointed to that someone being the husband. The jurors believed that as well. The husband was ultimately found guilty of murder and is currently serving time in prison for second-degree murder.

10

BURNIN' DOWN THE HOUSE
Arson

Fire. Fire is mankind's earliest fetish. Since the first lightning strike of a tree witnessed by man, he has forever been obsessed with this primordial heat. It has been such an obsession that it was even thought to have been one of only three elements in existence, earth and wind paling in comparison. Modern man has been no different. We love our fire so much that on our greatest occasions we shoot it into the air and have it burst into glorious flames as we stand underneath it and cheer. We love fire so much that we created a capacity to house and control its flames in order to throw it at our adversaries. And we have even loved fire so much that for over one hundred years, one of the best ways to stay "cool" has been to carry a fire-making device in your pocket and, when the mood strikes, light the end of a paper tube and breathe the heat into your lungs, blowing the smoke out with delightful avarice. Yes, it can be said that we love our fire.

Some love fire too much. For whatever reason, arsonists get a thrill and emotional fulfillment, resembling that of sexual gratification, not only from starting their fires but also from watching them burn. As a matter of fact, most firefighters themselves join the force due to an overwhelming predilection toward fire. If you don't believe this, try watching something burn within earshot of one—they will make unbelievable orgasmic noises that would make even Meg Ryan's character, Sally, blush with envy. Others just choose fire as a means to an end, to cover up and/or disguise a crime. Regardless of the cause, fire creates an extraordinarily difficult challenge for the crime scene investigator.

The United States has the highest rate of fire deaths among developed countries. In 2003 alone, 4,036 people lost their lives in fires. Of those deaths, 305 were the result of arson. At the academy we teach a week of arson investigation to give our students the base knowledge necessary to make key decisions if they are ever called to a fire scene. We don't teach them to be fire investigators. We show them how to recognize key pieces of evidence typical of foul play and when to call for the assistance of fire experts when on a scene. Most people believe that fire will destroy anything and everything, leaving no evidence behind. This is a myth. Fire cannot destroy all of the evidence of a crime, whether it is a metal gas can or a human corpse. If trained properly a CSI should be able to notice key elements at a fire scene that can determine whether a crime has occurred.

Normally, anything involving fire is taught separately to fire personnel alone. This is true for a couple of reasons. One, fire scenes are traditionally left to fire investigators who respond to the scene. Unless there is a dead body found, the police will usually be left out of the investigation. Second and more important, in our experience we've found that policemen and firemen generally don't like each other. Policemen think firemen are crazy, sitting around all day, polishing their shiny red truck, waiting for the bell to ring. When they finally get their once-in-a-blue-moon call, they jump into their truck, only to run headlong into a blazing inferno. On the other hand, firemen think policemen are insane. They believe that all cops do is drive around and around the city, stopping off for the occasional dozen doughnuts, only to be spit on and shot at by every drunken lunatic on the street. We've witnessed this exact debate between two warring public servants at the academy, and it's eerily similar in complexity to those made famous by Lincoln and Douglas. Well, maybe not quite that good.

Most of this is just good-natured ribbing. But there is an underlying element of animosity. We believe that it is of extreme importance for the two factions to work together and learn from each other. We employ actual firefighters and fire investigators at the academy to teach this part of the program, throwing them into the middle of the lion's den each and every session. After four days of hard work, the class always has a new perspective on the life of fire personnel.

Our students spend the first day learning about the characteristics of a fire from our resident fire investigator, Mike Dalton. Mike has been described as being larger than life—and he is. Mike is a big man and has an imposing presence, but he's as nice and Southern as the day is long. "Neater 'en crap" can be heard sputtering out of his watering mouth when he sees a fire in progress. He says it so much that it has become his catchphrase. It is a scientific term in Sevier County, Tennessee, home of none other than Dolly Parton herself. Mike brings a down-home perspective to fire scene investigation. He begins by teaching the students that there are four causes of fire: accidental, arson, natural, and undetermined. An accidental fire occurs without the deliberate action of a person. In contrast, an arson fire occurs when a person deliberately sets it. Arson fires tend to burn at a higher temperature than other fires because an accelerant is normally used. A natural fire is caused by acts of God, such as lightning. When the cause of a fire cannot be found, it is considered undetermined.

Before any investigation into a fire begins, it is important for the class to understand the concept of the fire triangle. For this part of the lecture, we bring in members of the Bureau of Alcohol, Tobacco, Firearms and Explosives (ATF). In order for a fire to burn, it needs fuel, oxygen, and heat. Without any one of these three items, there will be no fire. Fire is very similar to a living entity. Its food comes from the items it burns, like a couch or a chair, and its flames act like lungs, taking in oxygen. The flames grow upward and outward, taking in all available oxygen in the room. It needs oxygen or it will suffocate and die. Since firefighters can do little about fuel and oxygen, they try to eliminate the only other variable over which they have some control—the heat. Unfortunately, the water used to put out the fire makes the investigation even more difficult.

The investigation into any fire begins with the determination of who or what caused the fire. The first task is to determine the point of origin of the fire. The point of origin will be where the fire burns the

Illustration of a V pattern.

(Illustration by Pamela Johanns of Johanns design)

hottest and the longest. When a fire begins, it grows and burns in a conical pattern that will leave a V-shape pattern on the walls at the point of origin. There will be other defining characteristics as well. In houses, the Sheetrock will have calcinated, turning the surface into a powder consistency. The point of origin will also have more charring within the V pattern and the ceiling above will have much more damage than in other places. If the fire continues, it will consume its surroundings as long as there is enough fuel in the vicinity (fuel here is anything consumable, like a chair, newspapers, or end tables) and spread, following the path of least resistance. A fire, under normal circumstances, will burn from floor to ceiling. Once the fire has established itself, it will begin to roll across the ceiling, filling in all areas, burning now from top to bottom. As the heat in the room increases to over two thousand degrees, other items in the room will begin to "off gas." In order for solids to catch on fire, they must turn into gas. Off gas is what happens when solids in the room begin to give off steam.

An NFA burn cell rages to the point of flashover.

(Copyright © Jarrett Hallcox, collection of the National Forensic Academy)

When objects begin to reach their maximum heat resistance, they begin to vaporize and spontaneously combust due to the tremendous heat. This is called *flashover*. If the fire is allowed to continue, it will burn in this manner until it has consumed everything—top to bottom and bottom to top.

Learning about fire from a book is one thing, but for the lessons to really sink in, the students must be able to see it for themselves. Our students get an opportunity that only a handful of people ever get—to watch a fire burn a house in a controlled environment. Well, not a house per se, but a couple of three-walled rooms, furnished to the hilt. These three-walled rooms, also known as burn cells, were originally devised by members of the ATF to allow their investigators to visualize how a fire burns. Instructors from the ATF brought this idea to the academy and we incorporated it into the program. We have built a semipermanent twenty-four-foot-by-twelve-foot structure, divided by one wall down the center, creating two twelve-by-twelve rooms. Both of the rooms are open in the front so that the fire can be seen. In each room, and for each and every academy class, we completely recreate a real living space. Each room is Sheetrocked—floor to ceiling. That's not an easy task. One of us is six feet one, while the other comes in at a whopping four feet nine. That doesn't make hanging Sheetrock easy. But with cordless screwdrivers in hand and a little ingenuity, we hang the drywall.

We also carpet each room. At first we received old carpet from a local carpet store. When we rolled it out on our hands and knees to install it in the cells, it was always wet. Then the smell would waft up. Dog urine. The carpet was soaked in dog urine. Beggars can't be choosers. Nowadays we rip up carpet out of one of our crime scene houses to use in the cells. Then it is back to our favorite place, Goodwill, for more furniture. The rooms are completely decorated, down to the pictures we hang on the walls and the lightbulbs we put into the lamps.

On the day we bring the students to the cells, we arrange to have a large pumper fire truck on standby, just in case things get out of hand. We only want the cells to burn to the point where the fire rolls out of the structure. This is when the fire has completely engulfed the room and the flames have begun seeking more oxygen from the outside air. When it does this, the firefighters put the fire out.

The class stands parallel to the structure, about ten yards away, so that they can get a good view of the upcoming blaze. We burn each cell independently of the other, burning the first one naturally and the second one with a petroleum-based accelerant. This will allow the students to see how much impact an accelerant has on spreading a fire. There is always a minimum of two firefighters dressed out in full gear to control the fires that we set. One of the firefighters will go into the cell and set the fire and exit quickly so they can help operate the hose. The fire hose fully throttled with water is a difficult apparatus to control. We know this all too well, because we have tried to operate the hose at full pressure. It resembled something out of a Three Stooges film, the two of us being propelled backward and upward like rag dolls. Remember, one of us is four feet nine (guess which one). Needless to say, we don't put out the fires anymore.

The NFA burn cell.

(Copyright © Jarrett Hallcox, collection of the National Forensic Academy)

Firefighters put out the burn cell fifteen seconds after flashover.

(Copyright © Amy Welch, collection of the National Forensic Academy)

As the fire begins to boil out of the structure, the brilliant and mesmerizing hues of orange and yellow become apparent. As Mike would say, fire is truly "Neater 'en crap." When the fire finally bursts out of the room, the temperature within the cells is somewhere around eighteen hundred degrees. We know all of this because the ATF has set up an electronic temperature measuring unit called a thermal couples. These thermal couples run from the floor to the ceiling of the burn cells and out to a command post, where a computer collects the data. No one really knows how hot it is outside of the cells, but it makes us run backward pretty damn fast because of the extreme heat. After about fifteen seconds of the fire burning outside of the cells, the firefighters move in to put it out. Many times the fire department will put rookies at the nozzle so they can practice putting out a fire. They always charge up to the cell and turn the hose on full blast, with a direct and powerful stream straight into the heart of the fire. This seems logical, but it is totally wrong. The nozzle should be pointed toward the ceiling and opened just enough to create a wide-angle spray. This spray will cover the most surface area, allow the water to cascade down, and turn most of the room to steam. Once the steam subsides, the hose can then be turned onto visible fires and embers with a powerful spray.

The events are repeated on the other burn cell, only this time the person setting the fire pours an accelerant trail from the inside corner to the end of the structure. Then, with a handheld grill igniter, the accelerant trail is lit. This time the fire makes it out of the cell in under sixty seconds, compared to the room without accelerant, which can take up to fifteen minutes.

Even in a controlled training environment, fires can still be extremely dangerous, especially if you let your guard down. During one of the sessions, a rookie firefighter performed flawlessly, except for one minor detail. He forgot to put on his gloves. The end result: second-degree burns and a trip to the hospital. We sometimes forget how dangerous this forensic stuff really is.

When the smoke clears, the instructors walk the class through the fire scene. The instructors point out many of the clues discussed in class, V patterns, calcinations, and so forth. Even though the fire burned for only a few minutes, the inside of the cells are a total loss.

NFA instructor Mike Dalton lectures to Session Eleven students after the burn cell experiment.
(Copyright © Jarrett Hallcox, collection of the National Forensic Academy)

The couch is burned almost beyond recognition, as is the chair and the surrounding carpet. The walls have turned from white to dark gray, and when touched they flake like chalk. The students are told that because of the way a fire burns, smoke detectors are almost useless if they are in the upper corner of where a wall meets the ceiling (which is where most people put them). The smoke billows into an arc, away from the corner and toward the center of the room, allowing little if any smoke to actually reach the detector. Therefore, the best place to install a smoke detector is in the middle of the ceiling, insuring the smoke will come into contact with the detector. (*After seeing this the first time, we both went home and moved all of our smoke detectors out of the corners and put new batteries in them.*) Mike also points out a couple of interesting tidbits related to fire scene investigation. First, lightbulbs always melt and are pulled in the direction where the heat originates. If the bulb is not completely destroyed, it will leave a very visible clue regarding the fire. Second, if an accelerant is poured onto a carpeted area, the soiled area will burn faster and hotter, melting the "fireproof" backside of the carpet in whatever pattern the solution was distributed. This is almost always indicative of arson.

Once the students have had a chance to examine the smoldering remains, the class adjourns until morning, leaving us to look longingly at the charred remnants of our masterpiece. Forty hours of work turned to ashes in mere seconds. Before the next class begins, we have to pull down all of the burnt, wet Sheetrock, load it into the back of a truck, and haul it to the dump. We then have to gather up all of the furniture skeletons and get rid of them as well. Then the fun really begins, pulling out each and every nail in the wall so we can prepare to do this all over again in a couple of months, all in the name of science.

Fire Death

The next day at the academy, the students are given a treat of sorts. They get to meet our resident Ph.D. anthropologist-firefighter, who is affectionately known as "Dr. Death." Dr. Death, also known as Dr. Joanne Devlin, is a specialist in fire fatalities. How do you get to be a doctor of fire death? Well, you burn a lot of flesh, for starters. Human legs, arms, entire pigs, and hindquarters of cows all have had their final day at the hands of Dr. Death.

Flesh is its own fuel source, and no, there is no such thing as spontaneous human combustion. Fat is the number-one fuel in the human body and can burn slow and steady for a long time, depending on the amount of body fat a person has. This slow, steady burn creates little destruction to anything except for the outline of the body. If the fire burns through the fat, the skin and muscle will be the next to burn. The body has to become extremely hot, a sustained temperature of twelve hundred degrees, in order to dehydrate the skin and muscle enough for it to catch fire. The last to burn is the bone, or technically the bone marrow. The bone marrow begins to shrink with the intense heat and eventually shatters the vast majority of the rest of the bone.

FLESH AND BONE

All too often, killers burn the body in an attempt to destroy it as well as the evidence. Though the body cannot be consumed, fire can be used to confuse many things about a crime, especially the time frame. If human long bones (arm and leg bones) are discovered, there is a way to tell if the body had been burnt with flesh or without. This can be used to help corroborate a time frame when someone went missing. When bones are found warped in a fire, that means they were burnt when they were green, or flesh-covered. Bones that are found burned but straight means they were older and without flesh.

TYPES OF BURNS

Dr. Devlin continues her lecture on many of the other intricacies associated with fire trauma and death by telling the class about the four types of burns: thermal, radiation, chemical, and electrical. Thermal burns occur when an external heat source causes the skin to burn. Boiling water is a good example. Radiation burns occur from what else but radiation. A sunburn is technically this type of burn because UV rays are radioactive. Chemical burns occur when chemicals, like acids, come in contact with the skin. Finally, an electrical burn is caused by electrical current burning the skin. All four of these types of burns, when they take place on the skin, are calculated in terms of "degree" burns. There are five degrees of burns. A first-degree burn is merely a superficial burn, with only minor redness and no blistering whatsoever. Second-degree burns destroy the epidermis, the top layer of skin. There is also blistering associated with this type of burn. Third-degree burns are the absolute worst simply because it is the highest degree of burn that someone can sustain and still survive. With third-degree burns, both the dermis and epidermis layers are destroyed. The skin blisters and begins to peel off just like skin slippage during decomposition.

But the pain nerve endings survive intact. This is why a third-degree burn is so excruciating.

Fourth-degree burns char the skin and the underlying tissue completely, causing the skin to shrink and the body to draw up into the pugilistic pose. The extremities may even displace themselves from the rest of the torso. There is also the potential of the cranial sutures splitting and rupturing due to the brain turning into a liquid and boiling. The buildup of the steam causes the skull to split open and spout smoke just like a teakettle. Fifth-degree burns are simply the condition of the bones after cremation. All of the tissue is gone and only skeletal fragments remain.

Regardless of how long a fire burns or how hot it gets, the human body cannot be completely consumed by the flames. There will always be small pieces of bone left. Parts of the skull will burn to pieces the size of a quarter. In a crematorium, the ash that a family receives is the result of the burnt bone being put through an industrial-strength grinder. Fire, however, does eliminate all of the organic material in the bone, such as carbon. Burnt bone takes on the appearance of fine ceramic—bleach white and very fragile. If a body is found at a fire scene an autopsy is always performed, even if it is suspected that the person died as a result of the fire. The body should also be X-rayed for any metal shards, indicative of a gunshot. This can eliminate any doubt as to whether a person was killed by other means and then set on fire.

Another piece of fire-related trivia deals with the calculation of the total percentage of burned surface area a victim sustains on his or her body. In order to calculate this, the body is divided in half, lengthwise, and numerical values are assigned to various parts of the body. The human head counts as 4.5 percent of the total body. The torso counts as 18 percent. Each leg equals 9 percent, while each arm counts as 4.5 percent. If you add that up for the top half of the body and for the bottom half of the body, you get 99 percent. The missing 1 percent is the genitalia—*no jokes, please.*

For the crime scene investigator, it is important to recognize many of the aforementioned physiological changes and to be able to identify certain characteristics fire brings about in the human body, such as differentiating between the signs of decomposition and a second-degree burn. But it is also important for the CSI to remember that fire makes a positive identification of a person a challenge, to say the least. Fire can completely change the way a person looks. Race is almost impossible to conclude at a fire fatality, and so is age. Furthermore, subtle physical changes occur in low-grade fires that make it even more difficult to ID a person. In a ten- to fifteen-minute fire at 250 degrees, a person's hair can go from completely gray to blonde. In the same amount of time, but at a temperature of 400 degrees, a person's hair can go from brown to red. Because there are so many obvious, as well as subtle, changes to the body, it has been found that the best way to positively ID a person who died in a fire is through their dental records. The root of a tooth and the enamel almost always survive a fire completely intact, though they become very fragile and difficult to work with. Most crime scene investigators have never seen this before, and the best way to illustrate this fragility is to actually simulate a fatal fire. There is no better way to do that than to recreate a car crash fatality.

Car Fires

Car fires and car fatalities are an all too common occurrence. Every single year there are over 300,000 single-passenger car fires in the United States alone. Chances are a crime scene investigator will have to work a car fire with a fatality in his or her lifetime. There is not a lot known about how a car burns with regard to intensity and duration. This lack of knowledge hinders the CSI's ability to properly document a car fire scene. We are hoping to change that.

In conjunction with Dr. Devlin and members of the ATF, we are beginning to combine some of the training elements of the Forensic Academy into research. Each year we set three cars ablaze as part of the ten-week academy. These cars are also included as part of Dr. Devlin's continuing research into car fire fatalities. Within each of these cars we place thermal couples to record the temperature data for the duration of the burn. We also place animal remains within the vehicle. This training exercise gives our students a chance to recognize and understand the intensity and duration of automobiles fires, as well as to witness the fire's impact on soft tissue, bone, and teeth.

Believe it or not, this part of the course is the most dangerous training we conduct. Each hydraulic part on the car, once heated to a certain point, will explode with absolute unpredictability. The hydraulic struts blow, with little more fanfare than a small jump from the students. But the hydraulics used in items like hatchbacks and hood openers are scarier than hell. One time, we had a hatchback explode, propelling a bolt roughly three hundred yards and Lord only knows how high into the air. It eventually crashed through the back window of one of the student's cars and melted through the backseat, all the way to the floor.

Other cars have had us dancing around as if someone was shooting at our feet. Some models have hydraulic devices that support the headlights. When heated to an extreme temperature, these small metal rods shoot out through the glass headlamps, traveling approximately one hundred miles an hour. They have been known to embed themselves in firefighters putting out fires like this. That is why neither a firefighter nor a CSI should ever approach a burning car from the front.

But the most dangerous part of burning a car is, of course, the gas tank. We don't have the resources to take the tank off, and if we did, we would have to dispose of it "properly," which costs money—money that is not provided for in the grant. So, like everything else, we wing it and hope for the best. With our first few cars, we siphoned the gas out of the tank. This was not a great idea for two reasons: one, ingesting gas is not a good thing, and two, it leaves a pocket of gas fumes within the tank. Gas fumes or gas vapors are ten times more prone to ignition than liquid gas. Thus, after siphoning the gas, we had to fill the tank with water to force out the fumes. This was a very long process. Now we just skip the first part and go straight to the flushing process, flooding the gas out of the tank and onto the trailer we have rented to haul the car.

We haul the car out to wherever we will eventually burn the house for the class to work. Dr. Devlin arrives on the scene with her cooler, chock-full of animal remains to place in the car. Depending on what the vet school has to offer, we might end up with a raccoon or a dog, sometimes a cat. No matter the vertebrate that is used, we refuse, absolutely refuse to watch its limp remains make the journey from cooler to car. (Isn't it ironic that we can stand all day in a morgue watching humans being sliced and diced, but the moment we see poor little Lassie used as fuel we hit the road?) Once they are in place, we cut all of the visible hydraulics on the vehicle to prepare for the burn.

The class gathers around the car at a safe distance to watch the fire take place. We open the driver's-side door and trail charcoal lighter fluid from the floor of the car out onto the grass. The grass is then lit and the flame follows the trail, and then *whoosh*, the interior of the car erupts into a ball of flames. The fire burns all of the cloth interior first, then it moves on to the plastic areas of the car. The fire generally spreads in both directions from where it was set. We nervously wait for the fire to breach the rear of the car and approach the fuel door. The cap is removed so that all of the vapors can escape, but some of the fumes linger. What they say is true. Oil and water do not mix. This becomes abundantly clear when the gas tank begins to blow flames out through the fuel door like a flamethrower as the water begins to spit and boil furiously out of the same hole. Fortunately, there hasn't been any explosion. Knock on wood.

It takes about one hour for the car to completely burn out. This is when the class gets a closer look. The extraordinary heat the car produces turns all of the glass into liquid and leaves the tires nothing more than a tangled mass of metal wires. The majority of the flesh will have burned off of the animal remains, leaving a pseudo-cremated skeleton behind. The teeth are always fully intact and usually still in the jawbone of the animal. Dr. Devlin shows the class how to carefully identify and recover the remains. Essentially, recovering these ashy remains is like trying to carry cigarette ashes on a piece of paper without it blowing around. The students take a trowel and gently insert it underneath the remains, deep enough to create a bed of ash for them to rest on. They then place the jawbone and teeth in a plastic container with a lid. The class takes turns practicing recovering the animal remains. By the time they have all completed their task, the teeth and other remaining bones have been completely pulverized. Ashes to ashes, dust to dust.

A car burns with animal remains during our car fire exercise.

(Copyright © Jarrett Hallcox, collection of the National Forensic Academy)

NFA instructor Dr. Joanne Devlin recovers animal remains from a car fire.

(Copyright © Jarrett Hallcox, collection of the National Forensic Academy)

House Fires

In Knoxville, we tend not to do things halfheartedly. For each and every class, we furnish and set ablaze a house for the class to go back to and practice what they have learned. Of course, we do the usual things, like get the furniture, paint the walls, and cut the holes for the fireproof cameras. But we made a deal early on that we would participate in every part of the training—from burying bodies to blowing up cars, even to burning down houses. You see, not being officers, or doctors, or firefighters, we are always having to prove ourselves. The only way to be accepted in any of these groups is to "ride the bull." No matter how dangerous, we ride the bull. Unfortunately, Amy is too small to go into the house. Though she can get into the suit, it does not fit her snuggly enough to be safe. It fits me perfectly, and now I'm nervous. . . .

Standing there, with flames blazing, bursting through the windows and licking the power lines, I begin nervously to put the fire suit on. Dr. Devlin always brings extra gear just in case I want to suit up. The fire that rages behind me is a simulated college drinking game gone terribly wrong. You'd be amazed by how hot rum burns. This fire is the second one for the day. The one I am suiting up for, a gasoline-arson scene, will be next. I am standing in the yard in a large patch of mint that wafts through the air as I pace, awaiting help with my fire suit.

First, the pants and suspenders. The pants are large and thick, like heavy-duty clown pants. They even make you waddle a little when you walk. Next are the boots. The boots are oversized with steel toes. They are too big to walk in and keep your balance, and I never feel stable in them. Next comes the jacket, again too big and very thick. The fire protection hood comes next. This is to protect your neck from the heat. It encases all of your head and neck except for the face. Now for the fun part—the oxygen mask. The mask I wear is an older model. It looks like those WWII gas masks with a long tube connected to it in the mouth area. The mask goes on over my head and is pulled tight by a series of rubber straps. The long, elephant-like tube is for the oxygen tank. The oxygen tank is then hoisted onto my back, causing me to al-

A house fire burns brightly during an NFA arson exercise.

(Copyright © Amy Welch, collection of the National Forensic Academy)

Jarrett nervously gets into the fire suit with the help of Dr. Joanne Devlin.

(Copyright © Amy Welch, collection of the National Forensic Academy)

most lose my balance. I now have to navigate the end of the snoutlike tube into the socket that rests at my side. This will connect the lifeline of air into the mask. Once connected, though, it is completely airtight. So tight you cannot even inhale one ounce of air, and when you try, it sucks your eardrums deeper into your head. It seems like an eternity, but with a little help I turn on the oxygen and can breathe again. If you're remotely claustrophobic, never get into a fire suit.

I then grab my fire gloves, and last, but certainly not least, I grab the envy of all boys, the firemen's hat. Only it is not beautifully shiny and red, but scorched and yellow. And it smells. This is living proof that dreams don't always mesh with reality. Fully suited up, I prepare to take my first step. I feel as if I'm walking on the moon. I can't hear anything, I can't say anything, I can't see anything, and I am loaded down with over seventy-five pounds of the most awkward gear. I am nervous. Amy looks nervous for me. She says a few things to me, but I have no idea what she is saying. She watches the events unfold on the fireproof cameras that are stationed in every room. The cables connect outside to the command center, where the fires will appear on a video display. This is a much safer vantage point from which to participate.

The first thing you learn about fire is that there is no way to predict what it will do. With this in mind, I slowly make my way to the threshold of the door. After what seems to be the longest walk of my life, I finally join the other firemen in the room, schoolgirl giddy with anticipation.

Not more than two hours earlier, we had put together an artificial Christmas tree in the living room of the house. This has become a regular part of the class, because for some reason people tend to leave their Christmas decorations when they abandon their houses. We put them to good use. We even decorate it with lights, ornaments, and the traditional tree-topping star—the icing on the cake. Now instead of it being part of a glorious Christmas morning, it will become part of a tragic Christmas arson fire.

The previous night, Mike had come up with an idea to recreate a popular method of burning a house down. A small tea-light candle will be placed in the middle of the room and lit. Next, a piece of kite string, long enough to almost reach from the ceiling to the candle, is taped to the floor. A balloon that has been partially filled with camp fuel is tied to the other end. The ingenious contraption is an old arson/fraud trick whereby the candle is lit and the gas-filled balloon is set in a pendulum motion. Once the balloon comes to a halt, it will be just above the lit candle. This gives the arsonist plenty of time to flee the scene. Fortunately, our instructors are better at putting out fires than creating them. After about thirty minutes of battling with the balloon and several tealight candles, they doused the remaining gas into the corner and struck a match.

Immediately, the room fills with fire, raising the temperature to well over seven hundred degrees in a matter of seconds. The flames crawl up the wall, following the liquid that was tossed into the corner, reaching the ceiling in a tumultuous wave. I back up toward the door. "One thousand degrees," comes across the radio of the fireman standing next to me. Then, all of a sudden, the burning levels off. Fuel is needed not only to start the fire, but to keep it going. Fuel, in this case, a sofa, a stuffed chair, two tables, newspapers, and the Christmas tree, didn't get hot enough to sustain the blaze. The room had not gotten hot enough to burn off all of the excess fuel either. When this occurs, there is an unbelievable churning and writhing of a sable-black layer of gas on the ceiling. It is beyond comprehension and utterly thrilling to watch. I stand, inches away from this living, breathing poltergeist.

Two of the firemen in the room try to communicate with me. Charlie Brown's teacher is much easier to understand. Suddenly, one of them gets behind me and grabs my shoulders, forcing me to kneel. They had been telling me to get down behind the door.

This is not my first time in a burning house, though it is my first time being left alone and allowed to move freely. It is so easy to get lulled into a feeling of safety when the bright flames diminish. Yet the temperature remains at seven hundred to eight hundred degrees at the ceiling, and with just a spark all of the swirling gas can ignite and explode into a fire, sending flames the entire length of the house and raising the temperature to over one thousand degrees in a matter of seconds. And that's just what it does.

As I lie here on my stomach, behind the door that had been cut in half to help stop the spread of the fire, I glance upward only to see the gas explode into a raging, broiling fire, going out in every direction. The fire rapidly spreads across the ceiling, flying down the walls and across the floor, filling in every crack and escaping through every crevice possible. The fire completely engulfs my head in a split second, stinging my face around my neck. I almost hyperventilate. At about the same time, I hear someone yell, "Oh shit!" I lean over to look, and there is Mike Dalton, not more than five feet from me, hidden by the smoke. The fire had bit him too. I stagger to my feet and try to make my way out of the house, but the smoke is so thick and black I cannot see my hand before my face. I crawl along the perimeter of the walls until I reach the back porch. I bolt from the house and tear out of the fireman's suit that was beginning to suffocate me.

It is too dangerous for us to go inside immediately after the fire and the destruction, so we wait until the next day and go back after the house has cooled. It is an alarming sight being inside a home that has been set on fire. Entire rooms that were once decorated in hues of bright blues and pinks are now charred completely black. Lightbulbs in the ceiling have been contorted by the intense heat and pulled in the direction of the source. Desks and chairs are barely recognizable, all burnt until there was almost nothing left. Everything is still very damp from the water used to put out the fire. The ashes and water mix to create an unbelievable pastelike substance that the students will have to sift through. Fire scenes are the dirtiest to work.

The following day the students arrive and use their newly acquired knowledge of fire investigation to see if they can figure out what happened. A burned room can reveal much information when someone is trained to read the signs. At the house, the students are divided up into teams, each with a room to work. Gloves, dust masks, empty paint cans, and shovels are among the tools we provide. They work their scene just like any crime scene—photographing and documenting everything they find. In this scene they are looking for fire clues— charred furniture, V patterns, accelerants. Any piece of physical evidence that is found must be placed into a metal paint can and sealed with a lid. This insures that the evidence is free from any contamination. The students must determine where the fire started and the burn path it traveled within their room. The class will eventually present

Session Seven graduate Mike Velez records information at an arson scene.
(Collection of the National Forensic Academy)

their findings to the instructors in the form of case files. Once the case files have been turned in, the students get to watch the video from the fires to see for themselves if they got it right—and they always do.

We have been told by several of our graduates that the three days we spend on arson is better than the entire week the renowned National Fire Academy spends teaching the nation's top fire scene investigators. No comprehensive training program in the country has at their disposal the cadre of instructors that we have right inside our doors. But that's not what makes our training so special. It's the practical exercises. It takes a lot of work to set up and destroy everything we destroy, and for most places it's just not worth it. One would think that the National Fire Academy would at least burn a house for the students to see for themselves how a fire burns and spreads, but they don't. There are so many things to learn from a fire scene that cannot be visualized from a book. Criminals using fire as a means of covering up their

HOT POTATO

Laboratories do not always detect accelerants that were used in a fire. Accelerant-sniffing dogs, whose sniffers are more sensitive than even the most sophisticated laboratory equipment, don't always, either. If it is believed that an accelerant was used in a fire, it might be that the accelerant itself is undetectable. One such accelerant could be a bag of potato chips. It is possible to set a bag of chips on fire and throw it on a couch, creating an accelerant-like effect. The fat in chips make them extremely volatile when ignited (think of a kitchen grease fire). An accelerant-sniffing dog won't even detect the chips, and the labs won't be testing for them, either. The CSI should always question finding a couch with too many crumbs in the cushions.

tracks don't realize how much evidence is actually preserved, if the CSI just knows what to look for. It's like handing a linguist a set of hieroglyphics without giving them the Rosetta Stone. At the National Forensic Academy, we pride ourselves in giving the CSI the Rosetta Stone for every discipline, so they can decipher the clues for themselves.

ARSON

The Menendez brothers are not the only offspring in the world who ever killed their parents. In essence, it happens more than anyone would like to believe. And the kids don't have to be teenagers to commit murder, either. As life expectancies continue to rise, for many the quality of life steadily declines. Oftentimes, this puts a tremendous burden on grown-up sons and daughters to take care of their ever-aging parents—a job many people relish. For some, however, the job is just too hard and they find a way out.

Several years ago, an apartment fire raged out of control, damaging much of the complex and all but destroying the unit in which it originated. The residents of the complex were safely evacuated, except for one elderly, bedridden woman who perished in the unit where the fire originated—a unit she shared with her son. As arson investigators began to sift through the rubble, they discovered that the fire began on the bed where the woman had perished. The charred remains of the woman were sent off for examination.

The fire scene was suspicious from the start, considering that it began on the bed of an invalid woman who could hardly move and who apparently did not smoke. Fire investigators theorized that something, or more probably, someone, started the fire. That theory was ultimately corroborated by the medical examiner and the university anthropologists specializing in fire fatalities.

During the autopsy of the woman, it was discovered that one of the bones in the neck, the hyoid bone, was broken. This is traditionally an indication of manual strangulation. The ME sent his report to the university to allow the anthropologists to examine the bone. Their experience with the way bones break apart in a fire allowed them to conclude that the heat was insufficient to break the hyoid bone in the neck, thus agreeing with the determination made by the ME.

Upon receiving this report, investigators working the crime called in the victim's son in order to interrogate him on his possible involvement. At first he was appalled at the suggestion that he could have had anything to do with his mother's death. But after several hours of interrogation, concluding with showing the son the evidence provided by the doctors and anthropologists, who were in the room at the time, he confessed that he "had snapped" and strangled his mother to death. In an effort to cover up his crime, he set the bed ablaze and returned to work. Eventually he pleaded guilty to his crimes in exchange for a more lenient sentence, receiving fifteen years for the murder of his mother and fifteen years for the arson fire that he set. This case once again confirms that it is almost impossible to cover up any crime with a fire.

11

FIRE IN THE HOLE!
Bombs

From David Letterman dropping watermelons from atop the Ed Sullivan Theater to demolition experts bringing down the Seattle Kingdome, everyone, everywhere loves to watch things explode. This obsession can be traced back nearly one thousand years to the advent of gunpowder, one of the greatest inventions of the ancient world. Gunpowder changed the entire face of the planet and completely shifted the balance of power to those who possessed this magnificent incendiary device. Since the age of the Renaissance, nations have worked rigorously to create the biggest and most powerful bombs. And the same holds true today. But making bombs is not for the faint of heart. It takes a steady hand, a brilliant mind, and sometimes, a death wish.

The bombs portion of the class is our most unique offering at the academy. Not because of content, but because of the instructor, Sergeant Van Bubel. Bomb instructors are the stereotypical, crusty soldiers, transported straight out of the jungles of Saigon. All of these guys are "cowboys"—men who do things however they want to. Our instructor is no exception. Van is an ex-marine and is the head of the bomb squad at the Knoxville Police Department. He is also a firearms instructor, specializing in the deadly art of sharpshooting. He is a stoic

NFA instructor Van Bubel holds a lit det cord in his hand.

(Collection of the National Forensic Academy)

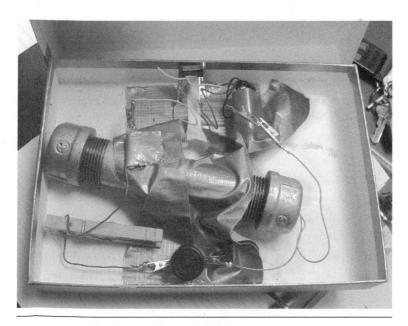

An improvised explosive device housed in a box meant to hold a Bible.

(Collection of the National Forensic Academy)

figure, with the customary graying crew cut, who always wears a scowl that would make most people wet their pants. We love him, but he scares the shit out of us.

We normally begin each day of class by giving the students a brief biographical introduction to their instructor. But not Van; he wants no part of it. Instead, he brazenly walks into the room, states his name, and goes into a tirade about our LCD projector. He then begins to yell at one of us, in a resonating baritone voice, about being tired of whatever seems to be agitating him on this particular day. The students' eyes begin to gloss over. After a moment of nervous fidgeting, he bellows, "I'm tired of this!" and jerks his marine fatigue jacket off of his body, revealing a back brace, outfitted with a dozen twelve-inch pipe bombs, attached to a handheld detonator. "Allah Akbar," he yells as he depresses the device, and the class jumps for cover. *Poof.* The faux flashbulb goes off and the class, now realizing the joke, begins to laugh a really, really nervous laugh. Van has a way of getting your attention. He then proceeds to tell the class that if the bomb had been real, we would all be dead. No kidding. Right after his fake bomb routine, Van will begin acting as if he is lost and doesn't know what to do next. "I'll tell you what," he says slyly, and this is where we cringe, "let's watch a cop die." The VCR immediately begins to display an image of an officer walking over to an object, presumably a bomb. As the officer leans over the device, it detonates, sending his now liquefied head against the back wall as the rest of his body falls lifelessly to the ground. Van, with an Eastwoodesque grimace, exclaims, "He's done inspecting it." The class looks on mortified.

There is a method to Van's madness. He believes in shocking the senses in order to make an indelible impression of the destruction and unpredictability of the devices that we will be handling over the next few days. Van moves right from "watching a cop die" into passing around real working bombs, including the device he was wearing, for the class to peruse. The only difference is that the bombs do not have the detonation devices attached, so they're relatively safe. All of this is his way of creating an environment of respect for the weapons of mass destruction. It is also a good way to clear the bladder. Van truly epitomizes the concept of hands-on learning. After all of that, it's time for a much-needed fifteen-minute break.

Explosions

An explosion loosely defined is nothing more than the rapid and sudden escape of gases from a confined space, followed immediately by extremely high temperatures, violent shocks, and, of course, a very loud noise. With all of the different types of bombs out there, they essentially fall into three categories: mechanical (like a steam boiler explosion), nuclear, and chemical. A mechanical explosion is usually an accidental explosion occurring at a work site. Everyone knows all too well about the devastation of a nuclear explosion, and with terrorism today, the deadly possibility of a "dirty bomb." Both of these types of explosions are relatively uncommon. That leaves the most common type of explosion—chemical.

Chemical explosive devices are the types used by terrorists and other cowardly wack-jobs with the intent to wreak havoc and instill fear, not to mention kill and maim. There are two types of these bombs: the purely chemical bomb and the chemical-reaction bomb. The Oklahoma City bombing is a perfect example of a chemical-reaction bomb, where fertilizer was combined with an oxidizer to create a deadly explosion. Purely chemical bombs are created with substances like TNT, black powder, or C-4, where a solid or liquid is converted into a gas. These bombs need a detonating device and not a chemical reaction to set them off. Both types of explosive devices can be just as powerful and just as deadly.

The effects of an explosion are unequivocally devastating beyond comprehension. The heat generated from an explosion can reach temperatures in excess of six thousand degrees, turning solid metal into molten liquid. The pressure exerted at the point of detonation can be as much as one million pounds per square inch, sending out shock waves at a whopping thirteen thousand miles per hour. But it is not these tremendous forces that kill the most people. It is the shrapnel that does the most damage. Shrapnel, including pieces of the bomb itself and other bits of metal placed within the incendiary device, can be propelled outward at over twenty-seven thousand feet per second.

Our students are taught that it is their responsibility to recover as much evidence as possible so they can determine not only what the device was, but also how the device was made. Because of the extraordinary heat at the scene, there will be no fingerprints left on the device or anything surrounding the device. Heat melts away or dries up both types of fingerprints. Furthermore, any trace evidence that might have been left will be destroyed by the blast itself, and if not, the water pressure of a fireman's hose will finish the job. The best they can hope for is to find a signature or clue about the device that gives the investigators some sort of lead.

Before any investigation or evidence collection can begin, students must first conduct a thorough search of the surrounding blast area. They are not searching for pieces of the bomb in question, but for the possibility of another bomb. Many extremists use secondary devices as their true method of destruction. These devices traditionally kill the persons despised most by terrorists, like police officers and other servants of the public. Only after this search has been completed can the investigation into the crime begin.

There are several things with regard to explosives and explosive devices that are common across the board. It is important for the CSI to recognize and understand these commonalities. For instance, most incendiary blasts send fragmentation, or frag, in a twenty-degree arc from the origin of the explosion. This helps the investigator formulate a starting point at which to begin the search. Once the initial frag has been discovered, the perimeter should be established 1.5 times larger than where the farthest piece was found. This is to ensure that no evidence will be trampled if pieces happen to have flown farther than the majority of the rest of the frag. When the debris field has been established and evidence collection has begun, certain inferences about the blast can be made through the careful examination of the pieces. For instance, if the bomb fragments are small and jagged, with a bluish discoloration, it is indicative of high brisance (shattering), typically associated with a device containing C-4 or tetrytol. On the other hand, if the pieces are long, jagged strips, then the explosive device was of a medium caliber associated traditionally with dynamite or a black powder pipe bomb sealed tight with end caps. If there are large chunks of metal found with square edges, a low explosive like black powder was probably used.

The word *fragment* is appropriate for what is found at a WMD explosion. Very small pieces are all that ever remain of the device. The detonator plugs of these IEDs (improvised explosive devices) often survive the blast, however. Detonator plugs, sometimes referred to as switches, are where the electrical circuit is completed, allowing the electricity to activate the device. The more expert bomb makers, like the Ted Kaczynskis of the world, continue to hone their skills over the years and learn to make their own bomb parts. Eventually, Kaczynski became so adept at bomb making that his signature switch was made out of wood—an unusual choice for a bomb. But not the most unusual.

Not long ago, a call came into the local bomb squad about a possible bomb that had been found in a building. The bomb techs responded and found a wrapped-up object that had been thrown through a window. The first investigator on the scene called into dispatch to alert that it was simply a false alarm. The head of the team questioned the conclusion and was informed by the rookie bomb tech that it couldn't be a bomb because he had stuck his finger into the device and it felt "squishy." "Bombs aren't squishy," he told the commander. Ultimately, the "squishy" device was found to be a condom filled with nitroglycerin, encased by three sticks of dynamite! A very deadly mixture, to say the least. As luck would have it, the bomber chose a name-brand condom that was tough and not prone to breaking, even when filled with nitro and hurled through a window. Bet you'll never see that on the back of the box.

Other less-sophisticated bomb builders use what can readily be purchased or obtained. The four most common manufacturers of these plugs are: Atlas, DuPont, Hercules, and the military. Each of these plugs has its own distinctive signature. The Atlas plug is a one-piece rubber design with an aluminum shunt. The DuPont is a two-piece white design that comes in vertical halves. These plugs have a copper foil shunt. The Hercules brand plug also comes in two white pieces, but the halves are horizontal and have a paper shunt. And last but not least, the military plug is a long piece of rubber, with four crimps that have a split washer as the shunt. Finding any of these pieces at a bomb crime scene might be the "fingerprint" of the maker. Hopefully, this will help lead investigators toward a specific group of people, or at least a specific locale. Armed with all of this information, the class prepares to be called out to our bomb scene—not knowing what to expect.

We blow up a lot of items at the National Forensic Academy, and getting all of this stuff is not easy. Blowing up a car each and every session, sending the autos to smithereens, takes some, well, let's call it bartering. We have destroyed our friends' cars, our coworkers' cars, stolen cars, cars confiscated in drug busts, questionably obtained cars—just about every kind of car. It's amazing what you can get for an NFA hat, a jacket, or a shot at a picture with Patricia Cornwell.

The one thing that all of our cars have had in common is that they do not run. That is, all except for one. Every group of friends has that one poor soul who is now and forever known as the Costanza of the group. We have that one friend. Fortunately for us he had purchased, along with his mother, dueling 1993 Dodge Shadows—without air, mind you. These cars are known to car connoisseurs everywhere simply by the letters *POS*. Our friend's POS was on its last leg, maintaining a steady trade-in value of nearly one hundred dollars. We convinced him that it was his civic duty to give us his POS so we could blow it up. This was still early on in the days of the academy and we were having trouble getting cars to blow up. To complicate matters, Patricia Cornwell was coming to town with a little network television show called *Primetime*. Oh my God, were we desperate! We were two days away from looking like complete fools in front of a large audience. Costanza gave in, with only three requests. One, he wanted an NFA jacket; two, he wanted to be there when the car blew up; and three, he wanted a picture with Ms. Cornwell. We would have promised him anything.

On the day we went to pick up the car, the brakes were locked and one of the tires was flat. Stupid POS! Those problems were quickly remedied with a sledgehammer and a can of Fix-A-Flat. After several attempts, we finally got the POS started and pointed in the right direction. With a large puff of white smoke, we took off. The first thing we did was to take the car to a car wash so it would look good when it made its television debut. We were pulling out all of the stops so that we would not look like a bunch of idiots trying to run a forensic school. We wanted everything to look just right, even down to picking up our first set of NFA hats on the day of the explosion.

With Ms. Cornwell, *Primetime*, our Costanza, and every local news station in tow, we were finally set to make our run on television. It's not like you get a second chance when working with bombs. The first lesson learned when dealing with incendiary devices is that they are unpredictable. We approached Ms. Cornwell and asked her if she would like to detonate the car. She excitedly accepted. Within a few minutes, Van's customary boisterous countdown began. We talked anxiously about how great this could be and also how bad this could go. We crossed our fingers. *Kaboom!* The car magnificently exploded, sending frag in every direction, hundreds of feet up and out. Everyone captured it on video, and most important, Ms. Cornwell still had all of her fingers and toes. Success!

Triumphantly, we all scurried toward the vehicle like schoolkids being let out for the summer—all the way, trampling into the ground hundreds of pieces of evidence. But it was worth it. We had pulled off the biggest and best explosion to date, initiated by one of the world's foremost fiction writers, detonated in front of millions of people. There was an inexplicable electricity in the air for everyone the rest of the day, even for Costanza, whose smile was a mile wide as we snapped a picture of him with his favorite author. Too bad his jacket did not fit.

The other items we blow up are a little more embarrassing to obtain. Mannequins have become an integral part of training at the academy. We purchase about two or three of these predominantly female mannequins each class from a local boutique downtown. They get the biggest kick out of selling us these fancy display mannequins to blow up. They also enjoy watching us drive away as three anatomically correct and very naked mannequins sit in the backseat of the Excursion.

Once back at the academy, we bring the mannequins inside to prepare them for detonation. After each male student in the class has had a chance to come by and make comments about wanting to borrow them for the weekend, we take the fleshy pink mannequins into the closet and shut the door. This is where we feel like putting on an eight-track of some 1970s porno theme. Because the mannequins come in pieces, we have to pop them together. But we found out early on that simply locking them together is not sufficient. To get the biggest explosion, they have to be glued. Picture it: there we are, locked away in a closet, dressing and gluing naked mannequins, holding their torsos tight to make sure the glue holds. Then we surreptitiously take the metal stands they each come with and thrust them into their buttocks, giving them the ability to stand erect. It's like a bad Russ Meyer film. Once they are dry enough to transport, we get to bring them out of the closet, to thunderous applause and catcalling, as we make our way down the stairs and into the Excursion.

On D-day, we amass at the Knoxville Police Department's firing range to blow stuff up. The firing range is way off the beaten path, down a long dirt road littered with large gullies and ravines—the absolute best roads to transport items like TNT, nitroglycerin, and C-4. Nothing, and we mean nothing, scares Van. Each class brings with it some new concoction of highly volatile ingredients placed on, under, or in some unfortunate receptacle. One of the more interesting creations Van has made in the past is a homemade hand grenade. Taking pieces and parts from a WWII-era hand grenade, Van jerry-rigs new explosives back into the device and fashions the pin back in place. All of his devices are created back at his lab (a.k.a. his basement) where his wife and grandson walk around with their fingers in their ears—just in case.

At the firing range, Van placed his homemade grenade under the hood of the car, with the pin attached to a twenty-five-foot piece of string. Just before the detonation of any device, Van yells "fire in the hole" three times, followed immediately by a countdown starting at four, three, two, one. . . . At "one," Van jerked the string, removing the firing pin. Nothing happened. Now the class and the two of us are hundreds of feet away and very glad to be, thank you. One of Van's colleagues, a bomb tech in his own right, begged Van to simply get back up on the ridge and shoot the device with a high-powered rifle. Not having any of that, Van waltzed nonchalantly back to the hood of the car, raised it up, grabbed the grenade, and calmly put the firing pin back into place to give it another go. The second time, the string pulled the firing pin out and the grenade exploded without a hitch—meaning the damn thing was live when he crammed the firing pin back down into the device. All anyone had to say after that was "balls of steel."

Most detonations go off without a hitch, to Van's dismay. The major explosion, and the one the class will be responsible for working, is the car. The car is detonated with two pounds of C-4, the legal amount to keep from cracking septic tanks. (Though it might seem that significantly more is used from time to time, we plead the Fifth when asked.) Van makes a pipe bomb and places it under the driver's seat within the vehicle. He then runs an electronic ignition switch about seventy-five yards away. This will be the device that detonates the car. While we scramble around making sure everyone has their earplugs, Van begins the countdown. With a flip of the switch, glass, metal, and other debris are cast magically into the air in roughly a 360-degree radius from the car. It appears at first glance that there is very little frag thrown a great distance. Yet small pieces of metal are found months later at least three to five hundred yards away.

It is the responsibility of the class to work the scene, flagging as many pieces from the car as possible. Fanning inward from the outermost perimeter, the students work their way toward the car. In reality, a crime scene of this magnitude would take a minimum of one week to work properly. We have one day. That is why the main objective is to focus not on the outside of the car, but on the inside. The class has no idea about the type of device that was used to blow the car up. It is up to them to find the pieces of the device and put the puzzle back together again. Of course, they don't know they are looking for remnants of a one-foot-long pipe bomb, filled with C-4 and sealed tight with two metal end caps, attached to an actual alarm clock, powered by a nine-volt battery. After the explosion, there is no more evidence found of the bomb than a small piece of the winding mechanism of the clock and several small pieces of the pipe no bigger than a penny.

The inside of the car is obliterated. There is a hole in the driver's side all the way through the car and into the ground below. The roof of the car is also bowed up several inches, with large gaping holes where metal has been shot upward. The steering wheel is completely de-

A car explosion casts fragments high into the air.
(Copyright © Jarrett Hallcox, collection of the National Forensic Academy)

stroyed, and it crumbles into several small pieces onto the floor of the car. It is a one-in-a-million chance that someone could survive such a violent act. In order for us to even enter the car, we have to pry the doors open with crowbars. The class then proceeds to shovel the debris into paint cans and sift through the pieces using large screen sifters. Once the class has worked the interior of the car, removing all of the door panels and searching for embedded pieces of the pipe, they move to the outside. All of us gather behind the car and shove it forward about twenty feet. This allows the class to look underneath where the point of detonation occurred. The blast makes about a six- to eight-inch divot where the force of the bomb was directed downward. Small pieces of the bomb are usually found buried in this area.

A WMD event is the absolute most difficult kind of scene to work because of the sheer destruction of all of the evidence. An event of this magnitude would have personnel trying to help the people involved and fire trucks spraying hundreds of gallons of water throughout the vehi-

Session Eleven students work the car explosion scene.

(Copyright © Amy Welch, collection of the National Forensic Academy)

The inside of the car is completely obliterated by a pipe bomb.

(Copyright © Jarrett Hallcox, collection of the National Forensic Academy)

A small fragment of the pipe bomb is found near the car.
(Collection of the National Forensic Academy)

cle. It is crime scene management's worse nightmare. The class has been taught to look for certain clues that help explain what caused the destruction, and every class finds enough of the bomb to tell what was used in the explosion. Most even find large enough pieces of the clock to be able to figure out how the device was created. But only one class found enough information about the pipe that was used to trace it back to where it was purchased. An end cap, with the size and serial number still visible, has been recovered during only one session of the academy. This just goes to show how unlikely it is to find enough of the evidence to put a good case together.

Improvised Explosive Devices

With the hard work behind us, we get to have a little fun. Van demonstrates a cadre of different incendiary devices to the delight of the class.

He starts with detonation, or "det," cord. Det cord looks like nothing more than rope, but it's much more than rope. When lit, one hundred feet of det cord will burn instantaneously, the entire length of the cord, traveling tens of thousands of miles per hour. It is very strong on its own, and when wrapped around a four-by-four piece of wood and lit, it can cut the board in half.

Next, we move on to chemical-reaction bombs. Van has several members of the class hold red plastic tubes filled with a substance that will remain a secret. He then pours another liquid solution into each of the red containers, and stirs it around with a pocketknife. The concoction is perfectly stable and needs only an electric jolt to set it off. Each of the tubes, now equal to one stick of dynamite, is placed into a PVC pipe. At the top of each PVC pipe's end cap, a small hole is drilled to allow space for det cord. These pipes are placed into a vest, with each piece of det cord connected together and hardwired to the electrical detonation box. The vest, now armed with the equivalent of at least twelve sticks of dynamite, is quite ominous, and most students shy away from its very presence. Yet we still have the occasional student put the brace on and model it for all to see.

While all of this is going on, we unload the mannequins that will be used to illustrate the magnitude of the back brace bomb. The intent is to simulate the destruction caused by a suicide bomber. We place the mannequins about a football field away from where we will watch the event. Van places the bomb on one mannequin and gives Margaret or Gertrude, or whatever names he has given them, one last good-bye. When the bomb is detonated, it is at least five times as loud as the car bomb due to the fact that it is not contained inside of anything. Believe it or not, mannequin pieces have landed near our feet. It's a good thing for us they are made out of fiberglass and not metal.

The mannequin that actually wore the bomb is utterly destroyed. The only discernable pieces remaining are part of the head and large pieces of the legs. The rest is dust. The other mannequins are intact, but wear the visible scars of the frag. The concussion has been so intense in the past that the hand from the exploded mannequin has embedded itself into the torso of another. Imagine what it would do to human flesh.

We cordon off the area and try to find pieces of the bomb. Nothing,

One of the NFA's "perky" mannequins awaits her demise.
(Collection of the National Forensic Academy)

absolutely nothing is left. Every piece of pipe, every piece of det cord, and all of the back brace are completely evaporated. The only thing we have ever found after this exercise is a piece of the back brace the size of a quarter. You're probably not going to convict anybody on that little piece of information. We move on to more destruction.

The most common bomb Van finds in our neck of the woods is contained in a swollen two-liter coke bottle. These chemical-reaction bombs are made by kids everywhere, trying their hand at petty destruction. Van demonstrates this device by having one of us hold the bottle that already contains the aluminum foil and drain cleaner, while the other pours in just a little water. This reaction takes about sixty to ninety seconds, depending on the outside temperature. On one hot summer day, as Van put the cap back on a two-liter bottle and began to shake it, it began to swell immediately. He threw it out of his hands at the same moment it exploded, spraying acid in all directions and shooting the bottle thirty feet. We were all very fortunate not to have acid sprayed into our faces since we were only a few feet away. We no longer perform this demonstration for obvious reasons.

That concludes the day with Van—almost. He usually ends up with an extra pipe bomb that he just must use. So he will grab anything in sight to blow up. This is when the class gets concerned. One rainy day, he decided to lay down a pipe bomb on the ground. We brought him a metal fence post that had a circular metal disk attached to the base. It weighed about thirty pounds. Before anyone could say anything or take cover, he put the post on top of the bomb and lit the fuse. We all started scrambling because no one, including Van, had any idea where that thing might go. With one mighty explosion, the post went sailing and landed about seventy-five yards away. "Don't tell anyone about that one," he said to us. We've never, ever said a word.

Lessons from the Unabomber

We have a lot of fun during the bombs portion of the academy, but bombs are a serious business. Ted Kaczynski, the infamous Unabomber, placed thirteen bombs across the country before he got his first kill. His first victim was an unsuspecting man who merely went to move a block of wood with nails sticking out of it. The wood had been strategically placed on a busy street so that it needed to be moved in order for cars to avoid getting a flat tire. The bomb went off in his face, sent the nails through his heart, and killed him instantly. An abhorrent act of cowardice.

In this turbulent, post-9/11 world, you should never, ever accept a suspicious package, move a suspicious package, or, most of all, open a suspicious package. We work in a building that at any given time might be littered with certified bomb techs, chiefs of police, district attorneys, and sometimes, children. There's even a university division of the Office of Homeland Security right downstairs, just below the academy. If there are any people on Earth that should know better than to move a suspicious package, it is the residents of our building. Yet someone picked up a small suitcase just the other day that had been placed inside the door. All it had was a note that read simply "for the music school." He took the suspicious suitcase back to the office, sat it down, popped open both of the metal locks, and found . . . a clarinet. Our building has been labeled as a point of interest for terrorists, so it could have been much worse.

The one thing that we have learned about bombs and bombings is that the only thing you can be sure of is that if someone really wants to bomb you, there is nothing, absolutely nothing you can do about it. No one can be vigilant enough each and every day to prevent it unless they decide to shut themselves off from the world—and even then, you're still not safe. T. S. Elliot once wrote, "This is the way the world will end, not with a bang, but a whimper." Unfortunately, we doubt that will be the case.

BOMBS

Working a crime scene has been equated to working a puzzle, piecing the evidence together to form a complete picture. Working a crime scene where a bomb has been detonated, however, is like taking a box of fleas and being told to put them in order by height. It is a difficult proposition, to say the least. Sometimes, the CSI just needs a little luck.

Being an heir to a $10 million real estate fortune can take its toll on a person. Thinking about all of that money, day in and day out, can drive some people to do just about anything—some even to murder. Twenty years ago, a young man in charge of his mother's fortune decided it was time to take over the family business. The business had begun losing money and the mother became worried about how it was being managed. As she dug deeper and deeper into her son's business practices, she uncovered a plethora of poor business practices, as well as other improprieties. The mother confronted her son about what she had found out and a heated argument took place on July 8. It would be their last argument.

The next day, her son had arranged for the entire family to participate in staking out a piece of property where his mother intended to build. This included himself, his sister, an adopted brother, and, of course, his mother. The son arrived in a white van on the day of the trip, parking extremely close to the Suburban that they would use for their journey. The sister noticed how her brother fiddled around for several minutes behind the van, with its cargo doors spread wide open. After about five minutes, he entered the residence, only to grab the keys for the Suburban and announce that he was going for coffee and would be back in a few minutes. The seven-mile round trip took over an hour.

When he arrived back at the house, the family boarded the Suburban for the trip to the property. Only instead of the customary seating arrangement, the son had decided to assign seats. Normally, he would drive and his sister would ride in the passenger seat because she got carsick very easily. The mother always rode in the back and the adopted brother was rarely, if ever, invited to tag along. Today would be different. He asked that the adopted brother drive and that his mother ride shotgun, while he and his sister rode in the back. The mother and adopted brother took their positions in the suburban as the sister climbed into the backseat of the vehicle. The son, who had helped his sister into the Suburban, went to close the door, but the sister wanted it left open for air until they were ready to depart. She would be glad she did.

The son seemed hesitant to get into the vehicle, and he made his way back toward the house to get a tape measure he supposedly forgot. While the son hurried to retrieve the tape, his brother went to turn the ignition. As he did, there was an immediate explosion that threw the sister back into her seat, completely engulfing her in the inferno. She dove out of the Suburban through the door she had left open and rolled on the ground, attempting to put out her clothes, which were on fire. On one of her rolls she noticed her brother, standing stationary in the middle of the yard as the events unfolded before his eyes. The next explosion sealed the fate of her mother and adopted brother. Of those who got into the suburban, she was the only survivor.

Immediately, the son became the primary suspect in the bombing of his family, especially in light of his suspicious actions, which his sister lived to tell about. Acting suspicious, however, does not convict one of a crime. Crime scene investigators and other bomb experts be-gan working the scene right away, attempting to recover as much evi-dence as possible. The recovered evidence showed that a pipe bomb filled with gunpowder and sealed with two end caps was the device used to blow up the Suburban. Evidence also pointed to an electrical detonator. Yet though this information told investigators what the de-vice was, it was still circumstantial at best in pointing toward the son. They needed a little luck.

From the analysis of the fragments that were recovered, investiga-tors were able to determine that the pipes used were twelve inches long and four inches in diameter. They were able to draw this conclu-sion for two reasons. First, the end cap fragments, though incomplete, were enough for the investigators to determine the circumference of the cap. Second, the threads found in the pieces of the pipe fragments matched the industry standards for twelve-inch pipe. Still, not enough evidence to charge the son.

Investigators continued working the case, looking into every clue, when one noticed a hardware store within a block of the suspect's of-fice. After searching through old receipts, the investigators found one receipt dated July 5 for the purchase of two four-inch end caps. They also found another receipt dated July 8, the day of the mother-son ar-gument, for the purchase of two four-by-twelve pieces of pipe. Now they were getting somewhere.

The CSIs immediately began processing the receipts and devel-oped very nice palm prints on both. At the same time, other officers obtained a search warrant for the suspect's house and took his major case prints to compare to the receipts. They matched to a tee. Coinci-dence? The jurors didn't think so, convicting the son on two counts of first-degree murder and one count of attempted first-degree murder. He is currently serving two consecutive life sentences for his crimes.

12

HAIR TODAY . . . COURT TOMORROW
Trace Evidence

There is no more disconcerting place on Earth than a prison. Vile, palatable wickedness hangs along every hallway like spiderwebs that cling to your head. There is an unimaginable culture that exists behind those rusty iron bars that even Hollywood has failed to portray accurately. Just like in any other culture, learned behaviors in prison are passed down from generation to generation. This oral history includes a whole cadre of things. We're not talking about violence; that's been done. We're talking about the miscreants. Their learned behavior is unmatched.

As law enforcement develops new scientific advances that put people behind bars, those behind bars continue to share ideas on how to beat the science. One of the newest problems on the street is of growing concern to the CSIs: Inmates everywhere are sharing tips on how to beat DNA tests. There's nothing scientific about their methods. Some have chosen the unenviable path of taking the blood from another person and washing their mouths out with it, so as to confuse a DNA test in prison. Others have chosen to simply share each other's semen and throw it around at a crime scene in order to confuse the cops about whose DNA is actually present.

The final week of training is about helping the CSI stay one step ahead of the criminals. Week ten brings with it a hodgepodge of train-ing that we group together and call Trace Evidence. Trace evidence in-cludes everything that doesn't fit in or is too small for a specific category. In most circles, DNA falls into this category, though it has grown so much over the last decade that it commands its own stand-alone discipline. Though we could teach it separately, we still include it as part of this block of training. Other types of evidence, like hair, blood swabs, bomb residue, glass particles, paint chips, glass filaments, gunshot residue, dust, dandruff, and metal bits are all lumped into the trace evidence discipline.

The trace evidence specialist is sort of thought of as the "geek" or "nerd" of crime scene investigation. They most closely resemble the specialists on the television show *CSI*, though they are not nearly as in-teresting. In fact, we have come to realize that the forensic discipline people choose to work in is closely related to their personalities. If, for example, you want to party, find a fingerprint expert. If you want to laugh, find someone who works with dead bodies all day. If you want to be aggravated, find a bloodstain expert. But if you want to be bored to tears, find a DNA instructor.

DNA is the hardest topic to teach a CSI. First of all, it can be very scientific. Translation: Cops will usually white-eye (police lingo for passing out) within one hour of the start of the lecture. But more im-portant, if you say the words *semen* or *ejaculate* or *sperm* in front of cops, you might as well have said it in front of tenth-graders. If you are an instructor in this field, you have to say it, but most never show it.

Though by this point in the class we have illustrated the uses of the alternate light source (ALS) one thousand times, we had one instructor who liked to use it for his own amusement. Semen will fluoresce under UV light.

One of the earliest instructors the NFA ever had took a break in the middle of a lecture, left the room, and came back after about fifteen minutes. Then we moved the class downstairs to an interior closet that was pitch-black with the door shut. We would bring down the alternate light source and have it ready to go in the closet for when the instruc-tor was ready for the experiment. The experiment was merely a demon-stration of how an ALS fluoresces when it detects semen. All of us packed into a six-by-ten room with the instructor, an alternate light source, and a mysterious Ziploc bag. We turned the lights off and the ALS on, and immediately the object in the bag began to glow like a fluorescent Christmas tree. Then the bomb was dropped. The instructor informed us that he had just masturbated on the T-shirt in the bag not more than thirty minutes earlier. It was as if someone had yelled, "Grenade!" Members of the class were actually trampled trying to get out of the door. We wish we could tell you that the instructor was kidding, but he was not. We no longer use him.

DNA

DNA has become a hot-button issue nationwide, ever since the Daubert hearings, when the courts began challenging fingerprint evidence on the grounds that fingerprint analysis was not founded on scientific principles. This created a backlash, and every type of forensic discipline has been subject to more and more scrutiny due to lack of standards—and with good reason. DNA is heralded to be even more precise than fingerprints in determining who did what. The way DNA is collected, preserved, and tested is critical in determining the outcome in criminal prosecutions by either helping to convict the guilty or exonerate the innocent. Tragically, poor procedures and standards at DNA laboratories have helped prosecute the innocent at an alarming rate by improperly sequencing a suspect's DNA. The problem had gotten so egregious that then U.S. Attorney General Janet Reno established postconviction DNA testing recommendations for the rest of the country to follow. Even as late as 2003, large DNA laboratories, such as those in Houston, Texas, were shut down because of procedural flaws, security lapses, and in some cases outright purposeful tampering with evidence— evidence that ultimately sent innocent people to the electric chair. All of this, though, starts at the bottom with the CSI. If the CSI doesn't know what to collect or how to collect it, then the process is flawed from the start. This is why we teach DNA at the academy.

DNA (deoxyribonucleic acid) is found in the cells of all living things. It can be extracted from hair, blood, semen, vaginal secretions, teeth, bones, organs, tissues, and saliva. It is up to the CSI to figure out which, if any, of these items might be present at a crime scene. Blood evidence is a perfect example. It cannot be assumed that any red stain found at a crime scene is blood. When confronted with a red stain, the first thing that a CSI performs is a presumptive test to confirm the actual presence of blood. But the presence of blood does not prove that it is human blood. The sample must be collected and sent to the trace evidence scientist to confirm whether it is human. This is done by adding what is called a Takayama reagent to the blood. This reagent causes the hemochromogen in the blood to form crystals, signifying that the blood is human, as opposed to a nonhuman animal. In the blood, DNA exists only within the white blood cells. The general rule is if the blood can be seen, it can be tested. The best way to take a sample of the blood is to moisten a regular Q-Tip in water and dab at the stain gently until the Q-Tip has turned red. The sample is then placed into a glass vial or tube that can be topped by a lid. As always, the CSI must wear gloves at all times!

Sperm is the most talked about body fluid with regard to DNA. In the average male's ejaculate, there can be as many as 600 million sperm. Sperm can survive for up to three days in the vagina of a living person, and has been known to survive for over three years in the rectum of a frozen cadaver. In order to perform a DNA test on sperm, there must be at least one hundred sperm heads collected. That means that the investigator must have the victim, living or dead, swabbed vaginally and anally, and if there is reason to believe oral sex took place, flossed. Hundreds of sperm heads have been known to survive between the cheek and gum for up to six hours after ejaculation. Flossing between the teeth is the best way to collect this evidence.

EXTRACTING DNA

With the class up to their collective eyeballs in DNA, we shift gears just a little. As we said before, every living thing contains the blueprint of life. Every dog, tree, and onion has DNA locked somewhere within its structure. The key is unlocking it. Though it might seem juvenile, we have the students extract DNA from an onion. The first time we did this, we were not sure if the idea was a good one or not. That is, until someone in the class said with an extremely puzzled look on his face: "Whose DNA is in the onion?" We knew extracting DNA would be a great learning experience.

DNA can be extracted out of any living thing. All you need is detergent, meat tenderizer, salt, alcohol, and whatever you want to extract the DNA from. We typically use an onion because it yields a nice strand. Here's how we do it. First, the students take about 100 milliliters of chopped white onion, one-eighth of a tablespoon of salt (a pinch will do), and 200 milliliters of ice-cold water. They put all of that into a blender and blend the mixture for about fifteen seconds. The blending of the mixture helps to separate the onion cells from each other. Then they blend the mixture on low for another twenty seconds, until the mixture looks foamy. The students pour the solution into another container and add one-sixth the amount of soap as there is solution. If they have followed the directions, it should yield about two tablespoons. The soap used can be virtually any liquid soap, but liquid dish detergent works best. Next, they swirl the soap throughout the mixture and pour the mixture into test tubes to about one-third full. They then take a pinch of meat tenderizer and sprinkle it into the test tube. The meat tenderizer acts as the enzyme, or catalyst, to speed up the process by cutting the proteins like a pair of scissors, freeing up the DNA. The mixture must be stirred very gently or the DNA will break apart. Finally, the students tilt the test tube and poor rubbing alcohol slowly down the inside of the tube until the tube is two-thirds full. If done correctly, the alcohol will form a layer at the top of the solution. Carefully, the students take a wooden stick—or preferably a small glass stirring rod—insert it into the top layer, and twist in one direction. Voilà, the DNA will curl around the rod. The DNA looks remarkably like, well, like sperm—a fact that the students do not hesitate to point out with a little *hand gesture*. We ignore the motion and move back to the lecture.

SOURCES OF DNA

Saliva is technically the last of the body excretions that DNA can be extracted from, and it is possible, but not probable, to extract DNA from tears, sweat, urine, fecal matter, and our favorite, vomit. Saliva is not generally deposited or collected directly. What is collected are items believed to contain a suspect's DNA. In other words, things that might have been in the perp's mouth. The obvious choices are things like cigarette butts, straws, chewing gum, toothbrushes, lipsticks, toothpicks, eating utensils, eye glasses, stamps, and envelopes. Stamps and envelopes are our absolute favorites. We probably should not give this away, but this is one of an investigator's best and least-known tricks. We cannot tell you the number of cases where an investigator has a DNA sample from a crime, but the suspect is in another state. That makes it difficult to collect their DNA unless you have a really long swab. The trick is superbly simple and brilliant. The investigator mails the suspect a letter indicating they need to be reached for an important message, usually involving money. Within the packet, there is a return envelope—one that must be moistened to seal. All the suspect has to do to get the money is send back the return envelope, which they usually lick to seal. This gives the investigator a much-needed sample, and if it matches, it gives the suspect a one-way ticket to prison.

Hair is one of the most common items used to get DNA. To get a good sample to use, the CSI needs the root. The root most often comes out at a crime scene during a struggle when hair is pulled out. CSIs who have to collect a sample of hair from a rape suspect often choose the pubic area to pull from. Not because they have to, but because it hurts. They'll take a pair of forceps and grab as much pubic hair as possible and jerk it out with excruciating delight. This gives them a good and bloody sample from which to draw DNA and compare.

As far as the rest of the body goes, it just depends on what the CSI finds. If human remains are found without much flesh, the bone marrow is the best choice to take a sample from. If at all possible, the rib bone or vertebrae should be used because more blood passes through these bones. But if the body still has its teeth, including the dental pulp, then the teeth are the best choice. Teeth are the most resilient part of the body. Baby teeth have even been used as secondary DNA in missing persons cases. If a possible ID cannot be made, teeth should be collected and sent to the lab whenever possible. Last but not least are the organs and tissues. If the body still has tissue, but no real blood to speak of, then the liver and spleen are the best choices. After that, the CSI would collect whatever organ was available and place it in a jar to preserve for transportation to the lab.

But what if there are certain organs already found in jars? In one of the most bizarre cases we have ever seen, an Indiana man, turned in by an anonymous phone caller, was practicing none other than the lost art of human castration. Castration, unbeknownst to us, is something that some men in the world are really into. These men have problems with the lumps and bumps of their own bodies and desperately want all of them removed because they want to be smooth. This includes the nipples, as well as the genitalia. These bumpless men, also known as smoothies, suffer from a condition known as genital dysphoria. Because of the embarrassment associated with castration, many of these men seek out what are called cutters. Cutters are underworld, unlicensed surgeons who perform everything from castrations to tongue splittings. Many of these cutters are very into S&M, and as part of their ritual share in the bounty of the man oysters that they have removed.

As one of the more notorious cutters, Edward Bodkin sold how-to videos. After a tip from his one-time roommate, CSIs responded to his residence and discovered nine baby-food-sized jars, each containing a mysterious fleshy substance. Ultimately, DNA experts discovered that the fleshy objects were indeed testicles from five different men. Upon Bodkin's arrest, he confessed to castrating five very willing men, though one castration still remained incomplete due to complications, hence the reason for only nine testicles. Bodkin was eventually charged with practicing medicine without a license and pled guilty to the charges, serving four years in prison.

Tissues, specifically skin, are similar to saliva in that often they are not left at the scene, but on an object. There are some obvious places skin can be found, like razor blades and earrings. Things like dandruff, if found in large enough amounts, can be used to extract DNA as well. Yet the best place to find a suspect's DNA, especially in sexual assault cases where a struggle has occurred, is underneath the fingernails.

Many a corpse have sent their killers to the electric chair by simply clawing the hell out of their assailants. Students are taught to always scrape under the nails of a victim for this reason.

The future of where DNA evidence is headed is exciting, to say the least. Already there is a national database that contains the typing of thousands of criminal DNA, called CODIS (Combined DNA Index System), set up by the FBI. This system allows laboratories to enter in a DNA profile of a suspect and match it to other possible cases. Though this system has been a success, some of the kinks still need to be worked out. Scientists are also working feverishly to improve a CSI's ability to work crime scenes. For example, Oak Ridge National Laboratory has developed a "lab on a chip," which will eventually allow the CSI to take a sample in the field and sequence it on the spot. Other inventions at ORNL include extracting the DNA from nothing more than a person's fingerprint. Science is truly advancing the field of forensics.

Collecting Trace Evidence

After all of the DNA material is presented to the class, we move on to the more practical application of trace evidence recovery. Before any discussion can begin about trace evidence, it is important to once again reiterate the Theory of Transfer, also known as Locard's Exchange Principle. Locard's Exchange Principle states that when two objects come in contact with one another, a transfer of material will occur between the objects. This principle applies to every discipline, but none more so than trace. Pieces of trace evidence are usually in effect transformed due to subtle or unobservable contact between two objects. For instance, a bomb explodes and the smoke plume travels toward a group of bystanders. The bystanders, though unaffected by the explosion, might have traces of bomb residue on their clothing. It is not up to the CSI to determine what the trace evidence is. That work will be done back at the lab, by scientists using very sophisticated microscopes and other devices. It is, however, the responsibility of the CSI to collect and package the evidence properly.

The students are taught standards for the collection of trace evidence. Specifically, there are six recommended methods: picking, lifting, scraping, vacuuming, combing, and clipping. Picking is using tweezers and like instruments to separate the trace evidence from other items. Hairs would be an example. Lifting trace evidence is using an adhesive material to collect the evidence off of items like clothing. Common household items like Scotch tape and sticky lint rollers can be used to collect this evidence. Scraping is the method used when evidence such as blood has dried on a coarse surface. For instance, with this procedure blood would be scraped off the side of a brick wall with the use of a clean utensil, like a scalpel, and onto clean paper.

Vacuuming trace evidence is another common but very controversial method. None of our instructors believes in the use of these micro-canister vacuums because they mostly collect things that are not evidence. If they do pick up something useful, it is either partly destroyed by the device or at the very least cross-contaminated with the other debris that is sucked into the vacuum. We own seven of these very expensive machines, and we have never used a single one—except to vacuum out our car.

Clipping for trace evidence is merely the clipping of finger- and toenails for analysis. Combing for evidence is literally the combing of the hair of an individual. This is typically done in sexual assault cases, where the pubic areas are combed looking for foreign objects like hair and skin. If you haven't realized it by now, trace evidence experts get assigned some very questionable tasks. Combing pubic hair, taking off toenail polish, swabbing anuses—and that's just the "fun" stuff. We didn't even tell you about digging through human waste, peanut by peanut.

Trace evidence is such a catchall category that it is difficult for us to comprehensively teach everything associated with it. The majority of all trace cases will involve either DNA, gunshot residue, explosive material, or hit-and-run evidence, with hit-and-run cases falling a close second behind DNA. The crime that most often contains nearly all of the elements of trace, like hair, fiber, flesh, paint, glass, and so on, is a hit and run. That is why we teach vehicle identification and hit and run together as part of our trace evidence course.

Vehicle Identification

Vehicle identification is a very specialized course for investigators. Normally, it would not be included as part of a forensic course, but certain elements of this discipline are very important for the crime scene investigator to understand. We bring in two of the best in the business, a husband-and-wife dynamic duo. They are well known coast to coast and have forgotten more about cars than Mr. Chevrolet ever knew. They are as good as they are entertaining. They teach the class two very important concepts with regard to vehicle identification: serial number restoration and vehicle glass identification.

The words *serial number restoration* evoke images of Southern "chop-shops," where stolen cars are hacked up and put back out onto the street with a new look. And for good reason. The vast majority of stolen cars have had the serial numbers filed down and often replaced with new, bogus numbers. But there is a way to bring out the truth. Serial number restoration is a challenging technique that only a few specialists have ever mastered. It takes time, patience, luck, and a little acid. The best way to restore serial numbers that have been filed down is to file them down even further, creating a mirror-smooth finish where the numbers once were. This seems counterintuitive, but believe us, it works. Our students smooth the metal out with fine-grain sandpaper. Next, the students open a bottle of hydrochloric acid, or HCL (it's best to test a spot first, but HCL works on most metals). Caution—this should be performed in a well-ventilated area, wearing the proper attire, including acid-proof gloves and goggles to avoid being burned. The students then take a toothbrush and dip it into the acid and brush it across where the serial numbers once were, in one smooth motion and in one direction. Eventually, a shadow of the old serial number will develop. It is important to always have a camera ready, because the number might appear for only a few seconds and then disappear forever. This is because during the stamping process, the metal molecules are dispersed in accordance with the amount of pressure used when stamping the letters and numbers into the object. Ultimately, brushing with the acid causes a reaction within these molecules to bring out the ghost impression of the serial number. Our students are not always successful because time and technique are the biggest hindrances. But when they are, they are amazed that they can take a smooth piece of metal with no visible markings and bring out numbers and letters that were once invisible. Though we practice on cars, serial number restoration can be used on any metal where the numbers have been filed down, including firearms. When everyone is finished with their project, we make everyone wash their hands in hot, soapy water. This is particularly imperative for the guys in the class. Regardless of how "acid proof" the gloves are, some invariably seeps through and is discovered the hard way, usually after a bathroom break. As our instructor says, "When it does, Mr. Happy ain't happy no more." We've had students make this mistake, and when they do, we can hear them all the way down the hall.

After about half a day of serial number restoration, the class moves on to studying vehicle glass. How to decode vehicle glass is one of the great secrets among crime scene investigators, and the secret behind this mysterious science will not be given away here. But we will give a little insight. Every piece of auto glass, whether it is original or replacement, has a wealth of information. It contains the manufacturer, the year it was made, the date it was manufactured, and the shift it was created on. If a piece of auto glass is found by an investigator, a well-trained CSI can glean a tremendous amount of information about the vehicle itself by having no more than an inch-by-inch piece. This is a particularly useful tool, especially when it comes to a hit and run. There are many, many cases where people witness a hit and run but cannot discern the make of the fleeing vehicle. If the right amount of glass is left, a good investigator can turn the information into a lead, and hopefully, into an arrest.

Our instructors pass around several pieces of glass from all kinds of vehicles, while the students practice identifying what cars they are from. We kid our instructors about bringing so many different car parts to our class, because if they are ever in a wreck, nobody will ever be able to figure out why there were a hundred cars in a one-car collision.

After each student has had a chance to examine each piece of glass, they are dismissed for the day. New instructors will come back in the morning and set up our hit-and-run practical exercise.

Of all of the mock crime scenes we create, this one probably makes us cringe the most. Not because it is gross or scary, but because it is not very realistic. As a matter of fact, it is so simplistic that it borders on being stupid—a fact that several of our students have been quick to point out. The scenario is simple: Someone hits a pedestrian with a car. Though there are probably a few people we could think of to stick in front of a moving vehicle, our grant does not allow us to kill anybody. Stupid federal regulations. Thus, as always, we improvise.

Armed with another NFA jacket as collateral, we go to the city pound to try to score two more cars. We need cars that have decent paint jobs, with their windshields still intact. We'll do the rest. First off, we simulate a head smashing into the windshield. Easy enough. A medium hit with a baseball bat does the trick. Next, to make it even more real, we need traces of humanity. We pull out Amy's hair—just for fun. Then we take the hair and pry up parts of the broken glass to embed the hair beneath the shards. If there is absolutely no wind, the hairs might be there the next day. This is also the point of the setup when we begin to question the reality of the scenario, but we continue.

With the head bashing the windshield simulated, we need to simulate something on the hood to make it appear as if a person was hit. Often there is an impression transfer left on the hood in accidents such as these. To create this impression, we take an old pair of Levi's and place the button facedown on the hood of the car. Using the baseball bat perpendicular to the hood, we drive the button down into the car. If done correctly, there will be an intelligible impression of the button left on the hood. For added authenticity, we take a shirt and shred it, using nothing more than a few threads to hang into the fenders.

The next thing we do is to break the headlights all of the way through and into the surrounding glass, breaking into the filaments themselves. These filaments should always be collected by the CSI and submitted to the lab for a very interesting reason. Say you pull out of your driveway and someone hits you with their lights off. When the po-

Session Four graduates prepare to collect hair from a broken wind-shield.

(Collection of the National Forensic Academy)

The button of a pair of jeans pressed into the hood of a car.

(Collection of the National Forensic Academy)

lice arrive, however, the person swears that you pulled out in front of him. Good CSIs are careful to collect the filaments, because trace evidence examiners can tell for sure whether the lights were on or off. This can be done through the use of special analysis that determines stretching, breakage, and oxidation, among other things, in the inside of the headlamps. Finally, the last thing we do on the top of the car is to take a can of spray paint and spray the end of the baseball bat and let it dry a few minutes. With the paint moderately dry, we simply drag the bat across the car, transferring the paint from the bat onto the car. It is possible to match this transferred paint to the car from which it came, if the object is ever found.

Currently, that is the setup for our hit-and-run mock crime scene. Yet all people who are hit are not necessarily thrown up onto the car. Many people are run over. Once, our instructors got the brilliant idea of taking our seven-thousand-pound Excursion and driving it up onto car ramps. (Note, the Excursion is one of the heaviest production vehicles made, and those flimsy car ramps are only meant to support a couple thousand pounds.) Nevertheless, we drove the vehicle up onto the ramps, fearing for our lives. Our instructors had made two simple requests for supplies for this particular scene. One was hair. Amy now pulls her hair out on her own and hands it to the instructors. The other requested item was bacon. Hickory-smoked bacon. We roll under the Excursion on mechanics dollies and put Amy's hair and hickory-smoked bacon in various nooks and crannies to recreate a scene where someone has supposedly been run over. We have to say that this is by far the silliest crime scene setup we have ever created. How realistic are a few hairs and some bacon underneath an Excursion? Who runs over people who are hickory-smoked anyway? We had a thought during the setup that maybe we should have improved on the scene and had the pedestrian be run over while carrying a chicken; we would have at least been able to fry some eggs on the manifold and eat breakfast. Ludicrous.

When the class arrives to work the scenes, we divide the group in half, sending each group to their respective car. The groups begin by taking a cursory look around each car, looking for defining characteristics associated with a hit and run, such as impression transfers, radial patterns in the broken windshield, and paint transfers. The first item usually collected is the hair from the windshield. This is done very gently with the use of tweezers. Since the hairs are very difficult to see, one of the students will obliquely shine a flashlight across the windshield as another one collects the evidence. This helps illuminate the hair, making it easier to be seen and photographed. The hair is placed into a small manila envelope for submission to the lab. Samples of the broken glass are also collected into small glass vials. This is done to compare it to any glass found on the victim. This will be performed back at the lab under a comparison microscope.

The paint transfers on the cars are collected by scraping a scalpel through the paint and into a glass vial. The procedure is then repeated for the actual paint of the car. This will give the trace scientists a sample to compare it to. The impression evidence is photographed and then generally cut out with a reciprocating saw and sent to the lab. Fibers on the car are collected just like the hair. The filaments on the vehicle can be collected by first unscrewing the mechanism that holds them in place. Next, the CSI would pull the filament out through the headlamp casing, which is accessed from underneath the hood. Fragile items, like filaments, need to be packaged in a box or jar that is large enough to support the item and to protect it from any more damage. With the filaments put into boxes, that leaves the bacon as the only evidence left to collect. We only set this scene up one time and refused to ever do it again, not because it was dangerous, but because it was silly. Though there are a lot of ways to collect the bacon, we have found that nothing works better than a warm, buttermilk biscuit. The bacon was collected by the students, who continued to be good sports. They pretended it was human flesh and collected it with either the tweezers or the scalpel and placed the specimens into the glass vials. If it were human flesh, it would then be refrigerated until it could be sent to the lab. With all of the evidence collected, we drive the Excursion off the ramps and head back to the classroom, one final time.

On the last day of class, we invite the renowned FBI Behavioral Analysis Unit to come and speak. The students have spent ten weeks on forensic science, and a lecture on profiling puts a defining stamp on the program. Technically, this has nothing to do with crime scene investigation in the traditional sense. But this particular lecture gives the class some insight on what to look for at a crime scene that might not be random or happenstance. Serial criminals often have patterns that differentiate them from the common criminal. For instance, a body displayed in a specific pose might suggest that a serial killer is at work. This reemphasizes the need to always properly document a crime scene, because investigators never know what they might ultimately be dealing with. It is possible that the crime scene they arrive at is the beginning of a serial killer's rampage. A CSI should always look at the crime scene in terms of what it is saying about a criminal. We're certainly not trying to make our students behavioral analysts. That would take years and years of training. Yet just learning how to look at a crime scene from a different perspective could make the difference in there being one Bundyesque murder or dozens.

The students make their last presentation at the academy on the trace evidence they collected back at the impound lot. It's a bittersweet presentation, juxtaposed against the desire to complete the task and the desire to finally get to go home. Not to mention a fight through a terrible hangover from the good-bye party the night before. Everyone struggles through it though, like the professionals they truly are. Ten weeks is a very long time to be away from home. Now, the emotions of leaving new friendships take over, and even though their last obligations to the academy are complete, many remain in their seats reflecting on what they have been through and what they have accomplished. Some of our graduates come prepared to give teary orations about their experience, a sort of cleansing of the soul. One even went so far as to allegorize her ten weeks at the academy to that of Dorothy, thrust into a forensic version of *Oz*. We didn't know whether to laugh or cry.

The next day is graduation, and for us it might be the last time we ever lay eyes on a few of the students in the class. For two and a half months we have been their principals, their teachers, their psychiatrists, their custodians, their tour guides, and most important, their friends. It is as if we have given birth and the kids have fled the nest. Slowly, everyone gathers their belongings, and leaves the room to kisses, hugs, handshakes, and tears. As the last person exits the class, we exhale a sigh of relief and turn the lights out on a job well done.

DNA

Using DNA in forensic science to match or eliminate a suspect has been around for decades. If the crime scene investigator has been properly trained, he should be able to recognize the sources of DNA at a scene and collect them as evidence. Blood, hair, semen, and saliva are common sources of DNA that are found at crime scenes. But there are many *uncommon* sources that can be present as well, such as animal hair. The bond between a child and a pet can be stronger than that between hydrogen and oxygen. Pets provide comfort, protection, and friendship. But sometimes pets can provide the evidence necessary to catch the bad guy.

In February 2002 the van Dam family of San Diego was enjoying a typical evening. Mom was out with some friends, and Dad was watching television while their seven-year-old daughter, Danielle, played with the family dog, Layla, a Weimaraner. After several minutes of wrestling with the dog, Danielle went to bed. When her father tucked her in he would have no idea it would be the last time he would see his baby girl. The next morning when her mother went to wake Danielle up, she was not in her room.

Immediately, Danielle's parents called the police to report her missing, and thus began a nationwide search for their daughter. It was as though little Danielle had vanished without a trace. Her dad stated that he had woken up in the middle of the night to let the dog out and noticed that the burglar alarm light was blinking. He found that a sliding door was open, and without thinking twice he closed it and went back to bed. At around 2:30 A.M. the mom returned home from her night out with friends. So as not to wake up the children, she made sure the bedroom doors were closed while she stayed up and chatted with her husband and friends. She never looked into the kids' rooms.

After only a few short days, the focus of the investigation fell upon a neighbor, David Westerfield, who lived only yards away from the van Dam home. After obtaining a search warrant, the police searched his home and RV and found several items of evidence, including small traces of blood and hair. The hair found in the RV turned out to be dog hair. It was taken to a lab and DNA tests confirmed that the hair belonged to a Weimaraner. Westerfield was arrested. Danielle's body was found six days later, nude and partially burned, off of a two-lane back road near San Diego.

The use of DNA testing for animal cases has been around since the early 1990s, when fish and wildlife officers would use it to catch poachers. The tests would help match feathers, tusks, and other animal parts with the poachers who murdered them. Animal DNA tests have also been used in animal abuse cases and in animal maulings. While DNA testing may not be the be-all and end-all of the investigation, it does usually help establish a connection between the victim and the suspect.

This technology has only recently been used in criminal cases. Seattle was one of the first cities to use animal DNA in a criminal case. The DNA from a pit bull that had been shot and killed, along with two other people, was found on a suspect's shirt. The suspect told the police he did not commit the shootings and was not anywhere near the crime scene at the time of the murder. After testing the blood on the suspect's shirt, it was concluded that the blood did match that of the pit bull. This crucial piece of evidence placed the suspect at the scene of the crime when the pit bull was killed. The suspect confessed and was convicted.

In the Danielle van Dam case, the Weimaraner hairs found in the neighbor's RV established the fact that Danielle was inside his RV at some point. The jury was presented with this and other evidence, and in August of 2002 they found David Westerfield guilty of the kidnapping and murder of Danielle van Dam. Seven days after the verdict was read, Westerfield was sentenced to die for those crimes. He is currently awaiting execution.

EPILOGUE

Seventy-five thousand. That's how many round-trip miles the average group of CSIs travel to spend two and a half months of their lives at the National Forensic Academy. And it all culminates with a graduation ceremony on the very last day. There are no mortarboards for the graduates to toss into the air or tassels to flip from left to right, just sixteen very proud men and women, along with a small group of their friends, relatives, and coworkers. Not to mention a couple of very tired NFA employees.

On the morning of graduation, we arrive at a local reception hall wearing blue jeans so we can set up our last scene for this particular session. But at this scene, we won't be throwing blood or setting anything on fire. After more than a dozen sessions we have this down to a science. We first hang the National Forensic Academy "Harvard of Hellish Violence" banner across the top of the stage. We then arrange the tables, making sure name cards are placed at the appropriate seats. Finally, we set up the audiovisuals, including speakers and a video screen.

The graduation ceremony itself is a semiformal affair, attended by several dignitaries, including university presidents and vice presidents, various chiefs and sheriffs, senators, congressmen, and sometimes even

Jarrett and Amy with Patricia Cornwell at the NFA graduation.
(Copyright © Sue Courtney)

Patricia Cornwell herself. Everyone is always treated to a light sit-down lunch before the ceremony begins in earnest.

At the proper moment, usually sometime around when dessert is served, we dim the lights and kick off the graduation ceremony with a video tribute to the NFA and its current graduating class. We follow the class around with a camera at different times, capturing the highlights of the course so that they will have something to remember their experience by. The students have never seen the video, and it always becomes one of the highlights of the program, providing a nostalgic look back over the past ten weeks. So much happens during the academy that many things are forgotten until they are displayed once again on the big screen. Everyone jumps at the chance to get a copy of the video so they can show everyone what they have been up to for the last few months. We already know they'll want it, and so we come prepared to give each of them a copy at graduation—a small token of our appreciation for all of their hard work.

Session Seven graduate Jessica Jones is presented the Dr. Bass Award by none other than Dr. Bass himself.
(Copyright © Amy Welch, collection of the National Forensic Academy)

When the video finishes, we introduce our guest speaker, who gives the keynote address to the graduating class. Then we bring Dr. Bass on-stage, who needs no introduction, so he can present the class valedictorian with an award named in his honor. The aptly named Dr. William Bass Award for Outstanding Work in the Field of Forensic Investigation is given to the student who receives the most votes for his or her contributions to the class. Then, after we say a few short words to the class one last time, we invite the class president to come onstage to speak to the group. Traditionally, the president gives a speech on behalf of the class and presents the academy with a plaque commemorating the graduating session. Back in the first session, one of the students had the brilliant idea to collect every department's arm patch and have them framed, along with a student roster and class photo. All of these items are placed under glass and mounted on a blue velvet background. Each plaque now hangs in the classroom as a living tribute to the hundreds

Jarrett and Amy pose for a picture with the plaque Session Seven presented to the NFA.

(Collection of the National Forensic Academy)

of graduates who have graced our doors. The plaques have gone through the same metamorphosis the academy has gone through, with each one being bigger and better than the one before it. It's also become a sort of "laying down the gauntlet" to the next session. Now the plaques contain artistic elements cut into the matte, not to mention various Latin quotes and class creeds.

Once the president has finished presenting the plaque to us, it's time for the class to finally graduate. We call the students individually, so they can walk across the stage, pause for a picture, and collect their diplomas. When the last student finishes his or her journey, the audience gives the entire class a round of applause. With that, the ten-week National Forensic Academy is complete.

After we finish saying a few more good-byes, we collect the plaque to take back to hang in the classroom. We've just about run out of room. During the course of an academy, we talk with the students about what it will be like to come back one day and visit their respective plaques in a new building that we have lovingly titled the Cornwell Forensic Science Institute. For now, though, the building is nothing more than a dream. The future for those who graduate from the academy is very bright. When they leave us to go back to their respective departments, they are considered by most to be part of an elite group of some of the best-trained CSIs in the country. Many begin new careers, heading up CSI units within their departments or creating new ones from scratch. Others go back to delve into their old cases, resurrecting leads with their newfound knowledge. It never ceases to amaze us how many e-mails we get from our graduates who actually put into practice what they learned while spending time with us. Even those who seemed to have slept through the academy call us back to tell us just how much knowledge they attained. Osmosis is a wonderful thing.

As for us, we don't know what the future holds. Budget cuts are at an all-time high, and even though we are working on a congressional act to become a line item in the federal budget, it has yet to see the light of day. But that's okay. Though more money would help make the NFA better, it is not money that makes the NFA great. What makes the NFA great is people; people who believe in what we are doing, including those of us who work there and those who have contributed in both big and small ways to its success. Success in anything can always be traced back to those who gave their sweat because they believed in something that was bigger than themselves. The National Forensic Academy has made a real difference in other people's lives and the communities in which they serve. And how often do you get to be a part of something as powerful as that?

Amy and Jarrett pose for a picture after responding to a call with sheriff's deputies from Brevard County, Florida.

(Collection of the National Forensic Academy)

GLOSSARY

AAFS American Academy of Forensic Science

accelerant a substance, such as gasoline, used to assist the ignition and spread of a fire

accumulated degree days (ADD) the collective total of the average daily temperature; used as an indicator in calculating time since death

adipocere the waxy, soaplike substance formed during the decomposition of a body; consists mainly of fatty tissues; sometimes referred to as grave wax

AFIS Automated Fingerprint Identification System

algor mortis the reduction of body temperature after death

alternate light source (ALS) a light source, other than a laser, that luminesces latent fingerprints, as well as body fluids; also referred to as the forensic light source

anthropology the science of the origin, development, and culture of humans

APIS Automated Palmprint Identification System

area of convergence term used in bloodstain pattern analysis; the area in space where the violence or bloodshed took place

argon laser an ion laser used to detect latent fingerprints

arson the deliberate and intentional setting of a fire

arterial spurting bloodstain pattern caused by blood exiting the body under the pressure of a punctured artery

asphyxiation death resulting from a lack of oxygen

ATF Bureau of Alcohol, Tobacco, Firearms and Explosives

autoerotic asphyxia a form of sexual masochism in which the oxygen flow to the brain is reduced by deliberate strangulation or suffocation in order to enhance the sexual euphoria of masturbation

autopsy the internal and external examination of a human body after death performed to determine the cause of death

ballistics the science of the motion of projectiles, specifically bullets

BDU battle dress uniform

BioFoam brand name of a foam used to make impressions

bloodspatter bloodstains on various surfaces

bloodstain pattern analysis the interpretations of the depth, size, dimension, shape, and orientation of the result of blood in motion

blowfly a metallic blue or green fly that is attracted to decomposing bodies, laying its eggs in the orifices or wounds, which will eventually hatch into maggots

blunt force trauma trauma or injury caused by a blunt object, such as a hammer

C-4 also known as composition-4; a high explosive in the variety of plastic explosives

cadaver a dead body; usually referring to one used in dissection

cast-off pattern bloodstain pattern caused when blood from one source travels to another source, such as blood from a weapon to a wall

CBC Cyanoacrylate Blowing Contraption developed by Arthur Bohanan; machine used in superglue fuming a body

CODIS Combined DNA Index System; the Federal Bureau of Investigation's database of criminal DNA profiles

crime scene the location where a crime occurred

CSI crime scene investigator

CSM crime scene management

cumulative degree hours (CDH) the collective total of the average hourly temperature; used as an indicator in calculating time since death

cyanoacrylate generic name for the adhesive substance more commonly known as superglue

Daubert hearing a term from a civil case entitled *Daubert v. Merrell Dow Pharmaceuticals* (1993); the opinion of the court set a precedent for the admissibility of scientific evidence in federal court

decomposition the decay of organic materials

dental stone a gypsum-based casting material

distal transverse crease the crease above the proximal transverse crease on the palm, also known as the heart line

DNA deoxyribonucleic acid; the genetic material found in cells

drip pattern bloodstain pattern caused when a drop of blood drips into another liquid, usually more blood

EDTA ethylenediaminetetraacetic acid; an anticoagulating agent or blood thinner

electrostatic dust lifter device used to lift dust prints off of various surfaces

entomology the study of insects; knowing the type of insect and its stages of development are indicators of time since death

expirated blood bloodstain pattern caused by blood being blown out of the nose, mouth, or a wound as a result of air pressure

femur the thighbone

fibula the small bone of the lower leg

fingerprint the pattern created by the ridges in the skin of fingers, thumbs, palms, toes, and soles of feet

fire triangle the three things necessary for a fire to burn: oxygen, fuel, and heat

flashover point during a fire when the intense heat causes surrounding objects to spontaneously combust and ignite

floater a body found in water

flow pattern a bloodstain pattern caused by blood that has dropped in a trail

FORDISC Personal Computer Forensic Discriminant Functions, a computer program that classifies adults by race and sex using any combination of standard measurements of bones

forensic light source (FLS) term used for all light sources, including lasers, that are used in forensic science

forensic pathology the study of how and why people die

forensic science the application of scientific principles and methods to the investigation of crime

humerus the bone in the upper arm

hyoid small, horseshoe-shaped bone in the neck; usually broken during strangulation

hypothenar fatty part of hand near the pinky finger

IABPA International Association of Bloodstain Pattern Analysts

IAI International Association for Identification

IED improvised explosive device; a homemade device that is designed to cause death or injury by using explosive material

impact spatter bloodstain pattern created by an impact

impression evidence impressions or marks formed by contact with an object; usually refers to footwear or tire-track impressions left on a surface, such as dirt

interdigital fleshy area of palm just below each finger

laser outside edges of the palm, also referred to as the "karate chop" side

latent fingerprint fingerprint made by the deposition of the fats and oils found in the skin; usually invisible to the human eye until enhanced by such methods as applying fingerprint powder

lividity also known as livor mortis; *see* livor mortis

livor mortis the postmortem pooling of blood within the body due to gravity; causes skin discoloration

Locard's Exchange Principle principle stating that when two objects come into contact with each other a transfer of material will occur between the two; *see* Theory of Transfer

longitudinal radial crease the large, lower horizontal crease on the palm

luminol chemical used to detect the presence of blood; can detect blood that has been diluted; crime scene investigators use it to detect blood that has been cleaned up

maggot the wormlike larva of a fly, such as a blowfly, commonly found in decaying matter

major case prints a recording of all of the ridge detail in the hand that includes the palms, joints, tips, and sides of the fingers; usually taken of suspects of major crimes

manner of death also known as MO; the way in which death was caused; manners of death include homicide, suicide, natural, accidental, and undetermined

mass spectrometer a mass spectroscope that records data electronically

methamphetamine a synthetic drug used as a stimulant

mummification the shriveling and drying of a dead body

nanometer one-billionth of a meter

ninhydrin a chemical used to detect latent fingerprints; it binds to the amino acids found in fingerprints

ORNL Oak Ridge National Laboratory; a national science and energy lab funded by the Department of Energy

osteology the study of bones

petechial hemorrhage very small hemorrhages that occur beneath the skin, typically in the eyelids; common result of strangulation or asphyxiation

physical evidence any object that can link a suspect to a crime scene, a suspect to the victim, or a victim to a crime scene

postmortem occurring or performed after death

postmortem interval also known as time since death, the period of time between death and discovery of the body

PPE personal protective equipment

proximal transverse crease the large, middle horizontal crease on the palm, also known as the head line

pubic symphysis the section of the pelvis where the right and left pubic bones join; can reveal information about the age of a skeleton

pugilistic pose the distortion of a body that is being burned caused by the contracting of the large joints and muscles of the body; the arms and legs will curl inward up toward the chest; also called the boxerlike pose

pupa the third stage in the life of an insect between the larva and adult stages; also called the nonfeeding stage

putrefaction the decomposition of the soft tissues in the body

radius the outer (away from the body) bone of the forearm

rigor mortis stiffening of the muscles of the body after death

satellite pattern a bloodstain pattern caused when blood that was originally part of a bigger stain leaves that stain through some type of force

sharp force trauma trauma or injury caused by a sharp object, such as a knife

SLR single lens reflex, a type of camera in which the reflecting mirror retracts when the shutter is released

starburst skin flap where the thumb connects to the hand

SWG-STAIN Scientific Working Group in Bloodstain Pattern Analysis; practitioners that meet regularly to discuss the leading theories and practices in the field of bloodstain pattern analysis

swipe pattern bloodstain pattern created when an object that is already stained with blood comes into contact across an object that is not stained

tache noire drying of the eye that results in a black line across the cornea

Tardieu spots brownish black round spots that occur in areas of the body where large amounts of lividity has collected; caused by capillaries rupturing within the body

thenar fatty part of the palm near the thumb

Theory of Transfer theory stating that no one can enter a location without bringing in and depositing some type of evidence and that no one can leave a location without taking some sort of evidence with them

thermocouple device a thermoelectric device used to accurately measure temperatures

tibia the large bone of the lower leg

time since death also known as the postmortem interval; the period of time between death and discovery of the body

TNT trinitrotoluene; used as a high explosive

Total Station an electronic distance-measuring device used to determine angles and distances from the instrument to points to be surveyed

trace evidence types of physical evidence that are deposited at a crime scene such as hair, fiber, soil; also includes evidence that can only be detected by special processing, such as DNA

trajectory the path a projectile, such as a bullet, makes through space under the friction of forces such as gravity and wind

transient evidence evidence collected at a crime scene that is very fragile and may not last very long, such as DNA

ulna the inside (near the body) bone of the forearm

ultraviolet light an invisible band of radiation at the upper end of the light spectrum

V pattern a thermal pattern formed by a fire as it burns against a wall; usually indicates origin of fire; in the shape of a V

volatile fatty acids the major end products of microbial activity in the digestive tract resulting in a fluid; used in determining time since death

wipe pattern a stain created by an object coming across a bloodstain that already exists on another object; this type of pattern would occur if, for instance, someone were to "wipe" a nonbloody hand through a bloodstain

WMD weapons of mass destruction

WHO'S WHO IN
FORENSIC INVESTIGATION

crime scene investigator typically the person who oversees the processing and investigation of a crime scene

crime scene photographer a crime scene technician who is highly skilled in the art of photography

crime scene technician the person who identifies, collects, preserves, and transports evidence from a crime scene

document examiner the person who conducts analysis on documents and document-related evidence from a crime scene; typically performed in a laboratory setting

evidence technician *see* crime scene technician

firearms/tool mark examiner a person who examines and identifies firearms, bullets, cartridges, ammunition, and other gun-related evidence at a crime scene; this person is also typically skilled in the identification and classification of tool marks found at a scene

forensic anthropologist an anthropologist who applies the knowledge and methods of anthropology to the law, usually in cases of identifying human remains

forensic pathologist a pathologist who determines the cause of death by the examination of wounds, injuries, and tissues relevant to criminal activity

latent print examiner a person who can not only recover latent print evidence from a crime scene but can also process the fingerprint evidence using complex techniques; the latent print examiner is also skilled in latent print comparison

medical examiner (ME) a physician who determines the cause of death of the deceased

pathologist a physician trained in the cause of death by disease determined through examination of body fluids, cell, and tissue samples

RESOURCES

Books

Bass, B. & Jefferson, J. (2003). *Death's Acre: Inside the Legendary Forensic Lab the Body Farm, Where the Dead Do Tell Tales.* New York: G.P. Putnam's Sons.

Bass, W. (1995). *Human Osteology: A Laboratory and Field Manual.* Columbia, MO: Missouri Archeological Society.

Bevel, T. & Gardner, R.M. (1997). *Bloodstain Pattern Analysis: With an Introduction to Crime Scene Reconstruction.* Boca Raton, FL: CRC Press.

Brenner, J.C. (2004). *Forensic Science: An Illustrated Dictionary.* Boca Raton, FL: CRC Press.

Brogdon, B.G., Vogel, H. & McDowell, J.D., eds. (2003). *A Radiologic Atlas of Abuse, Torture, Terrorism, and Inflicted Trauma.* Boca Raton, FL: CRC Press.

Casey, E. (2000). *Digital Evidence and Computer Crime: Forensic Science, Computers and the Internet.* San Diego: Academic Press.

Cornwell, P. (2003). *Blow Fly.* New York: G.P. Putnam's Sons.

DeForest, P.R., Gaensslen, R.E. & Lee, H. (1983). *Forensic Science: An Introduction to Criminalistics.* New York: McGraw-Hill.

Dimaio, V.J.M. (1999). *Gunshot Wounds: Practical Aspects of Firearms, Ballistics, and Forensic Techniques.* Boca Raton, FL: CRC Press.

Dix, J. (2000). *Color Atlas of Forensic Pathology.* Boca Raton, FL: CRC Press.

Dix, J. (2000). *Time of Death, Decomposition, and Identification: An Atlas.* Boca Raton, FL: CRC Press.

Eliopulos, L. N. (1993). *Death Investigator's Handbook: A Field Guide to Crime Scene Processing, Forensic Evaluations, and Investigative Techniques.* Boulder, CO: Paladin Press.

Fisher, B. A. (2000). *Techniques of Crime Scene Investigation.* Boca Raton, FL: CRC Press.

Geberth, V. J. (1996). *Practical Homicide Investigation.* Boca Raton, FL: CRC Press.

James, S. H. & Nordby, J. J., eds. (2003). *Forensic Science: An Introduction to Scientific and Investigative Techniques.* Boca Raton, FL: CRC Press.

Kubic, T. & Petraco, N. (2003). *Forensic Science: Laboratory Experiment Manual and Workbook.* Boca Raton, FL: CRC Press.

Olsen, R. D., Sr. (1978). *Scott's Fingerprint Mechanics.* Springfield, IL: Charles C. Thomas Publishing Company.

Osterburg, J. W. & Ward, R. (2000). *Criminal Investigation: A Method of Reconstructing the Past.* Cincinnati, OH: Anderson Publishing Company.

Redsicker, D. R (2001). *The Practical Methodology of Forensic Photography.* Boca Raton, FL: CRC Press.

Saferstein, R. E. (2001). *Criminalistics: An Introduction to Forensic Science.* Upper Saddle River, NJ: Prentice Hall.

Siegel, J. A., Saukko, P. J. & Knupfer, G. C. (2000). *Encyclopedia of Forensic Sciences.* San Diego: Academic Press.

Steadman, D. W. (2003). *Hard Evidence: Case Studies in Forensic Anthropology.* Upper Saddle River, NJ: Prentice Hall.

Websites

American Academy of Forensic Science
www.aafs.org

Association of Firearm and Tool Mark Examiners
www.afte.org

Bodies We've Buried: Inside the National Forensic Academy, the World's Top CSI Training School
www.bodiesweveburied.com

Death's Acre
www.deathsacre.com

Federal Bureau of Investigation
www.fbi.gov

International Association of Bloodstain Pattern Analysts
www.iabpa.org

International Association for Identification
www.theiai.org

International Crime Scene Investigators Association
www.icsia.org

National Forensic Academy
www.nfa.tennessee.edu

Patricia Cornwell
www.patriciacornwell.com

Oak Ridge National Laboratory
www.ornl.gov

Outdoor Anthropological Research Facility, a.k.a the Body Farm
http://web.utk.edu/~anthrop/index.htm

ACKNOWLEDGMENTS

Years ago, I came across an old proverb that says the only way to leave a lasting legacy is to do three things: plant a tree, have a child, and write a book. This book completes the trilogy. I have, for over ten years, practiced writing, creating everything from a complete screenplay to well over fifty poems. Writing a book, however, was always my dream. Being able to achieve one's dream in life is a very emotional experience and one that does not happen without a lot of help and encouragement.

To my mom and dad, Judy and Jerry Hallcox, I would like to thank them for all of their support through the years. They always treated my brother and me like people and not shadows that should be looked at and not acknowledged. They gave me every opportunity they could afford and taught me that I could do anything that I thought I could do. Thanks for always believing in me.

To my brother, Justin Hallcox, and my uncle, Larry Hallcox, for keeping me grounded while writing this book. Their incessant teasing kept the whole thing in perspective.

To Amy Welch, the coauthor of this book, I would like to extend my gratitude for believing in a project that most people cannot even fathom undertaking. If it had not been for a chance encounter while working at the academy, this book would never have been created. The synergy that we had while writing this book was unmatched and I will be forever grateful for your friendship.

But most of all, I would like to thank my adoring wife, Kolloia, and wonderful daughter, Kaylie, who supported me over the last three years as I sought to fulfill one of my life's ambitions. They never said a word as I delved deeper into the book and they stood behind me throughout all of the frustrations and celebrated with me through all of the joys that this project has brought with it. To Kolloia, thanks for always loving me, and always being patient, even when God knows it was hard. And to Kaylie, my little Peach, the toughest little girl in the world, always remember, no matter what happens, "Daddy loves you!"

—*J.J.H.*

I would like to thank my amazing husband, Steve, for never doubting my ability to write a book and for supporting me throughout the three-year process. There were many late nights and lost weekends that went into the writing of this book. If it hadn't been for his unconditional support of what many thought was a crazy idea, I never could have done it. Steve, thanks for chasing me when we were eight years old. I love you!

I would also like to thank my family for their never-ending support of everything I've ever done. My parents, Garry and Sara Mick, always told me that I could achieve anything I put my mind to. My brother Adam, on the other hand, always told me that I could do *almost* anything, except reach something on the top shelf. I love you guys! I also want to thank my Nanny and Papa, Minnie and the late Don Arbaugh, for always being two of my biggest fans. I love all of you!

I also want to thank Jarrett, not only for having the idea for this book but for asking me to coauthor it with him. It's amazing how every once in a while the planets will align and things seem to fall into place. It's been a crazy adventure, one that has fostered a lifelong friendship, and I wouldn't trade our experience for anything.

—*A.M.W.*

Special Thanks
First of all, we would like to thank Dr. and Mrs. Bill Bass for their friendship and support of this book and for the foreword that Dr. Bass so graciously agreed to write.

We want to give special thanks to Patricia Cornwell. It is not every day that a world-renowned author chooses not only to support your book with a quote but also to offer her friendship throughout the process. We owe her a debt of gratitude that we can never repay.

We would also like to thank Samantha Mandor, our editor, and all of

Berkley Books, who took a chance on a couple of unproven and unheard-of writers. Thanks for believing in us and giving us the chance of a lifetime.

And last, but certainly not least, we would like to thank our agent, Laurie Abkemeier. This book would not have happened if it had not been for her. By sheer happenstance we met this "Angel," who saw us as a diamond in the rough and decided that we could pull off the impossible. Her patience, hard work, and undying enthusiasm are the real reasons this book happened in the first place. We will never be able to thank Laurie, and for that matter, everyone at DeFiore and Company, enough for their contributions regarding this book.

—*Jarrett and Amy*

INDEX

ABOUT THE AUTHORS

Jarrett Hallcox is the director of the National Forensic Science Institute (NFSI) and is responsible for all of the day-to-day activities of the National Forensic Academy. He has a bachelor's degree in political science and history and a master's degree in public administration from the University of Tennessee. He has been featured in national and international media coverage of the NFA, including *Popular Science*, Court TV, the *London Daily Telegraph*, and CNN. Originally from Michigan, he resides in Knoxville with his wife and young daughter.

Amy Welch is the forensic training coordinator for NFSI. She coordinates, along with Jarrett Hallcox, the day-to-day activities of the National Forensic Academy. She is in charge of the one-week courses, such as bloodstain pattern analysis, that the Academy takes across the nation. Amy also coordinates all alumni activity and forensic research projects for the Academy. She has assisted in a variety of media stories on the NFA, including those featured on Court TV. She graduated from Ohio University with a bachelor's degree in psychology and a master's degree in social work. Originally from Chillicothe, Ohio, she currently lives in Knoxville with her husband.